INSTRUCTIONAL ASSESSMENT

An Essential Path for Guiding Reading Instruction

Edward E. Gickling, Ph.D.

Todd A. Gravois, Ph.D.

Verlinda Angell, Ed.D.

**ICAT
PUBLISHING**

Gickling, Edward, E., Gravois, Todd, A., & Angell, V.

Instructional Assessment: An Essential Path for Guiding Reading Instruction

ISBN: 978-0-9835399-4-0

INSTRUCTIONAL ASSESSMENT

An Essential Path for Guiding Reading Instruction

This timely text brings relevant assessment practices into harmony with learning and teaching by ensuring that the assessment process is firmly anchored to the same principles that guide effective instruction. In general terms, Instructional Assessment provides educators with practical approaches that result in effective reading instruction for students of all ages and reading levels. In specific terms, Instructional Assessment is targeted at reducing the instructional and curriculum mismatches that hinder the learning of struggling students.

This comprehensive resource delineates the process of assessing the reading performance of students across different reading dimensions: comprehension, metacognition, language development, word recognition, word study, responding, and fluency and flow. Chapter by chapter, this authoritative text provides the empirical basis for instructional assessment and culminates with specific strategies that can be used with individuals, small groups and entire classrooms of students. Helpful reproducible tools are included throughout the material.

Edward E. Gickling, Ph.D., is recently retired after a distinguished career as Professor of Special Education, University of Tennessee, Knoxville, and University of Nevada, Reno, as Executive Director for Professional Development, Council for Exceptional Children, and as a national consultant working with schools and state departments of education across the United States. He resides in Draper, UT.

Todd A Gravois, Ph.D., formerly Research Associate Professor at University of Maryland, is President of ICAT Resources, Inc., and consults with schools, districts, and state departments of education in aligning support services for teachers and students.

Verlinda Angell, Ed.D., Professor Emeritus, Reading/Literacy, Graduate Studies Southern Utah University, is a Personal Learning Coach with Academic Answers, Austin, TX.

To Chuck Hargis, a life-long friend whose historical knowledge of language and reading development helped anchor our work. To Jim Tucker, a visionary mentor and leader for his unwavering support that enabled our work to be applied on a large scale. To Sylvia Rosenfield, a devoted scholar for believing in our work and for being a constant voice of encouragement. To Don Fleming, for his sharp insights and poignant questions that gave us additional experience to refine our work. To Lynne and Alicia Gravois for their tireless editorial and production efforts that helped bring our work to life. And to the untold number of classroom teachers, support personnel, and local, district, and state officials who enabled us to share, interact, and learn from each other, we are forever grateful!

Contents

Chapter 1

Assessment in the 21st Century: Fulfilling the Promise

*When are we going to stop weighing
the lambs and start feeding them?*

(Jonathan Kozol, 2006)

WHERE WE ARE

We live in an era where the evaluation of student performance is paramount and where the yardstick of success is passing rigorous learning standards. Such practices adhere to the belief that favorable learning outcomes will be achieved as schools clearly identify what students are to learn, align curricula and instructional practice to achieve specific learning standards, and systematically assess and monitor student progress. The major premise propelling this belief is that schools and teachers will alter their instructional practices as a function of setting higher learning standards and that achievement will increase as the result of students meeting higher standards. This is evident beginning with the passage of *No Child Left Behind,* continuing with *Race to the Top* and now seen in the *Common Core Standards* .

Despite the development of rigorous learning standards, legislation of student outcomes, and creation of special programs to meet the learning needs of a diverse population of students, Stiggins (2005) notes that there is scant evidence that schools are becoming more effective. No doubt there are schools that achieve extraordinary outcomes, but these schools are the exceptions, not the norm. For most schools, a few students perform at very high levels while the majority of students continue to maintain grade-level progress. Regrettably, a sizable percentage of students continue to flounder and remain at the bottom of the achievement ladder. Their poor performance routinely appears among the high-stakes test scores of the 68 million students tested annually to satisfy federal requirements (Scherer, 2005). The demand imposed by high-stakes testing does not end here. Students are increasingly required to take practice tests and quarterly assessments, all in preparation for taking annual year-end state tests. This excessive disposition for test preparation and testing is rooted in the misconception that constantly "weighing the lambs" (i.e, measuring student progress) will naturally improve learning outcomes (Kozol, 2006).

Reflecting upon where we are, we are mindful that "every path...even those with the best of intentions could end up further and further removed from the struggles of those they purported to serve" (Obama, 2004, p. 140). This view in many ways captures the current state of educational assessment. Educational assessment as routinely practiced has become removed from supporting the learning and instructional needs of students it purports to serve, especially those who repeatedly struggle and who are at risk of academic failure. In attempting to make schools more accountable, increasing numbers of students are the casualties of our high-stakes testing system which often forces them to repeat ineffective instruction or requires them to receive alternative instruction. Although the law previously stipulated that no child was to be left behind, the over-reliance on testing marginalizes students who perform at the bottom of the learning continuum—allowing many to view such students as being less diligent and by fiat as deserving to fail.

Relying on traditional forms of assessments that focus on evaluating student performance to identify student deficiencies, followed by a heavy reliance on the use of tutorial programs, has not altered the plight of low-achieving students. Instead, assessment results merely confirm what teachers already know about certain students and extra tutoring merely provides schools with a stopgap solution rather than being truly preventative. For struggling students to benefit from schooling, they need to achieve success by experiencing improvements in their own learning. Assessment must have a direct role in making this happen. It must inform instruction to ensure that instruction is delivered effectively and efficiently to struggling students.

This chapter provides a context for understanding how assessment has served education, and where changes are needed if assessment is to serve instruction better. While we recognize the link between instruction and assessment is not where it should be, there are encouraging signs this connection is improving. For example, current special education regulations acknowledge the importance of providing appropriate instruction to students who experience learning problems. Beginning with the passage of P.L. 94-142 (1975) and with each subsequent special education reauthorization, the law stipulates that the quality of instruction the student receives must be considered prior to initiating eligibility procedures. The law furthermore states that the quality and appropriateness of instruction must *not* be assumed, but instead verified. The recent introduction of the concept of Response to Intervention (RTI) represents the latest attempt to ensure that quality instruction occurs for students who struggle academically in the regular classroom (IDEIA, 2004). Another indication that things are improving is general education's willingness to expand and embrace a more instructionally relevant role for assessment (e.g., the concept of "assessment *of* learning" versus "assessment *for* learning").

Popham (2006) notes that the genesis of assessment *of* learning and assessment *for* learning came from the work of the United Kingdom's Assessment Reform Group (Black & Wiliam, 1998). Assessment *of* learning is characterized by traditional approaches which test students on what they have learned after periods of instruction have elapsed. Such approaches typically focus on evaluating and comparing student performance to core learning standards. In contrast, assessment *for* learning concentrates on encouraging teachers to interact directly with students by jointly reflecting upon on-going classroom data in order to better inform instruction. This form of assessment focuses on gaining a clearer understanding of the work the student is performing and allowing his or her teacher to provide timely support.

Distinguishing between assessment *of* learning and assessment *for* learning has helped clarify the two major approaches to assessment. The terminology has also shifted the focus from using assessment as the way to improve teaching to using assessment data as the way to improve learning. The rationale behind this shift is based on the belief that "students would be better served if educators embraced learning rather than teaching as the mission of their school" (DuFour, Eaker, & DuFour, 2005, p. 5). This emphasis coincides with the development of core learning standards which require schools to clearly define what students are to learn, to reliably assess what they have learned, and to intervene in a timely manner when students are experiencing difficulty (e.g., Common Core State Standards, CCSS, National Governors Association, 2010). Schools are no longer places where students are simply taught, but are places where professionals share their expertise and willingly accept responsibility for seeing that each student learns and succeeds, with the long-term goal of having students be college and career ready.

A THIRD PURPOSE OF ASSESSMENT

Beyond the practices of assessment of learning and assessment for learning, we see the urgent need for assessment to travel a more precise path in supporting learning and teaching. This third path is viewed as having three major objectives: (1) to create and manage the instructional match for the student, (2) to provide the student with timely instructional feedback, and (3) to monitor and evaluate student progress.

As recorded in the final stanza of President Lincoln's Gettysburg Address, President Lincoln used three small words to capture the significance of preserving the nation. These same small words, *"of," "for,"* and *"by,"* have garnered explicit meaning in identifying the major purposes of assessment. The preposition *"of"* refers to "the results of," as in how did the student perform after instruction was provided? The preposition "for" refers to "the reasons for," as in how are the results of assessment to be used to inform teaching and learning? The preposition missing from the current conversation concerning how assessment serves instruction is the word *"by."* This word provides even more meaning within the context of assessment because it refers to "the route by," as in the path followed to achieve meaningful assessment. As described below, each purpose of assessment has a different perspective as applied to instruction.

Assessment of Learning

Practices falling under the umbrella of assessment **of** learning concentrate on monitoring and evaluating student performance once a specific period of instruction has been provided. Informal, teacher-based assessments (such as quizzes, unit tests, term projects, and final exams) and formal state-based assessments (such as annual testing of grade-level standards, normative/standardized testing, and universal screenings) are included in this category. These assessment practices are often described as summative, since the information gained provides schools, teachers, students, parents, and the general public with summaries of how students have performed. The National Consortia's Partnership for Assessment of Readiness for College and Careers (PARCC) is a recent example of this summative form of assessment aligned with Common Core Standards (CCSS).

While federal and state officials view this form of data-driven accountability as the single best vehicle for closing the achievement gap, results of high-stakes testing for various reasons have not reduced the achievement gap (Valencia & Villarreal, 2003; Toppa, 2005). Annual tests designed to measure the performance of students do not provide data specific enough to inform instruction. Nor are resulting data available in a timely fashion to have any bearing on classroom instruction. When available, this information rarely informs teachers beyond what they already know. In Popham's (2006) words, such assessments are "instructionally insensitive—that is, they're unable to detect even striking instructional improvements when such improvements occur" (pp. 82-83). In summary, data from assessment *of* learning offer little useful information when it comes to actually informing instruction. Their primary use revolves around scoring, grading, evaluating, and comparing student performance.

The Sequence of Assessment of Learning

Practices that are categorized as assessment *of* learning have a specific starting point and flow often leading to annual state testing (see Figure 1.1). The instructional purpose served by this form of assessment is one of monitoring and evaluating student progress. Assessment *of* learning is rooted in learning tasks that are representative of grade-level standards or benchmarks. Curricula coverage for each grade level is organized to reflect the school district's pacing guide aligned with the standards. Students are expected to keep up with the ongoing curricula coverage as outlined and taught in conformance to the school district's pacing guide. When it is time to take the annual state test (e.g., CCSS), students are encouraged to do their best. Of course, the scores students receive from taking such high-stakes tests are used to determine which students pass and which students fail.

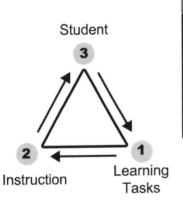

Sequence of Assessment Steps:

1. Start with the state benchmarks.
2. Follow the district's pacing guide aligned with the benchmarks. Focus instruction on achieving the benchmarks.
3. Students do your best! Try to keep up!

Figure 1.1 Sequence of Assessment of Learning

The limitations of assessment *of* learning are evident. While learning standards indicate the grade-level competencies states want students to achieve, relying on this form of assessment to determine progress ignores the fact that students have different entry points, they differ in their amount of skill acquisition, and they learn at different rates—all factors that work to the detriment of struggling students. Even when teachers are aware that certain students are lagging behind, they are reluctant to alter their instruction for fear of not having sufficient time to cover the required curriculum in preparation for their students taking annual state tests. This narrow view of assessment encourages a one pace, one-size-fits-all approach to grade-level instruction (Cooter & Cooter, 2004). At the same time, little flexibility is given to students who exhibit different learning trajectories and who constantly struggle and need additional learning support.

Assessment for Learning

This form of assessment is often referred to as formative assessment, and by far is the oldest form of assessment. It reflects a broad range of activities such as direct observation, questioning, discussion, student drafts, portfolio reviews, use of rubrics, informal reading inventories, fluency checks, pre-tests, and non-graded quizzes. These assessment activities provide teachers with ongoing snapshots of how students' performance aligns with the expected learning outcomes. Data from these activities enable teachers to identify where their students are in relationship to the skills and key concepts set forth in the state's learning standards (McNamee & Chinn, 2005) and now in the common core state standards.

Assessment *for* learning may be as informal as directly observing how a student engages a task and having a discussion with the student about his or her thinking regarding the task. However, making assumptions about the student's level of understanding based on how and where the student functions is insufficient. As Burns (2005) notes, spotting correct or incorrect responses is easy. It is much more difficult to gauge and understand the student's reasoning behind his or her responses. Instead, teachers need to delve into the student's thinking in order to gain insights into how the student actually views his or her own learning. Students need to be able to discuss their degree of understanding and to explain their thinking regardless of whether it is flawed or not.

When it comes to informing instruction, relying on assessment *for* learning is far superior to relying on assessment *of* learning. Black and Wiliam's (1998) meta-analysis of research on formative assessment found improvements in students' test scores on class tests as well as on external examinations, confirming the ongoing benefits of using assessment *for* learning. Popham (2006) lauded such benefits as well, stating that they provide "a marvelous, cost effective way of enhancing student learning. Solid research evidence confirms that it works, assessment experts endorse it, and teachers adore it" (p. 82). His main fear, however, was "that the big tests [assessment *of* learning] will drive out the little tests [assessment *for* learning] that can demonstrably help students learn" (p. 83).

The Sequence of Assessment for Learning

Assessment *for* learning serves to provide students with timely feedback and re-teaching as needed in preparing to take annual state tests. Figure 1.2 depicts the sequence and flow of assessment *for* learning. The starting point for assessment *for* learning is the state's learning standards (e.g., CCSS). These assessment forms start with the learning tasks and are used to determine where the student functions relative to each standard. They involve "a careful analysis of the enabling knowledge and sub-skills the student must acquire to master a higher curriculum aim" (Popham, 2006, p. 82). Instruction is targeted at helping the student achieve each curriculum aim or benchmark. Frequent feedback is given as part of ongoing classroom instruction with re-teaching occurring whenever the student needs additional instruction to master each curriculum aim.

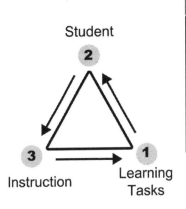

Sequence of Assessment Steps:

1. Start with the state benchmarks.
2. This is where the student functions. These are my benchmark targets.
3. This is how each target will be assessed.
   This is what the student has learned.
   These are the skills I need to re-teach.

Figure 1.2 Sequence of Assessment for Learning

Even with the myriad advantages of formative assessments, their use has not been sufficient to narrow the learning gaps of most poor readers. The central problem is not so much that teachers are not able to pinpoint gaps in student learning, or to be able to analyze the errors students make, or to know how to break tasks down into their component parts. Instead, the basic problem is that both assessment *of* learning and assessment *for* learning continue to focus on teaching that requires fitting the student to the curriculum rather than fitting the curriculum to the student.

Historically, the onus for learning or failing to learn has fallen on the student. When there are only a few students who repeatedly struggle while most students are able to achieve grade-level proficiency, the tendency is to view those students who struggle as having learning deficiencies, or worse still as having learning defects. In these circumstances, classroom instruction is assumed to be appropriate. Our educational system has been all too willing to treat problems in learning as a student's choice—or a result of an internal deficit beyond the student's control. In this erroneous view, the student is seen as the one who must decide if success is within his or her grasp and if putting forth the extra effort to learn is worth it (Stiggins, 2005).

Although we agree that student learning is an appropriate measure of the school's effectiveness, the defining characteristic of effective instruction is the ability to facilitate student learning. Teachers are well aware that instruction is the real engine that drives effective learning and teaching. We share Sparks' (2005) view "that the quality of our teaching is the most important thing in determining the quality of learning that students experience" (p. 169). To focus on student learning at the expense of teaching is as much a mistake as to place the focus on teaching at the expense of student learning. Rather than separating the two, we strongly believe that the primary purpose of assessment is to create successful instruction as a precursor to successful learning, which is why we continually couch assessment in the language of instruction.

Assessment by Instruction

Our perspective is that instruction is the path through which meaningful assessment occurs—hence the concept of Instructional Assessment (IA) or assessment *by* instruction. When assessment is viewed in relation to instruction, the vast majority of assessment activities are seen as emanating directly from the daily instruction students receive in the classroom. It is the instantaneous feedback that alerts the classroom teacher as to whether instruction matches or fails to match the learning needs of each student. From our viewpoint, establishing and maintaining appropriate instructional experiences for students is the first and foremost purpose of instructional assessment.

Unlike typical approaches to assessment, Instructional Assessment (IA) focuses on students' day-to-day success within the context of classroom instruction. Instead of dwelling on where a student is struggling, IA targets the creation and maintenance of optimal conditions for both learning and teaching. Without the presence of these conditions, the data derived from assessment are likely to be spurious. The advice written into the *Standards for the Assessment of Reading and Writing* (1994) reinforces the importance of this position:

> The quality of information is suspect when tasks are too difficult or too easy, when students do not understand the tasks or cannot follow the directions, or when they are too anxious to be able to do their best or even their typical work. In these situations students cannot produce their best efforts or demonstrate what they know. Requiring students to spend their time and efforts on assessment tasks that do not yield high quality, useful information results in students losing valuable learning time. Such a loss does not serve their interests and is thus an invalid practice (p. 14).

Too often educators attribute poor assessment results to weak student performance without considering the appropriateness of the task and its accompanying instruction. Unfortunately, the cycle of mismatched curriculum and instruction perpetuates most students' learning struggles—a cycle which ultimately appears in the form of inadequate achievement. Further, while such assessment results are reported as valid, they are fundamentally flawed because the necessary conditions for achieving valid results were never established in the first place.

Pearson (2006) wrote that assessments should reflect, and not lead, curriculum and instruction. This statement can be understood from two different perspectives. It is true that instructionally sensitive assessments are needed to accurately indicate how well the student is responding to curriculum and instruction. However, it is equally true that instructionally sensitive assessments are needed to accurately reflect how well curriculum and instruction are appropriately matched to each student's prior knowledge and entry skills.

The Sequence of Assessment by Instruction

Assessment *by* instruction takes a different path from the other two approaches to assessment. Its primary purpose focuses on creating and maintaining the instructional match. As depicted in Figure 1.3, the assessment sequence begins with the student. More specifically, it begins with ensuring instructional-level conditions exist, allowing the student to perform at his or her best.

Once valid assessment data are acquired, instructional decisions are based upon what the student knows and is able to do. New learning tasks and strategies are scaffolded to match the student's instructional level, ensuring that the student is able to function and achieve success. Long-term goals are always kept in mind, but assessment and instruction are managed incrementally under strategic, instructionally-matched conditions to assure that the ongoing data are valid and reflect precisely what the student knows and can do. While the assessor and teacher never lose sight of the grade-level benchmarks, they always approach the benchmarks with respect to where the student currently is able to function successfully.

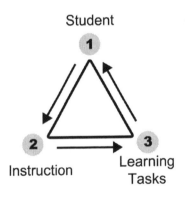

Sequence of Assessment Steps:

1. Establish instructional-level conditions within the learning task being assessed to determine precisely what the student knows and can do.
2. Set goals by scaffolding on what the student knows and can do. Select strategies based on what the student knows and needs.
3. Manage the instructional match to ensure that student success occurs with each learning task. Do not lose sight of the benchmarks but approach them with respect to where the student is able to function successfully.

Figure 1.3 Sequence of Assessment by Instruction

WHERE WE NEED TO BE

The three different assessment approaches (i.e., *of, for,* and *by*) described in this chapter all converge at the point of student learning. However, each assessment approach has a different starting point, has a different mission, and impacts instruction in a very different way. For example, year-end assessments (assessment *of* learning) are adequate to determine the proficiency levels of most students because their academic skills match the grade-level demands of curriculum and instruction. Formative assessments (assessment *for* learning) allow the assessor and teachers to make course corrections for certain students by providing timely feedback, re-teaching, and allowing for extra learning time. For students who repeatedly struggle, though, neither approach to assessment has proven precise enough to keep students from falling further and further behind. However, when Instructional Assessment (IA) and formative assessment activities are combined, curriculum and instruction can be aligned and effectively managed, thus enabling the struggling student to achieve continuous optimal growth.

SUMMARY

While educational assessment practices serve multiple purposes, our message is that assessment's major role is one of supporting the delivery of effective instruction. In specific terms this involves: (1) creating and managing the instructional match, (2) providing the student with timely and useful feedback, and (3) monitoring and evaluating student progress. The first priority involves securing the conditions that enable the student to perform optimally. Next, the role of assessment becomes one of providing confirming and corrective feedback. After these two purposes are stabilized, then and only then can assessment's third purpose, that of monitoring and measuring student performance, be considered valid. These three purposes must be aligned in this manner for assessment to serve the instructional needs of students.

Historically, when considering how assessment practices have served instruction, it is obvious that the typical sequence of screening, diagnosing, and progress monitoring, as routinely practiced, is not aligned with the successful delivery of instruction. Conversely, the extent to which assessment practices create and maintain optimal learning conditions largely determines how well the student will perform and achieve. If we are serious about closing the achievement gap and raising the academic level of the struggling student, then the starting point to bring about this change must center on creating and maintaining the instructional match. It is only when curriculum and instruction are strategically matched to the entry skills and prior knowledge of the struggling student, and delivered under optimal conditions, that learning and teaching will truly benefit the student.

The Latin derivative of assessment means literally to "sit with" (Wiggins, 1989), as in sitting with the student. Such opportunities allow the assessor and teacher to determine the student's entry skills and to gain insights into how the student is processing information related to the assigned learning task. Data obtained from these authentic opportunities are used to establish instructional-level conditions that enable the student to perform at his or her best. Classroom management, organizational skills, grouping practices, accommodations, and aligning instruction with the common core standards are vital. However, these variables are secondary to ensuring that the instructional match exists during the ongoing assessment and teaching process.

If schools are to become effective learning communities, where teachers work together to inform and to improve their instructional practices, then the vision of what meaningful assessment entails needs to change. Since the practice of monitoring and evaluating student progress does not contribute directly to delivering effective instruction, this narrow use of assessment needs to be strategically withheld until the instructional match is firmly in place, and once confirming and corrective feedback have become routine. Instead of perpetuating assessment practices that compare and rank students with little regard to how instruction bears down upon them, assessment should always focus on ensuring that optimal learning conditions exist for the student as a precondition to establishing and maintaining the instructional match.

Chapter 2

Broken Child or Broken Match:
A Matter of Choice

*Each year our knowledge progresses, each year we push back the
curtains of ignorance, but there remains so much to learn. Our
theories are only dancing shadows against a hard wall of reality.*

Haunted Mesa, Louis L' Amour (1992)

Educational assessment has historically been used for comparative and placement purposes, the rationale being that instruction is best served when students are aptly placed. Students who meet grade-level expectations have remained in regular classroom settings, whereas students who lag behind have been singled out to receive special instruction elsewhere. Our thinking about the pros and cons of this practice, however, relates directly to the choices we make based upon our beliefs and assumptions. We can choose to believe that a student's learning difficulties are inherent to the student—thus the concept of the "Broken Child"—or we can choose to believe that the vast majority of learning difficulties that students exhibit are created by mismatched curriculum and instruction—thus the concept of the "Broken Match." A person's beliefs and assumptions are fundamental to how the learning needs of struggling students are actually viewed and addressed. These assumptions influence whether resources and services are provided, whether solutions are pursued and, sadly, whether a solution is even thought possible. This chapter explores the concepts of the broken child and the broken match, including the belief system and assumptions upon which they are based. Further, we describe how beliefs and assumptions predispose how assessment is practiced and how data are interpreted.

THE CONCEPT OF THE BROKEN CHILD

Fortunately, the majority of students experience ongoing success in school, with many performing at very high levels of academic proficiency. However, there is a large percentage of students who are constantly at risk of failing academically. These students, regardless of how hard they work, still perform at the bottom of the achievement ladder. Learning is challenging and frustrating because they make such limited progress when compared to the achievement of other students. Faced with the lack of progress, parents, teachers, school officials, and support personnel are confronted with the same lingering question: *What is wrong with the child that is causing the child to fall behind and fail when other children are progressing and achieving grade-level success?*

Educators often describe these children as being different—a view that is not the same as acknowledging that students learn in different ways and at different speeds. It is a more deep-seated belief that something is inherently wrong with how the child learns (Harry & Klingner, 2007). This perception assumes that since the student lags behind and has trouble learning that somehow the child is broken, a view repeatedly reinforced through the use of labels such as minimal brain dysfunction, central processing disorders, dyslexic, and specific learning disabilities. The fact that a sizable percentage of school-age children have real difficulty acquiring basic skills, comprehending, retaining information, and keeping pace with their age-related peers merely perpetuates the general perception of inherent differences. The metaphor of the broken child is a haunting reminder of the struggles far too many students face each school day. Inwardly, they want to know why they feel like such failures, and why they are unable to learn and perform as well as their age-related peers.

Faulty Assumptions of the Broken Child

Students who struggle in school are not new to education nor are the desires of teachers to help them improve and achieve. Historically, though, our system of education has first required that students who struggle and lag behind be deemed as deficient learners before receiving support. Title I, special education, reading support, and other similar programs are all rooted in the same belief that faltering academic progress is due to inherent differences. Believing that the lack of student progress is due to some sort of inherent deficit or defect is based on a number of faulty assumptions that directly influence how assessment and instruction are viewed and practiced with regard to these students.

Faulty Assumption 1: Learning problems reflect internal deficits

Since most students make suitable grade-level progress when provided with typical classroom instruction, the assumption is that something must be internally wrong with students who habitually struggle when receiving the same instruction. This belief adheres to a medical viewpoint for explaining students' learning difficulties— that is, deficiencies or deficits exhibited in students' learning *(illness)* need to be correctly identified *(diagnosed)* and addressed *(treated)*. As a result, the "refer-test-place" model has pervaded education for nearly a half a century, and has become the preferred method for providing support services. This approach, though, has failed to consistently demonstrate positive results. For example, nearly 35 years of study have provided no assurance that appropriate instruction occurs as the result of being placed in special education for the mildly handicapped (Allington & McGill-Franzen, 1989; Allington & McGill-Franzen, 1996; Dunn, 1968; Glass, 1983; Hattie, 2011; Kavale, 1988; Lipsky & Gartner, 1987; Skrtic, 1991; Walmsley & Allington, 1995; Wang, Reynolds, & Walberg, 1987; Will, 1986).

Faulty Assumption 2: Students who struggle require specialized services

Over the past 30 years, regular classroom teachers have been led to believe "I don't have the skills," and/or "that it isn't my job" to teach the most challenging and less able students (Algozzine & Ysseldyke, 1983; Walmsley & Allington, 1995). The assessment and instruction of these students was considered best left to the learning specialist. Naturally, the emergence of the role of the "specialist" reinforced the belief that less able students learn in unique ways and require professionals with special preparation beyond the training available to regular classroom teachers (Allington, 1994). The assumption that struggling students learn differently has diverted attention away from the fact that the learning problems experienced by most students are directly attributed to how curriculum and instruction are routinely selected and taught (Skrtic, 1991). This viewpoint has led to the next faulty assumption.

Faulty Assumption 3: Curriculum and instruction are neutral

Although learning represents the interaction between curriculum, instruction, and the student, the lack of learning is generally assumed to be the fault of the student, holding curriculum and instruction harmless. However, students who fall behind do not want to fail—most failure is imposed upon them. Such students have become casualties of an increasingly rigid system of education that basically expects everyone to make the same uniform rate of progress given the same pace of instruction (Gickling & Havertape, 1981; Hargis, 2006; Rosenfield, 1987).

Unable to keep pace with the lock-step nature of grade-level instruction, many students are victimized by how curriculum and instruction are delivered. Although the onus for failing to keep pace has fallen upon the student, rarely is the curriculum, and how it is being taught, viewed as a contributing factor. Our grade-level system of instruction has been largely content to assess the performance of struggling students without taking into account how curriculum and instruction affect their poor performance.

Faulty Assumption 4: Individualization means one-to-one instruction

The frustration voiced by classroom teachers most often stems from trying to provide individualized instruction for each student. Unfortunately, these teachers have interpreted individual instruction to mean one-to-one instruction, a view that is far too narrow. This view regrettably has perpetuated the false assumption that instructional services for struggling students should primarily be delivered by the specialist. However, the concept of individualizing, in its most basic form, represents creating and maintaining optimal learning conditions for all students. Getting the conditions right for learning and teaching ensures that all students are able to acquire the knowledge and skills to be successful. As discussed in the forthcoming chapters, creating individualized instruction can be accomplished when teaching multiple students at the same time.

Faulty Assumption 5: Failure is required before services can be provided

Our educational system has historically been one of imposed failure before support can be provided. To receive support a student must fall behind and experience a degree of failure before access to special programs are justified. Instead of emphasizing prevention and/or early intervention, the traditional eligibility process first requires a level of deficiency to be manifest. This prolonged delay has resulted in increased frustration and less learning. A more sobering way of viewing the entire "refer-test-place" process is to understand that it legitimizes student failure. Once failure occurs, it is the same failure that provides the foundation for justifying the system of labeling disabilities and for entitling students to receive additional educational support.

Education's Bypass System of Support

Faulty assumptions have influenced how educators and policy makers view the learning needs of struggling students and have dictated how assessment and instruction should be practiced and funded. The result has been the creation and maintenance of a system of "add-on" programs (e.g., supplemental reading, after-school tutoring, etc.) designed to serve students who perform outside the so-called normal bands of achievement and adaptive behavior. While this is an accepted approach, its outcomes have been less than stellar, resulting in little coordination and planning as well as fragmented learning (Allington & McGill-Franzen, 1989). What is ironic about this approach is that students with less skill are placed in disjointed programs where they are expected to overcome their learning problems while students with more skill receive the benefit of more stable and consistent instruction (Slavin & Madden, 1989).

Moreover, add-on programs serve to bypass input from regular classroom teachers concerning the planning for their struggling students. Instead of seeking their input, this system of support encourages teachers to refer students for special assessment and services. Once officially referred, the system assumes responsibility for evaluating and placing these students. As these events unfold, planning decisions concerning instruction in the regular classroom are "bypassed" in favor of the student receiving either small group or one-to-one instruction outside the regular classroom setting (see Figure 2.1).

This "bypass" system diverts attention away from the classroom setting, creating the impression that classroom teachers are no longer responsible for or capable of providing such students with the best instruction. More and more of the instruction of these students is directed by specialists. At the same time, the vital role that regular classroom teachers and regular classroom settings play in the social and learning development of the students is minimized. The craziness of the bypass system is that while its structure wields increasing influence in the instructional planning of these students, it diminishes the classroom teacher's role in their planning, even though these students continue to receive the vast majority of their instruction within the classroom. For example, Cunningham and Allington (1999) estimate that for those students who receive "specialized" instruction outside the regular classroom, 75-85% of their school day is actually spent within regular classroom settings.

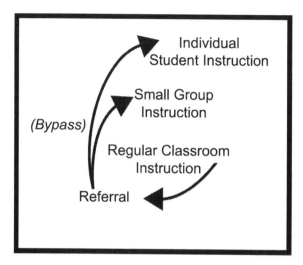

Figure 2.1 The Bypass System of Support

We are by no means suggesting that individual and small-group instruction has no benefit. On the contrary, there will always be the need for individual and small group instruction. We are instead saying that pullout services need to be scaled back in favor of providing more support directly within the regular classroom. Providing in-class support is far more efficient and effective in helping classroom teachers expand their assessment and instructional skills, especially when teaching their most vulnerable students.

Whether the bypass system of pullout programs continues to dominate education in the future depends to a large extent on how two competing issues are resolved. First, the pressure school officials and teachers face in preparing an increasing number of students to pass annual high-stakes tests in order to satisfy ever-changing federal mandates (e.g., CCSS) perpetuates pulling students into specialized programs separate from classroom instruction. It is understandable why school officials want classroom teachers to maintain a rigorous instructional pace aligned with the standards. It is also understandable why the regular classroom teacher is reluctant to take time away from instructing their entire classes to work with individual students.

The pressure directly competes with the second issue—teachers' professional sense of responsibility. They recognize the necessity of helping students work toward achieving the CCSS and providing them with intensive intervention when needed, as stated in the 2004 reauthorization of IDEIA. They support the principle of inclusive education and the practices associated with differentiated instruction and they desire to work collaboratively to achieve the goals these principles and practices espouse.

Whether the current multi-tiered systems of support (i.e., RTI and MTSS) will change the bypass system of support remains to be seen. If the RTI process ultimately encourages classroom teachers to be more reflective and to become actively engaged in creating instructionally-matched conditions for their struggling learners, then a great deal will have been accomplished. However, if RTI simply means more intensive screenings, identifying more students as deficient, and pulling more students out of the classroom for extended tutoring for the purpose of having students pass grade-level benchmarks, then nothing substantially will have changed.

THE CONCEPT OF THE BROKEN MATCH

Unlike the broken child concept, the broken match reflects what happens when learning tasks and their related instruction are well beyond the student's ability to function. The concept reflects a gap or mismatch between the student's prior knowledge and entry skills and the demands imposed by the spiraling nature of curriculum and instruction. As the learning gap widens, so does frustration. Although able to learn bits and pieces, the student is still unable to connect sufficient amounts of new information effectively with what he or she already knows. Unlike the metaphor of the broken child, the broken match poses a very different question: *Why is it so difficult to establish and maintain the instructional match for the struggling student when the instructional match is the cornerstone of effective learning and teaching?*

Creating a favorable instructional match for students involves bringing curriculum and instruction into alignment with respect to what the student knows and what he or she can do. The challenge for the assessor and teacher is to consistently manage the variability that occurs routinely within curriculum and instruction to enable the struggling student to perform at optimal levels.

Instructional Variability

While a wealth of information exists concerning what makes instruction work, findings from the Beginning Teacher Evaluation Studies (Denham & Lieberman, 1980) serve our purpose to illustrate this subject. Instead of waiting for end-of-year test results to assess student performance, the BTES researchers developed an immediate and effective process for determining the quality of student learning, a process they identified as Academic Learning Time (ALT). High ALT is "the amount of time a student spends engaged in academic tasks that s/he can perform with high success" (Fisher, et. al., 1980, p. 8). High ALT situations exist where the student has a good grasp of the learning task and makes only occasional careless errors. Conversely, low ALT learning situations exist where the student fails to understand the learning task and responds at a chance level. Without going into detail, the ALT model provides a relevant approach for assessing student learning by directly observing the student's level of high ALT within the general classroom setting on a regular basis.

The BTES model includes five general teaching functions: diagnosis, prescription, presentation, monitoring, and feedback, as shown in Figure 2.2. These five functions are subdivided into 15 instructional variables—13 which affect student achievement positively and two which affect student achievement negatively. For our purpose we focused only on the teaching function of diagnosis, and on the two variables negatively associated with student achievement. Although limited in scope, the various diagnostic functions reflect how well classroom teachers know their students in terms of what they can and cannot do.

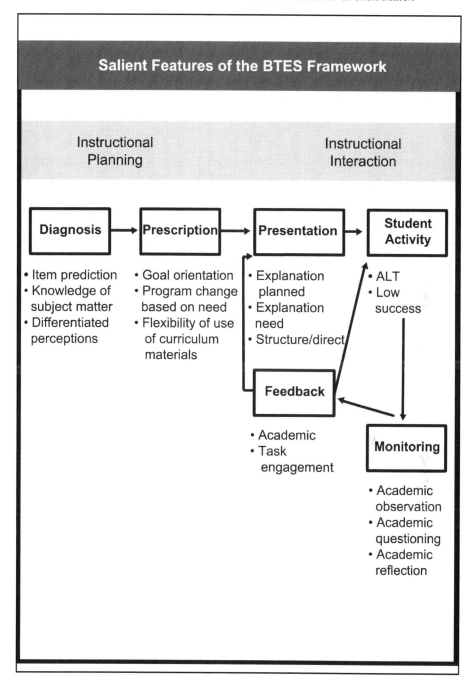

Figure 2.2 The 15 variables used in the BTES operational framework   (See Denham & Lieberman (Eds.), *Time to Learn*, page 79)

The research results showed that student achievement improved when teachers were able to accurately predict what their students could do and successfully identify what their students needed.   Such teachers were less likely to prescribe materials that were too hard for them, which resulted in students consistently demonstrating higher levels of task engagement and task success. This was not the case for teachers who lacked good diagnostic skills.   Students of these teachers were less engaged, experienced less task success, and had lower achievement levels (Romberg, 1980).

The two variables negatively associated with student achievement were "explanation need" and "low success." Explanation need referred to situations where students did not understand their learning tasks, made frequent mistakes, and needed additional explanation.   As Romberg (1980) observed, "one would hope…that explanation would be given in a manner timely enough to reduce overall confusion and increase the percentage of time coded as high success" (p. 86).   However, when additional explanation and assistance were given, the students who struggled remained confused.

> The explanation did not solve the problem since, in the long run, the student had little high success. Frequent need for explanation may be a signal that changes are needed in the student's instructional program, either in the difficulty of the assignments or in preparation for seatwork (Fisher, et al., 1980, p. 21).

A key finding was that, although added explanation and tutorial assistance may help students complete various learning tasks, apparently added explanation masks the fact that much of instruction remains innappropriately matched. As a consequence of needing additional explanation, this type of temporary fix fails to result in long-term academic success. The fact that extra explanation and tutorial assistance are constantly needed during instruction is a signal that students are not making the kind of connections that promote understanding. The resulting conclusion is that relying on the repetitive type of intervention to achieve minimal success illustrates how curriculum and instruction are easily misaligned, which in turn prolongs the broken match.

As would be expected, mismatched tasks and mismatched instruction result in low success. Regrettably, students experiencing low success are the very students whose abilities, prior knowledge, and learning rates are ignored when teachers are pressed to maintain grade-level progress. This does not imply that struggling students do not try to stay engaged; instead, it merely substantiates the fact that because of their lack of prior knowledge and skills they have real difficulty connecting what is taught with what they already know and are able to do.

The BTES remains one of the most detailed and comprehensive databases assembled involving the relationship between allocated time, task-engaged time and student achievement (Borg, 1980), and its findings remain particularly appropriate and valid today. With the emphasis on increasing educational standards and achieving annual yearly progress as measured by high-stakes testing, the fate of students who need excessive explanation and who receive low success is largely predetermined. These students are summarily assigned to after-school and summer tutorial programs or have to repeat the grade they failed for the purpose of raising their test scores.

Curriculum Variability

The variability of instructional delivery is only exceeded by the variability of curriculum materials. There are tremendous differences in the amount of curricula to be covered in different classrooms, as well as the amount of time given to covering different areas of the curriculum (Wiley & Harnischfeger, 1974). In addition to the amount of coverage, there is variability in the difficulty level of the curricula across and within grade levels, and across and within content areas within the same grade level (Doran & Fleischman, 2005; Popham, 2005). Similar variability is routinely found among and within reading materials. Genre, language concepts, and vocabulary vary enormously within grade-level materials and also within books that purportedly represent the same reading level of difficulty. This type of variability can also be found from page-to-page and from paragraph-to-paragraph within the same story.

Such variability in curriculum has always been present and denotes why educators need to carefully select the use of reading material when assessing and teaching children with limited prior knowledge and reading skills. Lane's (1975) original readability research, for example, found that the difficulty levels of primary-grade basal readers varied from one to three years (see Figure 2.3). Even greater variability was noted in the difficulty levels of intermediate-grade reading materials. These ranges only increased with each ascending grade.

Further, the language and concepts vary as well. In analyzing children's literature, Cunningham and Stanovich (1998) found that children's literature contains more sophisticated vocabulary than nearly every form of oral language. They further acknowledged "that the level of vocabulary in story books for preschoolers is at approximately the same level as speech between college graduates" (p. 38).

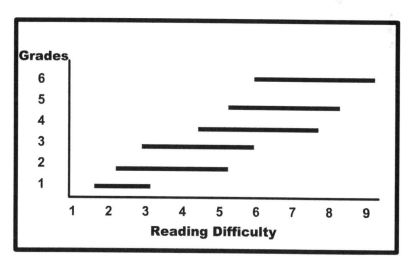

Figure 2.3 Estimated ranges in the difficulty levels of basal readers and trade books used in grades one through six (Lane, 1975)

Student Variability

Just as reading materials vary greatly, so too do students' reading skills. Carillo's (1964) classic research illustrated the overall range and variability of students' reading achievement test scores across first through eighth grade (See Figure 2.4). A close examination of the results shows that the reading test scores of first-graders ranged from a readiness level to third grade while the test scores for second-graders ranged from a readiness level to fourth grade. For each succeeding year the ranges in students' reading performance widened (see also Hargis, 2006).

More striking is the variability found in the reading performance scores of students considered to be average. The heavier bars embedded in each horizontal line in Figure 2.4 denote the scores of the middle 50% of each grade-level membership. Even average students demonstrated an ever-increasing range of scores from year to year. Hargis (2006) extended this research showing that an ever-increasing range of scores occurred for ninth through twelfth grade.

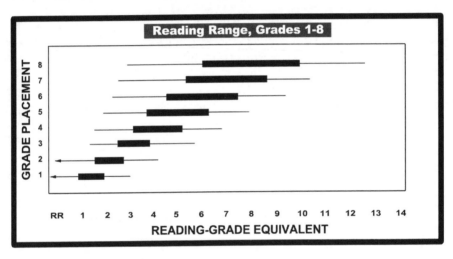

Figure 2.4 **Range of reading achievement test scores of students in first through eighth grade (Carillo, 1964)**

MANAGING THE VARIABILITY: THE CHALLENGE IN TEACHING

The variability existing across instruction, reading material, and student performance can challenge any teacher's ability to create suitable instructional matches for struggling readers. The ever-expanding content and language concepts, along with the fluctuating vocabulary demands of printed material generally, exceed the prior knowledge and entry skills of these students. A vicious cycle ensues with each succeeding reading lesson. The lack of reading skills combines with the challenge embedded within curricula, and instruction perpetuates that problem. As more mismatched instruction occurs, fragmented learning increases and gaps in learning widen, setting the stage for the next mismatched learning experience.

Providing appropriate instruction for struggling readers requires acknowledging that most of their learning problems are the result of poorly matched curriculum and instruction, rather than resulting from internal deficits. Those who cling to the concept of the broken child fixate on what is wrong with the student, believing that internal deficits are the issue. This is a faulty perception. In reality, the student is the most stable variable within the teaching/learning equation. To be more precise, what a student knows and what a student is able to do remains constant, and represents the key starting point for teaching and learning.

It is unfortunate that educators keep focusing on what they want the student to know, while ignoring what the student is able to do. Quality assessment and instruction prevent this from happening by identifying precisely what the student knows and can successfully do. While achieving the state common core standards is the ultimate goal, the ongoing focus of IA is to maintain an appropriate instructional match to ensure that optimal learning and teaching conditions exist and that student success is constant.

INSTRUCTIONAL ASSESSMENT (IA)

Effective management of the multiple variables that contribute to student learning is an essential assessment condition. While formative assessments are better able to inform instruction than summative assessments, neither achieves the goal of improving the quality of teaching and learning for most struggling readers. Nor do these forms of assessment enable teachers to manage the extensive variability that routinely exists within curriculum, instruction, and the limited entry skills of struggling readers.

IA on the other hand, provides the precision to manage this variability. Its structure encourages teachers and students to work collaboratively, to share their insights, and to use assessment data strategically to benefit both learning and teaching. The foundation of *IA* is one of determining the student's prior knowledge and entry skills and strategically using the data to manage the assessment process within appropriate levels of challenge. Assessment used in this manner allows the assessor and teacher to create the conditions that promote optimal student performance.

Furthermore, IA is consistent with the best practices of assessment as articulated within the *Standards for the Assessment of Reading and Writing* (1994). These standards stress the appropriate use of assessment, whereby the interest of the student must remain paramount.

> Assessment must serve, not harm, each and every student…We must recognize that assessment experiences, formal and informal, have consequences for students.....They have profound effects on students' lives. They may alter their educational opportunities, increase or decrease their motivation to learn, elicit positive or negative feelings about themselves and others, and influence their understanding of what it means to be literate, educated and successful.

First and foremost, assessment must encourage students to reflect on their own reading and writing in productive ways, to evaluate their intellectual growth, and to set goals. . . . In this way, students become involved in and responsible for their own learning and better able to assist the teacher in focusing instruction. Past assessment practices, particularly normative practices, have often produced conditions of threat and defensiveness for students. Constructive reflection is particularly difficult under such conditions. Thus assessment should emphasize what students can do rather than what they cannot do (p. 13).

A New Set of Assumptions

A new set of beliefs and assumptions have replaced old and ineffective beliefs and practices which failed to narrow the achievement gaps of struggling youngsters. These new beliefs and assumptions encourage targeting instruction at students' entry skills, providing direct and immediate support to teachers within the regular classroom setting, and developing collaborative professional relationships that support classroom teachers in providing direct instruction to their students.

Assumption 1: All students are ready to learn

Saying that all students are ready to learn does not mean that all students are ready to learn the same things at the same time and at the same pace. Nor does it mean that all students should receive the same intense instruction when entering school. As Allington (2001) indicated, there is an increasing recognition that acquiring reading facility is relatively easy for certain students and much more difficult for others. We know students vary a great deal in their ability to acquire new knowledge and skill (Caine & Caine, 1994; Carillo, 1964; Cook & Clymer, 1962; Hargis, 2006). To capitalize on their varying abilities, schools should be ready to accurately assess what students know and what they are able to do in order to tailor instruction to match what they are ready to learn.

By mandating that all students meet grade-level standards, policymakers have ignored the fact that students enter with different learning experiences and perform at different levels. While it is appropriate to have expectations, it is not appropriate to expect all students to perform at the same level at the same time (Hargis, 2006). Children are always learning and are always anxious to succeed, but they learn infinitely better when instruction is built around what they know and when the pace of instruction matches their learning rates. Ensuring that individual differences are accounted for enables students to work more systematically toward achieving the higher standards that schools desire.

Assumption 2: The instructional match is the foundation for learning

For years educators have believed that the way to help students succeed was to focus on their learning difficulties. The focus was on determining what was wrong with the student that inhibited learning. Only rarely did educators consider curriculum and instruction as possible sources of students' learning problems. We now realize that most learning problems reflect an inadequate match between a student's prior knowledge and entry skills and the ever-increasing demand made by the instructional setting (Gickling & Havertape, 1981; Rosenfield & Gravois, 1996). We realize that creating an appropriate match requires assessing the entry-level skills of the student in order to peg instruction to the student's instructional level (Rosenfield & Gravois, 1996).

Assumption 3: The student-teacher relationship within the general education classroom is the critical setting for intervention

A healthy student/teacher relationship within the classroom contributes to student learning. However, as Marzano and Marzano (2003) noted, students' academic success has little to do with the teacher's personality or with the friendship the teacher forms with students. Real success depends upon the teacher's ability to provide clear expectations and sound guidance, create cooperative learning environments, and respond in a timely way using appropriate interventions when the student is struggling.

Researchers refer to these teaching attributes as effective classroom management (Wang, Haertel, & Walberg, 1993; Marzano & Marzano, 2003; Marzano, Marzano, & Pickering, 2003). Rosenfield (1987) described these attributes as managing learning. We prefer to think of them as instructional management. Effective teachers are able to maintain control and discipline in their classrooms as an essential condition for learning. However, it is the teacher's effectiveness in managing instruction that is the primary factor contributing to student learning. How well teachers are able to match curriculum and instruction to the prior knowledge and entry skills of students is what truly enables students to achieve academically.

Assumption 4: Waiting for students to fail is unacceptable

Although there is wide agreement that early intervention provides the greatest possibility for success, educational practices have historically imposed severe delays before students are eligible to receive extra support. During these waiting periods little is accomplished except solidifying students' feelings of resentment and failure, including the possible mounting tensions and estrangement between students, parents, and teachers. Failure does little to help students succeed in the classroom and basically has no diagnostic value (Hargis, 1982). Waiting does little to address the real problem, which is that students need immediate support when struggling rather than being held hostage by the waiting game. Tucker (1988) paints a poignant picture of this flawed practice in the following allegory.

ISN'T THAT SPECIAL

The setting is a restaurant. It is the only restaurant in town
and there is only one item on the menu. You order the item
and finish it. You are still hungry, so you order more.

Waiter: I'm sorry, but that's all you can have. It's been determined by the Diet and Food Board that one serving is all that a normal person needs.

You: But I'm still hungry. Is there nothing you can do?

Waiter: There is one option. We have a very small serving room in the basement by the furnace, but it is only for malnourished persons.

You: Let's say that I'm malnourished then. Just point me to the basement.

Waiter: Before you can eat down there, you have to be evaluated by the malnourished examiner to determine if you are truly malnourished. Would you like me to refer you to the malnourished examiner?

You: How long will that take?

Waiter: We have only one examiner for this area, and he already has a heavy backlog of cases of suspected malnourishment. It will be at least two or three weeks before he can see you.

You: What! Three weeks! I'll starve by that time. Isn't it sufficient that I'm hungry?

Waiter: It's the law. The special malnourishment waiter downstairs cannot serve you unless it is verified by a team representing a number of disciplines that you are indeed malnourished.

You: This is unbelievable! I'm hungry, that's all. What kind of an evaluation can tell you more than that?

Waiter: As I understand it, there are any number of reasons why you may appear to be hungry or feel hungry. It is important, for example, to know how your mother fed you when you were young. Also, the examiner will go over all of the foods of the world to get some idea of what kinds of foods you may have missed in your life.

You: Does that mean you have those items on the menu in the basement?

Waiter: No. The menu down there is the same as it is up here. The only real difference is that down there the one item on the menu costs twice as much as it does up here.

You:	Let me get this straight. I'm hungry. In order to get anything else to eat, I have to wait three weeks to be evaluated in terms that are irrelevant to either my current hunger or to order the only existing item on the menu. Then if I am deemed sufficiently malnourished by a team of examiners, I will get the same food that you have on this menu, but I will have to pay twice as much for it. Have I left out anything?
Waiter:	That's about it.
You:	Why?
Waiter:	It's the law. Wonderful opportunity for the malnourished folks, don't you think?
You:	It may be okay for the malnourished, but it doesn't do a thing for the hungry.

© Tucker, 1993. Used with Permission

While this allegory contains several key points, its central message is that feeding students when they are instructionally hungry should not be delayed. Knowing that a student is struggling academically is sufficient reason to alter instruction. Requiring students to struggle and fail before services are provided is irresponsible, inhumane, and should not be tolerated. Sadly, teachers are also often forced to wait for failure before receiving assistance. Even with the creation of tiered structures, teachers are left isolated unless the student's learning difficulties become sufficient to warrant attention.

Assumption 5: Problem-solving improves through professional collaboration

We know there are no quick fixes for students who perform near the margins of school failure. But when faculty members share ideas and work collaboratively they "can more easily succeed in providing a strong learning community for students, particularly for those at the margins" (Rosenfield & Gravois, 1996, p. 16). When faculty members work together for the benefit of struggling students, professional collaboration becomes the cornerstone of problem-solving activity. Such activity is the heart of developing professional learning communities (DuFour, Eaker, & DuFour, 2005). Schools become places where teachers and students continually learn from each other and where the organizational structures within the school enable both students and teachers to ask for and receive timely assistance.

Requesting assistance, though, needs to expand beyond meeting the learning needs of students. It should also provide opportunities for professional growth, as illustrated by the following teacher's requests:

I need three or four of you to observe me several times during the semester. The part I think I really need help on is getting the kids to ask questions as we go along. I don't feel comfortable doing this just yet and I know you do it much better (Dolan, 1994, p. 147).

Nowhere is the need for professional collaboration manifest more than in working with students who experience reading difficulties. It is important to realize that reading assessment and reading instruction are not the purview of one specific discipline. Reading cuts across all disciplinary boundaries, as most rely on printed material as the principal medium of instruction. Elmore (2003) reiterated the need for interdisciplinary activity to strengthen our professional practices by offering these words of advice:

> Schools that are improving seldom, if ever, engage exclusively in role-based professional development—that is, professional learning in which people in different roles are segregated from one another. Instead, learning takes place across roles. Improving schools pay attention to who knows what and how that knowledge can strengthen the organization (p. 10).

While expertise is greatly appreciated in the teaching of reading, the task of improving and accelerating the reading skills of struggling students can no longer be the job of only the specialist working in isolation, removed from the action of the regular classroom. We have been down that road far too long without large-scale success. Most students who are at risk of reading and academic failure spend the majority of their instructional time within the regular classroom. For their instruction to be meaningful, additional support needs to take place in the classroom and be coordinated with what is being taught. There is simply too much fragmented learning when students go back and forth between regular and special programs to hope to narrow the achievement gap.

The expertise needed for effective assessment and instruction exists within the combined talents of teachers and support personnel. To activate these talents, changes in how schools are structured need to occur that allow for the inclusion of all students. Greater collaboration within and across regular classroom settings is necessary in order to support improved reading assessment and literacy practices of everyone.

SUMMARY

The fact that we have students who struggle in schools is not in question. However, our beliefs and approaches to support these students is a debate worth having. Two views of children who constantly struggle in school were put forth in this chapter, the view of the "broken child" and the view of the "broken match." For far too long education has been beholden to the broken child mentality. The result has been assessment practices aligned with the medical model, and support systems that bypass the classroom teachers. It is only when achievement falls below grade-level norms that such programs emerge as safety nets for failing students. While safety nets may meet the immediate needs of struggling students, they fail to improve the instructional skills of classroom teachers in meeting the increasingly diverse learning needs of all students.

We present a different set of assumptions and thereby a different choice-- that of the broken match. As practitioners, we have a choice whether to follow the traditional assessment path that focuses on student deficits or to follow the path of creating instructional matches. Our preference is the latter. We reaffirm Rosenfield and Gravois' (1996) belief that "looking for deficits within a student benefits neither the teacher nor the student in reaching the ultimate goal" (p. 8). If educators are to achieve the goal of reaching every student, then assessment's role must focus on ensuring that curriculum and instruction are matched so that students achieve continuous success and perform at their best.

Chapter 3

The Instructional Match: The Central Feature of Quality Learning and Quality Teaching

Success can be facilitated for children by classroom teachers who know what an instructional match is, how to use assessment data to discover it, and how to manage instruction and curriculum to maintain it.

(Papandrea, 2003)

If we are serious about improving learning and instruction then assessment practices must be concentrated on creating and maintaining instructional conditions that support the student who struggles. Assessment is far more productive when the learning conditions enable the student to function optimally and receive meaningful feedback before monitoring and evaluating the student's performance. From our viewpoint, far too much attention is placed on monitoring and measuring the performance of students and on singling out students who fall behind as being learning deficient. This practice occurs to the detriment of observing how students learn and creating the conditions that enhance their learning (Edwards, Turner, & Mokhtari, 2008). In this chapter, we describe the genesis of this viewpoint beginning with our formative work in curriculum-based assessment (CBA, Gickling, 1977) and its evolution into what we now refer to as Instructional Assessment (IA).

Gickling realized early in his career that assessment was not serving instruction as it should, but observed two seemingly incompatible issues. The first issue involved the educational establishment's predisposition to use assessment primarily to identify students' deficiencies and then to hammer away instructionally in an attempt to correct such deficiencies. This occurred without understanding how curriculum and instruction exacerbates students' learning difficulties. Collecting data simply to identify a student's deficiencies was an insufficient role for assessment, especially since the data failed to lead to better instruction and improved achievement.

The second issue centered on ensuring that students received instruction that matched their instructional reading levels—levels where both learning and teaching could be maximized. The importance of the instructional-level concept was never questioned. Starting with the work of Betts (1946), the reading literature presented a history of the need to match materials and instruction to the student's functional reading level. Common sense indicated that reading tasks should contain appropriate margins of challenge in relationship to the student's individual reading skills sufficient to enable the student to demonstrate his or her best efforts (Gravois & Gickling, 2002, 2008; Gravois & Nelson, 2015). Matching reading materials at the student's instructional reading level has been one of the most enduring concepts in the literature

(Hargis, 2006). Simply stated, students learn best when reading tasks are not too hard or too easy.

Although the importance of matching reading materials and instruction to the entry-level skills of students had been firmly established, implementing this practice on a daily basis had proven extraordinarily difficult for teachers of struggling readers. The gaps between students' reading skills and the ever-changing vocabulary demands of grade-level materials resulted in frequent frustration. Of course, the problem of matching materials to reading needs is not new. Variation in instruction, the language and concepts of texts, genre, and the ever-shifting levels of vocabulary constantly keep these students off balance in their capacity to read. Informal reading inventories, readability formulas, and the leveling of books had been developed to address these disparities, all with varying degrees of success. However, none of these practices provided teachers with the consistency needed to create and maintain the instructional match for the truly struggling reader.

THE TURNING POINT

The turning point for understanding how to address these problems came to Gickling in 1975 while observing a student teacher's language arts lesson as part of a university teacher training program. The student teacher was teaching a repetitive cursive writing task that required a third grader to trace and copy various letters of the alphabet, names of months, and days of the week. Her instructions were explicit. The student was to trace a single letter before copying the letter on the line below. Similar instructions were given for tracing and copying the names of months and days of the week. The student began to trace and copy the first few letters and then proceeded only to copy the letters without first tracing as directed. Noting that he was not following the directions, the student teacher reminded him to "trace first and copy second," to which he replied, "Oh, I forgot." A similar pattern occurred in tracing and copying the names of months and days of the week. He would trace a word, copy it, then continue to copy the names of the months or days of the week only to be reminded to "trace first and copy second." This writing task and how the student responded is shown in Figure 3.1.

From observing the penmanship it was evident the student did not need additional practice tracing. His letter formations and handwriting were legible, but the student teacher continued to follow her lesson plan to trace first, not seeing what the student could do. This episode crystallized the difficulty classroom teachers confront in matching learning tasks to students' instructional levels. Traditional assessments routinely fail to identify what students know but instead focus on what students do not know. To be instructionally relevant, assessment must chart a different path—a path that focuses on identifying precisely what students know as a pre-condition for planning and delivering instruction.

A related observation indicated that the student teacher lacked experience with analyzing and problem-solving. For example, the student's construction of individual letters appeared not to be a problem. The breakdown occurred when copying the days of the week and months of the year. While he traced each word correctly, letter omissions were made during copying, but what was he doing? What

Figure 3.1 Cursive tracing and copying activity of a third-grader

was the pattern that resulted in *May* being written as *May* and *February* being written as *Febuay*? Further analysis disclosed that he was using the stem of a preceding letter to form the stem of the adjacent letter. For example, he used the down-stroke of the letter "a" as the first up-stroke for the letter "y" as when writing *May*.

This particular episode clarified the challenges faced by classroom teachers when trying to create instructional level conditions for struggling readers. Equally important, it redefined how assessment data could best be used to facilitate effective learning and teaching. This experience demonstrated how an overemphasis on correcting students' learning problems not only leads to over-teaching, but unintentionally increases student frustration. While classroom teachers are concerned about their students, our observations further confirm that within most classroom settings, teachers routinely over and under adjust as they attempt to match curriculum and instruction to students who are struggling.

This and related experiences forged a fundamental change in how we viewed the purpose of assessment and its role in informing and guiding instruction. The key to regulating the variability found in curriculum and instruction was not to focus on what the student did not know, but to focus on what the student did know. As our work progressed we realized the importance of actively interacting with students to gain insights into their learning and thinking. These related experiences caused us to focus and frame our work around five key assessment questions:

- What does the student know?
- What can the student do?
- How does the student think?
- What does the student do when unsure?
- Now what do I do as a teacher?

These questions over the years have helped us maintain a vigilant instructional focus. In more specific terms, these questions have helped guide three decades of research and practice studying the importance of creating and managing instructional-level conditions in order to improve the learning and achievement of low performing students (see, for example, Gickling, 1977; Gickling & Armstrong, 1978; Gickling & Havertape, 1981; Gickling & Rosenfield, 1995; Gicking, Shane, & Croskery, K.M., 1989; Gickling & Thompson, 1985; Gravois & Gickling, 2002, 2008; Thompson, Gickling, & Havertape, 1983; Tucker, 1985).

CURRICULUM CASUALTIES

A fuller appreciation of the literacy issues germane to the concept of the instructional match requires an awareness of how the oral and print processing skills must align with the expectations of curriculum and instruction. For struggling students there is often a misalignment of their oral and print processing with the demands of curriculum and instruction. Failure to understand, confront, and resolve these misalignment issues results in instructional experiences that accumulate to produce curriculum casualties—students who fall further and further behind and are ultimately viewed and labeled as disabled (Gickling & Armstrong, 1978; Hargis, 1982).

Hargis (1989) noted that language processing requires both comprehension and production. However, before language can be comprehended and produced, the child must first attain an explicit knowledge of its spoken form. After comprehending spoken language the child then needs to learn to read and interpret its printed form and then be able to reproduce its spoken form in written form.

Figure 3.2 denotes four scenarios that commonly occur when we fail to adequately address both the oral and printed language skills of students. At the oral-processing level, the student may not have acquired the language and conceptual base to understand what is being taught or, in a second scenario, a student may possess the skills to listen to and understand the language and concepts being taught but never receive the content due to insufficient reading skills. At the print-processing level, a third scenario exists when students lack the necessary entry skills required to read the material. In the fourth scenario, the instructional pace simply moves too fast for the student to keep up. The learning gaps portrayed in these scenarios only grow wider unless targeted action is taken.

Effective instruction requires that both the oral and print processing dimensions of language be assessed as a way to effectively match curriculum and instruction to the current skills of each student. As a general rule, instruction in print processing (i.e., reading and writing) needs to work in concert with the development of oral language (i.e., listening and speaking) for meaningful learning to occur.

Ongoing assessments must focus on the ability of the student to process both oral and printed language. Otherwise, students who have the ability to understand grade-level content, but are unable to read it, will be denied access to its content.

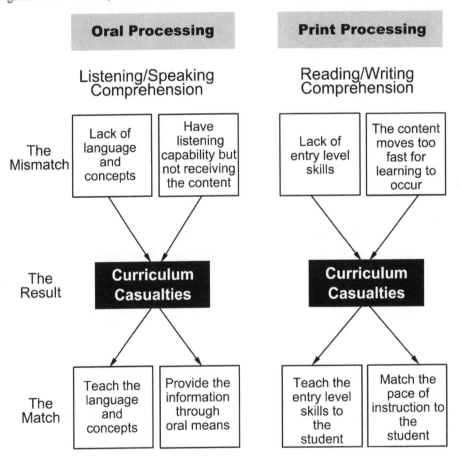

Figure 3.2 Oral and print processing effects on student listening, reading, and writing performance

Such a practice merely ensures that the student will fall further and further behind in mastering what is being taught. When a student lacks sufficient reading skills, yet possesses the oral language skill to understand grade-level content, opportunities to participate in oral presentations should be made available. Oral presentations (e.g., read-alouds, partner reading, etc.) ensure that the student will receive the same content and concepts offered to their more capable reading peers. Comprehension should always be the primary consideration when addressing any oral and print processing concern.

THE LEARNING TRIANGLE

Three variables largely influence learning--the student, instruction, and the learning task (Bloom, 1976). These three variables are depicted in Figure 3.3 as the points of the learning triangle. How well these three variables are synchronized determines if, what, and how much academic gain is actually achieved by the student. Unfortunately, when a student struggles, the natural tendency is to become fixated on the student as the cause for the lack of learning. The ensuing discussion becomes narrowly centered on the student and on student-related variables. In contrast, instruction and the learning task are usually ignored as contributing factors even though these two variables are under the teacher's direct control. When faced with the struggling learner, educators typically spend 90% of their time focusing on only 1/3 of the variables that influence learning. More disturbing, the time is spent on discussing the one variable (i.e., the student) over which they have the least control. For this practice to change, teachers and related school personnel need to gain a better

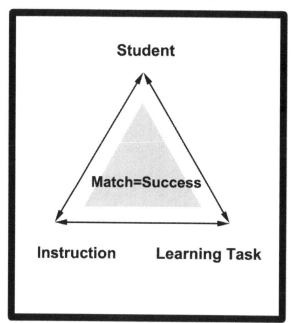

Figure 3.3 The Learning Triangle

appreciation of the importance of all three learning variables and their relationship to one another.

Student Variables

Student variables comprise all that the student brings into the learning situation and, to a large extent, dictate what the student is able to produce in the form of meaningful outcomes. Student variables include both internal factors associated with learning, such as processing skills, interest, and motivation to learn, as well as ecological factors, such as socioeconomic background and family support. While interest, motivation, and personal experiences are important factors that influence learning, they are often over-emphasized at the expense of attending to a student's prior knowledge.

Prior knowledge refers to the skills and experiences that a student possesses and reflects the content skills and mental schemata the student uses to connect new learning to existing knowledge (Shapiro, 2004). These "pre-sets" for learning--prior knowledge, prior experiences, and entry skills--are central to all learning. Dochy, Segers, and Buehl (1999) and Wolfe and Brandt's (1998) research confirmed Bloom's (1976) observation that success in current learning is highly contingent upon the cumulative knowledge the student has gained from previous experiences. Conversely, the lack of prior knowledge, or its inaccurate use, can adversely affect how the student learns and what the student acquires (Shapiro, 2004). To paraphrase Bloom (1976), no matter how well the teacher prepares, manages the class, or delivers instruction, the lack of prior knowledge is generally reason enough for the student to struggle with mastering the learning task.

Slavin (2003) noted that students do not spontaneously use prior knowledge to connect new situations to existing information. The fact that they do not automatically generalize requires the assessor to actively engage the student to gain an accurate understanding of the student's prior knowledge. Although activating prior knowledge is increasingly recognized as an important function of effective teaching, it is often ignored as part of the ongoing assessment. In contrast to traditional assessment practices that require all students to be tested the same way regardless of their prior knowledge and skills, IA deliberately honors and incorporates students' prior knowledge into the assessment and instructional process.

Instructional Variables

The second major influence on learning is the instruction provided to students. Instruction reflects the delivery system teachers use to provide students with formal and informal opportunities to learn. It represents the interplay that occurs between the teacher and the learner as the teacher guides the learner through various learning experiences (Thompson & Gickling, 1992). As a component of the learning triangle, the importance of instruction cannot be overstated. As Sanders (1998) succinctly noted:

Of all the contextual variables that have been studied to date (indicators of school socioeconomic status, class size, student variability within classrooms, etc.) the single largest factor affecting academic growth of populations of students is differences in the effectiveness of individual classroom teachers. When considered simultaneously, the magnitude of these differences dwarfs the other factors (p. 27).

Students flourish under the guidance of highly effective teachers. More importantly, the group benefiting most are low-achieving students, as highlighted in the 1998 spring issue of *English Update* (see also Chetty, Friedman, & Rockoff, 2011). Figure 3.4 displays the Terra Nova Achievement Test scores of first-graders in five different states: California, New Jersey, New York, Texas, and Wisconsin. In this research, students taught by highly effective classroom teachers were compared to students taught by typical classroom teachers. Composite reading scores consisted of both passage reading and vocabulary development while word-analysis scores reflected decoding skills.

As shown in Figure 3.4, the gains made by low-achieving students taught by highly effective teachers consistently surpassed the gains made by low-achieving students taught by typical classroom teachers. As noted by the researchers, "the lowest achieving students in the most effective teachers' classrooms out-scored their peers in the more typical classrooms to a significant degree" (*English Update,* p. 9). Furthermore, the word-analysis scores of low-achievers surpassed those of average achieving students, whereas their composite reading scores were nearly equal to those of their average-achieving peers.

Highly effective teachers are catalysts for real learning. They strive to match each new learning task at the instructional level of each student and help each student make meaningful connections between their prior knowledge and skill and each new task being taught. Effective teachers organize and manage the learning environment to maximize the use of instructional time in meeting the varied needs of their students. They provide appropriate guidance and sufficient practice to allow students to master the skills and concepts taught and they expect continuous academic improvement from their students.

Task and Curriculum Variables

The final variable central to learning is the task itself. Curricula "can be understood as an array of interrelated instructional activities that facilitate the acquisition of complex skills, strategies, and knowledge" (Allington, 1990, p. 1), whereas learning tasks include the individual assignments and activities making up different areas of the curricula. Such tasks represent the ongoing work students are expected to master in order to acquire the knowledge and skill provided through the various content areas taught in school.

Bloom's (1976) theory of school learning not only exemplifies the central role of the learning task, but conceptualizes the learning task as a mediating variable (see Figure 3.5). Bloom's research reinforced the idea that the task a student was assigned was not a "neutral" variable. Rather, Bloom perceived that the student's cognitive

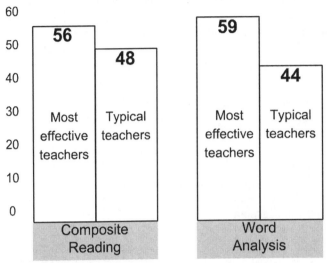

n=30 for the most effective teachers, 29 for the typical teachers

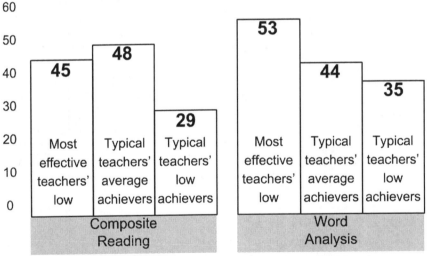

n=10 for the most effective teachers, 9 for the typical teachers

Figure 3.4 Differences in student reading performance comparing highly effective versus typical classroom teachers

and affective entry behaviors interact directly with each new learning task, as does the quality of instruction the student receives. Success is determined by how well the student's entry behaviors and the teacher's instruction match the demands of the learning task.

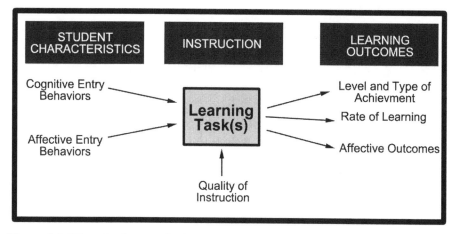

Figure 3.5 Bloom's theory of school learning

Cognitive entry behaviors are the prerequisite skills the student has attained relative to the learning task at hand; affective behaviors are the student's motivation to learn. Sufficient entry behaviors enable the student to connect new information meaningfully to what is known. Tasks convey the expectations of the curriculum and influence the instructional flow. These factors, along with the student's responses to the task requirements and flow of the curriculum, largely determine student-related outcomes—i.e., the level and type of achievement, rate of learning, and feelings about one's self as a learner.

The successful completion of task after task creates important antecedents for further learning. This cycle of success promotes a motivation to learn, stimulating the student's affective entry behaviors to learn (Borkowski, 1990; Meichenbaum & Biemiller, 1990). Variations in a student's cognitive and affective entry behaviors, together with the quality of instruction the student receives, are major reasons why student-learning outcomes are so varied.

CONDITIONS OF QUALITY LEARNING AND QUALITY TEACHING

Managing and aligning all three variables to establish the instructional match is essential for meaningful instruction and student achievement to occur. A successful match emerges when the three variables work in concert and in harmony (Gickling, 1990; Gickling & Havertape, 1981; Gravois, Gickling, & Rosenfield, 2011). Although the points of the learning triangle represent the critical variables, it is the reciprocal interaction between these variables that creates the right condition to optimize learning. This reciprocal interaction on a task-by-task basis largely determines whether students are successful, or whether they struggle and/or fail in school.

The Central Role of Prior Knowledge on Learning

The importance of prior knowledge on student learning is well documented, starting with the work of Bloom (1976), and supported by subsequent research (e.g., Wolfe & Brandt, 1999; Dochy, Segers, & Buehl, 1998). For example, in reviewing over 100 studies, Dochy, Segers, and Buehl (1999) concluded that the amount of learning variance accounted for by students' prior knowledge ranged from 25 to 81 percent. Tobias (1994) reported similar findings, with prior knowledge accounting for between 30-60% of the learning variance.

Building on these research findings and our concept of the learning triangle, Figures 3.6, 3.7, and 3.8 depict how student learning is influenced by different levels of prior knowledge. As shown in Figure 3.6, prior knowledge routinely accounts for as much as 50-60% of the learning variance for the average student. In this scenario, the variables of curriculum and instruction, and the general grade-level pace in which they are delivered, allow average students to perform at reasonably high levels. These students typically possess sufficient prior knowledge and skill to match the ongoing curricular demands of grade-level instruction. Instruction can be estimated to account for between 25-35% of the learning variance, while the mediating effect of learning tasks accounts for 5-15% of the learning variance.

Combining the student's prior knowledge and entry skills with the alterable variables of instruction and learning tasks is central to establishing the instructional match. Practically speaking, when these variables are matched, conditions for quality learning exist. These conditions enable learning experiences to become maximized—where the student's skill knowledge fits comfortably with the pace of instruction and the demands of the learning task (Rosenfield, 1987).

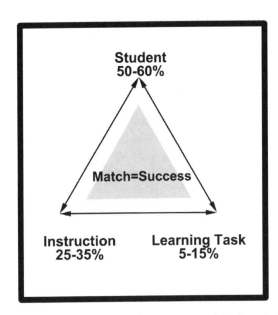

Figure 3.6 Estimated learning variance for average achieving students

The challenge of aligning these three variables rests with the teacher. The ability to create these matched conditions represents effective instruction. To reiterate, when the student's prior knowledge and entry skills are aligned with the instructional objectives and fit comfortably with the demands of the tasks, learning is the result. While quality learning exists when the instructional match is created, *quality teaching* exists when the teacher is able to create and sustain an instructional match for each and every student.

Quality Learning = Match = Success

Quality Teaching = Creating and Sustaining the Match = Success

But what about other types of students? While Figure 3.6 projects an overall picture of average achieving students, omitted from this picture are students not adequately challenged and students who are excessively challenged. We can hypothesize that, if prior knowledge were stratified based upon the highest and lowest achieving students, then the influence of the remaining two variables on learning outcomes would be strikingly different depending upon the prior knowledge of the students.

For example, high achieving students possess a great deal of prior knowledge and are able to draw upon a vast array of experiences. The prior knowledge of these students could account for as much as 80-90% of the learning variance (see Figure 3.7). Under these circumstances, the influence of instruction and task selection on the learning outcomes of these students would precipitously decrease, possibly accounting for as little as 5-10% of the learning variance. Such a depiction does not imply that teachers of these students are not important. It only suggests that the influence of curriculum and instruction is much less.

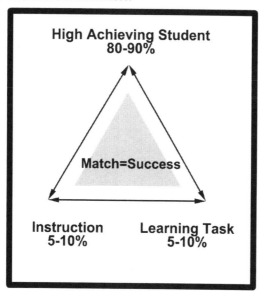

Figure 3.7 Estimated learning variance for high achieving students

Learning for high achieving students can at times appear effortless. As Smith (1978) observed, the more the student knows about a subject the easier it is for the student to dig deeper into the subject. Inasmuch as high achievers have more prior knowledge, it becomes easier for them to make new connections. They absorb new information and acquire academic facility quite easily, but they can also become bored due to the routine pace of classroom instruction and the lack of challenging content.

High achievers' extensive knowledge can be an asset for the teacher, but it also challenges the teacher to offer appropriate options and choices to sustain the instructional match. The key advantage is that teachers have more options when students have more prior knowledge and skill. They can draw from a larger repertoire of reading material and instructional objectives because these students have the skills to facilitate the instructional match.

The circumstances are reversed for low-achieving and struggling students. As depicted in Figure 3.8, the limited prior knowledge of these students puts them at a distinct disadvantage academically. Because of little academic success, their prior knowledge could account for as little as 15-25% of the learning variance, which means that the influence of instruction and task selection increases dramatically and could easily account for as much as 40-45% of the learning variance. Given these circumstances, the teacher's instruction and task selection bear a greater responsibility. Less prior knowledge not only increases the challenge for teachers to create matched conditions, it also restricts the choices and options they have available for selecting material and instructional objectives. The choices of materials and instructional objectives are often limited because the teacher must consider the entry skill of the student. Fortunately, though, when the match is strategically created and sustained, low-achieving students are the first to benefit from instruction provided by highly effective teachers (*English Update*, Spring 1998; Sanders, 1998).

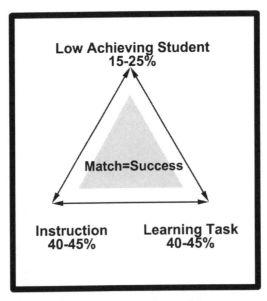

Figure 3.8 Estimated learning variance for low achievers

The evidence is clear that a lack of prior knowledge, a lack of attention to prior knowledge, and the failure to apply prior knowledge adversely affect how well students learn and progress in school (Shapiro, 2004). Even when students display sufficient prior knowledge, there is no assurance they will draw upon that knowledge and experience on their own (Slavin, 2003). This realization means that teachers not only need to accurately assess what struggling students know, they need to plan and actively use this knowledge as a routine part of ongoing instruction.

UNDERSTANDING APPROPRIATE CHALLENGE

Spady (1984) noted that "excellence occurs when the instructional system is able to provide the learner with an appropriate level of challenge and a realistic opportunity for success on a frequent and continuous basis" (p. 25). This is an apt description of Figure 3.3 where the legs of the learning triangle work in harmony to create an instructional system that provides the *learner* with an *appropriate level of challenge*. To be even more precise, appropriate levels of challenge should occur between each set of variables within the triangle--between the student and task, the student and instruction, and instruction and the task.

Unfortunately, understanding what constitutes an appropriate level of challenge has remained difficult for teachers to determine. This is especially true considering that teachers are expected to manage the challenge levels for multiple students from day to day within their classrooms. The concept of an appropriate level of challenge has generally been described as an "appropriate fit" or "comfort zone" where the student has the prerequisite knowledge and skill to learn from the curricula of the classroom and can benefit maximally from instruction (Rosenfield, 1987). Vygotsky (1978) described the concept as the "zone of proximal development" where learning occurs slightly beyond the student's entry skills and where the role of the teacher is to create challenge that exceeds this point but does not overwhelm the student.

While the concept of appropriate fit, comfort zone, or the zone of proximal development offers a general view of what a suitable level of challenge means, bringing the concept into instructional practice within the classroom has been elusive. The problem from our perspective is that beyond the concept, teachers have little sense of how to actually apply it. In contrast, our work has been dedicated to defining the concept in operational terms, thus enabling classroom teachers to create the conditions that optimize learning.

Defining Instructional Level Related to Reading

Prior to the introduction of Vygotsky's zone of proximal development, the reading community offered its own view of an an appropriate challenge, a view first researched by Betts (1946). Betts identified four discrete reading levels of challenge: *capacity, independent, instructional,* and *frustrational.* Reading capacity was described as the student's listening ability, whereas independent reading was described as easy or recreational reading. Instructional reading was described as the area where learning was enhanced and where "maximum development may be expected when the learner is challenged but not frustrated" (p. 449). Frustration resulted when comprehension started to deteriorate.

Betts (1946) operationalized these terms as a function of reading continuous text (e.g., passage reading). A *capacity level* was the highest level of material the student could understand when the material was read aloud to the student. A frustration level occurred when the student's reading error rate for word recognition and word meaning exceeded 5%. An instructional level occurred when the error rate was between 3-5%, and an independent level was where the error rate for word recognition and word meaning was less than 2 % (see Figure 3.9).

While Bett's original findings continue to permeate reading practices, it is interesting that only a handful of studies have been conducted to substantiate his research (e.g., Gickling & Armstrong, 1978). Recently, a study by Cramer and Rosenfield (2008) provided additional support for his concept. An important finding of their 2008 study was the need to consider the limitations of both word identification and word meaning when defining an instructional level in reading. They found that accuracy in word identification alone (i.e., word calling), versus the more encompassing concept of sight vocabulary (word identification with word meaning), was insufficient to promote comprehension, especially when working with traditionally underserved populations (e.g., minority, urban, etc.).

Experiencing frustrational and independent reading levels

The following passages contain identical information but different levels of difficulty. The first is written at a frustration level with only 80% known words and 20% unknown words, while the second is written at an independent level (98% known words and 2% unknown). Although you will be able to decode (i.e., pronounce) the fabricated words in the first passage and answer a few questions, the meaning of the passage will escape you. However, you will have no problem reading and understanding the second passage where the unknown vocabulary is limited to 2%. The concept of instructional level exists between the difficulty presented in the two passages.

THE BLIMBLAT

(80% Known)

Once when I was a yoder, my tomly and I were mayle in line to buy motts for the blimblat. Finally, there was only one plam between us and the mott counter. The plam made a big impression on me. There were eight utzs all probably under under the age of 12. You could tell ture did not have a lot of willen. Their pards were not yanker, but ture were clean. The utzs were well behaved, all of them mayle in line, two-by-two behind their potents holdin zibits. Ture were excitedly temering about the plums, fonts, and other yoks ture would see that noster.

It is important to recognize that, even at 80% known words, students can often engage and answer questions. For example, after reading the passage above, you would be able to correctly answer the following questions:

Who was mayle in line to buy motts?
How many utzs were under the age of 12?
What was not yanker?
What were ture excitedly temering about?

However, does being able to answer these questions convey a true understanding of the passage? Now read the passage written with 98% known words to compare how variation in task challenge impacts understanding.

THE CIRCUS

(98% Known)

Once when I was a teenager, my father and I were standing in line to buy tickets for the circus. Finally, there was only one plam between us and the ticket counter. This plam made a big impression on me. There were eight children, all probably under the age of 12. You could tell they did not have a lot of money. Their clothes were not expensive, but they were clean. The children were well-behaved, all of them standing in line, two-by-two behind their parents holding hands. They were excitedly temering about the clowns, animals, and other acts they would see that night.

(Adapted from Clark's Chicken Soup,
1997, p. 18)

Miller (2002) recounted how, in her early career as a first-grade teacher, the burden of word meaning and vocabulary impacted student learning. She noted how difficult it was for students to apply reading strategies when hardly any words were known. Likewise, she noted how difficult it was for students to apply reading strategies (e.g., decoding) when students knew nearly every word and had complete understanding. The preceding passages highlight the type of challenges teachers routinely face when trying to match instruction to the needs of both poor and capable readers.

Defining Instructional Level Related to Discrete Practice

The second research area involving the instructional level concept relates to tasks that address discrete skills (e.g., learning letters, sounds, sight words, math facts). Research originating during the 1970's and early 1980's expanded the concept of instructional level to include the conditions necessary for drill and practice activities. Observations of teachers who effectively manage the amount of challenge during rehearsal and practice activities at a ratio of approximately 80% known to 20% unknown show they are consistently able to increase the retention of information and elevate students' performance (Archer, et al., 1987; Shapiro & Elliott, 1999).

A recent literature review in this area found more research focusing on drill and practice activities than on actual reading. Most of these studies were designed to determine the "best" ratio of known to unknown sight-words for students (Burns, M.K., 2004; Gickling & Thompson,1985; MacQuarrie, Tucker, Burns, M.K., & Hartman, 2002; Neef, Iwata, & Page, 1980; Roberts & Shapiro, 1996; Roberts, Turco, & Shapiro, 1991). Depending upon the particular study, student population, and the nature of the practice tasks, these studies provided a range of ratios to use for achieving the best conditions for drill and practice. Although these studies resulted in different findings, in general any ratio below 50:50 known to unknown sight-words was likely to frustrate the student while a ratio of 90:10 did not provide sufficient challenge.

Defining Instructional Level Related to Working Memory

"Working memory is what you are paying attention to at any given point. So everything you are mulling over, making a decision about, or are learning, is at first in working memory" (O'Neil, 1996, p. 8). All new learning first appears in working memory. Before it is possible to organize and to store new information into long-term memory, it is processed in working memory. However, there are characteristics (limitations) to working memory that directly impact a student's ability to effectively and efficiently process information (Dempster, 1981; Miller, 1956; Pascuel-Leon, 1970). These characteristics include: (1) a limited capacity which gradually increases with age (see Figure 3.9), (2) a short-term focus needing total attention, and (3) a shut down feature when overloaded (Miller, 1956; O'Neil, 1996). Violation of any of these characteristics not only adversely impacts the student's ability to learn and retain new information but contributes to partial/fragmented learning.

Considering the variety of instructional and curriculum activities facing students, and taking into account the student's working memory capacity, Figure 3.9 summarizes the research-based guidelines for establishing instructional-level conditions. For reading continuous text, a general sight-word accuracy ratio of 93-97% known words with a 3-7% challenge is the preferred level. An accuracy ratio of 70-85% known items with a 15-30% level of challenge is the preferred level for drill and practice.

The Optimum Window for Learning

Figure 3.10 integrates the research on instructional levels and working memory to create an "optimum window" for student learning. This window provides a concrete way to conceptualize appropriate challenge when assessing and instructing students. The left-hand columns denote the student's age and related working memory capacity. For example, a three-year-old can generally process one new item at a time, a seven-year-old three new items at a time, and a fifteen-year-old or older can generally process seven new items at a time—plus or minus two (Miller, 1956; Willingham, 2009). Although these are general findings, they represent good starting points when

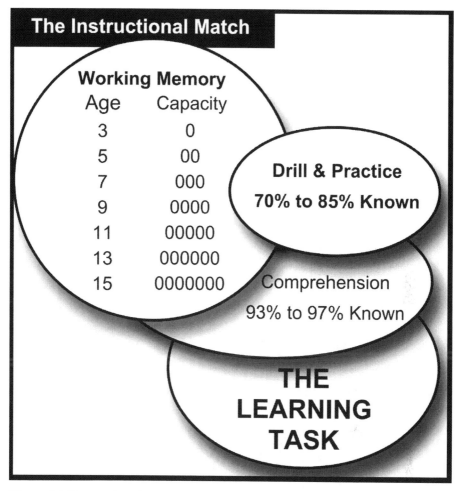

Figure 3.9 Researched Guidelines for Instructional-Level Conditions for Reading and Drill Activities

working with students.

These age-related guidelines do not imply that first-graders can learn only three new items per lesson or that fifth-graders can learn only five. Instead, they suggest that new information needs to be strategically organized and presented in limited sets so as not to overload working memory. Another way of saying this is that the amount of new information school age children can process comfortably at one time generally ranges from three to seven discrete items depending upon the age of the child. As illustrated in column three of Figure 3.10, these ranges are what Kirschner (2002) considers "cognitive load" or the size of the learning set. The fourth column displays the percentage of known sight-words routinely needed to comprehend reading material as described by Betts (1946). These numbers and percentages form the perimeter of what we refer to as the "optimal window of learning."

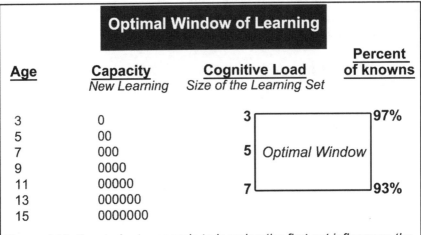

Figure 3.10 Optimal Window of Learning

It is important to stress that the guidelines depicted in Figure 3.10 should not be considered rigid and unchanging. Instead, they represent starting points for considering the amount of new information that can be introduced related to the developmental age of the student. The values suggest that new information is learned more efficiently when the information is strategically organized and presented in small learning sets. Individual differences in student learning are accounted for by observing how quickly the student learns a new set of information and then adjusting the size of the learning set to match the student's comfort level. When a decision is made to teach the student one set, or to teach more than one set, what is important to remember is that optimal learning and teaching conditions occur when the limits of working memory are not violated.

RESEARCH ON MATCHED INSTRUCTION

It is important to understand that creating matched conditions for students is more than a theory; it is a researched concept that influences student success. In studying the impact of task difficulty on struggling students, Gickling and Armstrong (1978) altered the task-related behavior of four first-graders and four second-graders by varying the challenge levels of their language arts tasks. The research was conducted over a seven-week period with each student participating in 21 one-hour sessions three days per week (i.e., Monday, Wednesday, Friday). The first six sessions consisted of assessing each student's prior knowledge and entry skills and gathering baseline data. The remaining 15 sessions were divided equally into three treatment conditions— frustrational, instructional, and independent. Language arts tasks were developed individually to reflect the different treatment conditions for each student. Observations of on-task (task engaged), task-completion (work attempted), and task-comprehension

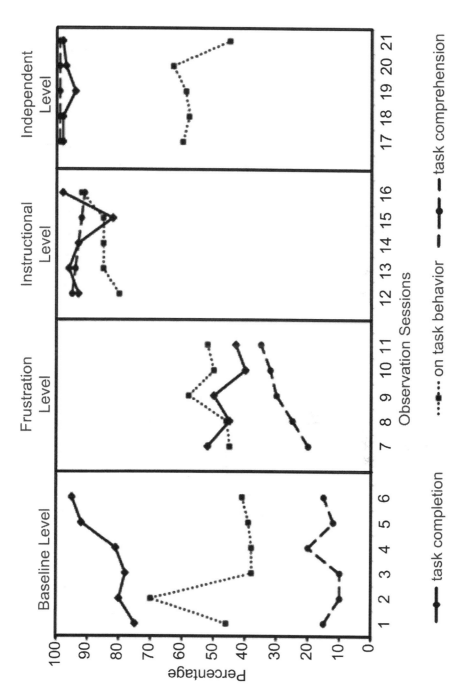

Figure 3.11 Effects of varying levels of difficulty on three task-related behaviors

(work understood) behaviors were conducted and data collected and converted into percentages. Figure 3.11 displays the mean percentages recorded across each of the observed behaviors during baseline and during the three treatment conditions.

As shown, the behavior patterns during baseline and frustrational conditions were poor and erratic, indicating the students had little understanding of their assigned tasks. Their task-related behaviors consistently ranged at or below the 50% level except in the case of work attempted. Instantaneous and dramatic changes occurred when instructional-level conditions were implemented. Task-completion rates averaged 96%, comprehension rates ranged from 87-94%, and on-task behavior ranged from 84-94%. In addition to high rates of academic behavior, it is noted that the three task-related behaviors were tightly clustered and stable.

Using a similar research format, Thompson, Gickling, and Havertape (1983) studied the effects of task difficulty by comparing students medically identified as Attention Deficit Disordered (ADD) with low-achieving (LA) and average-achieving (AA) peers. Two treatment conditions were the focus of the study (medication and type of instruction). On-task, task-completion, and task-comprehension behaviors were again the dependent measures. Table 3.1 displays the format and research schedule followed during the eight-week study.

The six ADD students were enrolled in six different elementary classrooms. The six low-achievers and the six average-achievers were selected from the same six elementary classrooms. The average-achievers were selected randomly from students functioning at grade level, whereas the low-achievers were selected due to their lack of academic progress. The ADD subjects received medication (M) or placebo (NM) under two treatment conditions: regular instruction (RI) or instructional-level conditions (CI). The low-achievers also received regular and controlled instruction, while the average-achievers, representing the controlled group, only received regular classroom

Subjects	Treatments			
Classrooms 1-6	Interval A weeks 1-2	Interval B weeks 3-4	Interval C weeks 5-6	Interval D weeks 7-8
ADD	M/RI........	NM/RI........	M/CI........	NM/CI........
LA	RI		CI	
AA	RI			
	Key $\underline{M}$ Medication phase $\underline{NM}$ No-medication phase $\underline{RI}$ Regular instruction phase $\underline{CI}$ Controlled instruction phase			
Observation Sessions	1 2 3 4	1 2 3 4	1 2 3 4	1 2 3 4

Table 3.1 Thompson, et al. (1983) 8 week experimental schedule

instruction. Direct observations of on-task, task-completion, and task-comprehension were recorded and converted to percentages similar to the study cited previously.

During Regular Instruction (RI), the ADD and low-achieving students exhibited similar lower levels of performance compared to the average-achieving students (see Figure 3.12). The one exception involved the use of medication on the on-task behavior of ADD students. Task completion rates (work attempted) remained in the 60-70% range for both the ADD and LA students but lagged behind the 85-92% completion rates of the average students. Task comprehension remained in the 60% range for the ADD students and in the 70% range for the LA students.

Under CI (instructional-level conditions), the performance patterns of the ADD and LA students rose substantially across all three task-related behaviors and were no longer significantly different from their average-achieving peers. Most importantly,

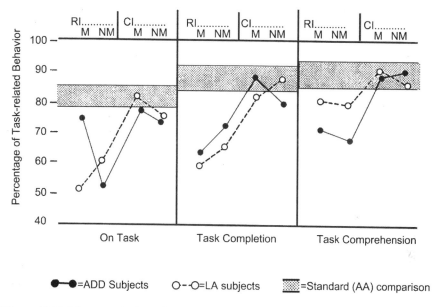

Figure 3.12 Mean on-task, task-completion, and task-comprehension percentages for ADD medicated (M) and non-medicated (NM) students and for low-achieving students under regular instruction (RI) and controlled instruction (CI) conditions

task comprehension remained firmly within the 80-90% range while task-completion rates remained within the 75-85% range. The effect of medication on ADD students did not appear to alter their task-completion or task-comprehension rates.

Together, these studies exemplify the profound effects that occur when struggling students are faced with learning tasks of varying levels of difficulty. More importantly, the studies demonstrate the positive outcomes that occur with knowing how to use assessment to create favorable learning conditions and knowing how to manage the conditions strategically to ensure learning success for struggling learners.

FUNDAMENTAL PRINCIPLES OF THE
INSTRUCTIONAL MATCH

Effective assessment and effective instruction are envisioned as integrated functions working fluidly to establish and support the development and maintenance of optimal learning conditions. This view holds that effective assessment and effective instruction are grounded on the same basic learning principles—principles that, when strategically organized and applied, support quality learning for the student. These principles are illustrated in Figure 3.13 in the form of a Roman arch, with each principle representing an essential building block for successful learning and teaching. Applied sequentially and strategically, they enable the student to perform at his or her best. Omission or violation of any one of the principles during either the assessment or instructional process contributes to the breakdown of the instructional match and can lead to poor assessment, instruction, and learning.

Activating Prior Knowledge

The pivotal role that prior knowledge plays in linking assessment to instruction was highlighted by the work of Bloom (1976). After conducting numerous learning and teaching observations, he concluded that students are not graded based upon what they learn in a particular course of study. Instead, they are graded based upon their lack of prerequisite skills before entering the course of study. Activating a student's prior knowledge is so important with regard to instruction that it is now considered the first step of an effectively taught lesson. Activating the student's prior knowledge, though, refers to more than simply recalling topical information. It requires helping the student strategically attend to the clues provided within the context of reading material, thus guiding the student's thinking to respond effectively.

Making Connections

New information is best acquired and used when it is linked strategically to prior knowledge and prior experience. The human mind constantly seeks to make connections between what is new and what is known. It takes in new information through the senses where it sifts, analyzes, and synthesizes the information in order to place it into meaningful categories (Wolfe & Brandt, 1998). When new incoming information is remote or alien to what the student knows, it has no meaning. When this happens, the information becomes irrelevant and quickly fades away (Crowley & Underwood, 1998).

Insufficient prior knowledge and experience often result in the student being quickly overloaded by the amount of new information to be learned, making it difficult to establish connections (Gravois & Gickling, 2008). In fact, it is not always easy to determine exactly what a student knows or how the student thinks when making connections. Chad's case illustrates this very point.

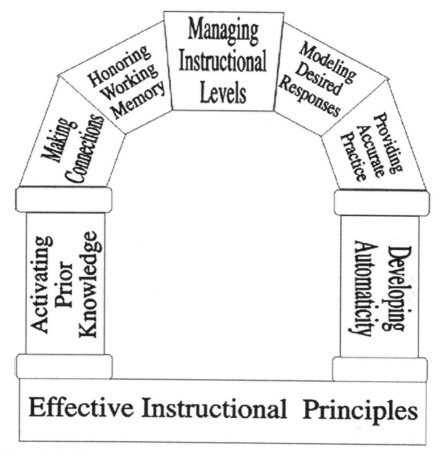

Figure 3.13 Effective learning and teaching principles

After reviewing the concept of alphabetizing with the second-grade class, Chad's teacher wrote the following words on the chalkboard: "Dog," "Cat," "Apple," and "Ball." She then asked her students to take out a sheet of paper and alphabetize the four words. Chad responded by writing the four words followed by writing four numbers:

Dog	3
Cat	4
Apple	2
Ball	1

Was Chad confused by the task? It initially appears that he was. Or are you the one that is really confused? Right or wrong, was there a pattern to his thinking? In terms of your own experience you would have chosen "Apple" as the first word, which is what Chad actually chose. Confused? Now look at the numbers from top to bottom. Number 3 was the first number Chad wrote, which referred to the third word down the list--the word "Apple." Number 4 was the second number he wrote and referred to the fourth word on the list--"Ball." Central to assessment's role is reflecting with students about their thinking. This determines precisely what a student knows as a foundation to designing and delivering instruction.

Honoring Working Memory

While making connections between new and known information is essential for learning to occur, the amount of new information needs to remain within the limits of the student's working memory to effectively maintain learning efficiency. Smith (1978) described working memory as being similar to a bottleneck where only a limited amount of fluid can flow through and be processed at one time. Similarly, too much new information causes processing to become backed up, disrupting and adversely affecting the student's ability to retain and use new information effectively (Gravois & Gickling, 2008). Further, this disruption causes some information to be lost, which contributes to partial and fragmented learning rather than learning that is connected and coherent. Likewise, if new information is not immediately acted upon, the short duration of working memory automatically clears itself.

Working memory is also strongly affected by emotion. Emotions can heighten awareness and strengthen the creation of new memory associations when positive learning experiences occur (Wolfe & Brandt, 1998), or emotions can have the opposite effect when associated with negative experiences. To the extent that the student becomes frustrated anxious, upset, or angry, these intrusive thoughts preoccupy the student's working memory (Jensen, 1998; O'Neil, 1996). Such thoughts seriously interfere with what the student should be learning, robbing the working memory capacity of the student.

Managing the Instructional Level

Efforts to activate a student's prior knowledge, to make meaningful connections, and to honor the limits of working memory converge at the instructional level. Fountas and Pinnell (1996) describe this level as the "Goldilock's Principle" where learning tasks should not be too hard, nor too easy, but just right. Wong, Groth, and O'Flahavan (1995) describe it as the level where the student can read with assistance but not independently. Managing instructional-level conditions represents the heart of the instructional match and is the keystone to the arch. Betts (1946) and Vygotsy (1978) identified this "sweet spot" conceptually by stating it is the favored teaching and learning place existing between independent and frustrational performance.

Performing within instructional-level conditions confirms for the student that he or she has the prerequisite knowledge and skill to engage the learning task successfully, which motivates the student to actively pursue the next new learning task

(Borkowski, 1990; Meichenbaum & Biemiller, 1990). The challenge for teachers, of course, is to manage each learning task at an instructional level so that the student is never pushed out of his or her comfort zone (Howard, 2009). It is the careful and wise management of instructional-level conditions that consistently enables the student to perform under optimal conditions.

Instructional-level conditions are not static. The concept does not refer to an assigned grade level or an assigned level of a particular book. Nor does it imply that students should all possess the same knowledge, perform at the same ability level, or work in the same material at the same rate. The concept instead refers to ensuring that favorable conditions exist that foster optimal learning and teaching. The instructional level concept does not inform teachers about what to teach per se. Its role consists of guiding teachers in a strategic manner to manage the challenge level contained in reading materials and learning tasks to insure consistent success and student growth.

The guidelines discussed here may need to be adjusted depending upon the comfort level of the individual student. These guidelines are built into the steps of the instructional assessment process and will be discussed in detail in subsequent chapters. The focus of the process is one of ensuring that an appropriate fit or comfort zone exists during the assessment and instructional process—a focus that is fundamental to literacy development.

Modeling Desired Responses

Demonstrating the type of responses desired of students when completing a task or mastering a skill allows teachers the opportunity to express their own thinking. Talking through the steps they themselves would pursue when approaching a particular task, or solving a problem, as Howard (2009) said, paves the way for students to apply this to their own learning. Modeling, however, will have little effect if the preceding principles are not considered and strategically applied. For example, in *Putting Reading First* (2002), it states, "by listening to good models of fluent reading, students learn how a reader's voice can help written text make sense....By reading effortlessly and with expression, you are modeling for your students how a fluent reader sounds during reading" (p. 26). However, modeling fluent reading is not likely to help the struggling reader become fluent if the challenge level of the material is too hard and instruction is not suitably matched.

Modeling does not help if the student's knowledge and entry skills are too far removed from what is being modeled. When this happens, there is a slim chance that what is modeled will be effective (Gravois & Gickling, 2008). Modeling of activities for struggling students needs to be precise, scaffolded, and presented in a step-by-step process consistent with where the student can function successfully. This means that modeling is most beneficial when it occurs under instructional-level conditions.

Providing Accurate Practice

Before new information and skill can become firmly implanted in the student's learning repertoire, adequate amounts of practice and repetition are needed. Research dating back over a century substantiated how students benefit from receiving guided practice, particularly struggling students (Mason & Bruning, 1999). "During guided practice, we step in and out of the learning process, providing just enough support to give students room to control their own learning and achieve increasing independence" (Howard, 2009, p. 50).

The old adage "practice makes perfect" in reality would be more appropriately stated, "practice makes permanent." To achieve "perfection" requires receiving both confirming and corrective feedback during practice. The student needs to know when practice is correct and needs to be steered in the right direction when veering off course (Guskey, 2003). In this sense, "perfect practice makes perfect." As a caution, when too much corrective feedback is given the student can easily lose sight of what the practice is to accomplish. As suggested in *Dancing with the Pen* (1987), feedback needs to be specific, targeted, and judiciously applied.

> Make it a discipline to choose one thing to teach, realizing that retention from conferences is high. The tendency when first working with conferences is to over teach, since the teacher feels it may be a week before she meets with the child again. Over teaching means the child leaves the conference more confused than when he entered (p. 64).

Confining corrective feedback to a specific skill or concept allows the student to focus on what is most important and provides the student with a better chance of acquiring the desired skill or concept. Once actively engaged, the skill and/or concept needs to be rehearsed and practiced in an integrated manner. Practice also needs to be provided in a variety of meaningful contexts to facilitate generalization.

Allington (1998) stated that students who are developing reading skills need enormous amounts of easy reading experiences where high levels of accuracy, fluency, and comprehension abound and where a ratio of 80% easy to 20% more difficult material is about right. We believe a similar ratio is about right when providing confirming and corrective feedback, with 80% of the time being devoted to students receiving confirming feedback and 20% of the time being devoted to corrective feedback. Blake (cited in Checkley, 2003) acknowledges that good teachers, when providing feedback, are like good coaches in that they do not watch their players practice something wrong and wait until practice is completed to correct their players; they offer timely on-the-spot support instead. For feedback to be effective it needs to be applied on the spot in a timely manner.

Developing Automaticity

The seventh and final principle involves elevating students' skills to an independent and automatic level. While gaining automaticity does not involve new learning, it does involve learning tasks that students can successfully engage in on their own (Howard, 2009). In every aspect of skill development there are certain skills that are so basic and fundamental that they need to become automatic; gaining certain reading skills is no different (LaBerge & Samuels, 1974; Pearson, 2006). Samuels (1979, 1997), for example, compared the training involved in developing a skilled reader with how athletes and musicians are trained using small units of activity practiced over and over until they are mastered. He also noted that, unfortunately, "in reading we are often too eager to have children cover a year's work in a year's time, so that some children, especially those having difficulty with reading, are moved too rapidly through a book, never having mastered a single page" (1997, p. 380). Like trained athletes and musicians, struggling readers need sufficient practice to become automatic at applying certain skills. Large quantities of rehearsal and practice are needed for new words, language concepts, and new information to work their way through working memory and become readily available to long-term memory.

Although the amount of repetition students need to achieve automaticity varies, Table 3.2 illustrates the amount generally needed for words to be recognized on sight by high, average, and slower students (Gates, 1930; Hargis, Terhaar-Yonkers, Williams, & Reed, 1988). In studying sight-word attainment, for example, Hargis and his associates noted that it does not matter if words are decodable or not, it still takes between 25 to 55 repetitions for a new word to become instantly accessible as a sight-word.

High Ability	**(IQ 120)**	**25 repetitions**
Average Ability	**(IQ 100)**	**35 repetitions**
Slower Ability	**(IQ 80)**	**55 repetitions**

Table 3.2 Suggested repetition requirements for sight-word attainment by ability

Collectively, these seven fundamental principles work together to create optimal conditions both for student learning and for teaching. When systematically applied, these principles provide the best path for ensuring that optimal conditions exist for gaining meaningful data during the ongoing assessment and instructional process. Whenever a concern is raised over the student's lack of academic progress, it is often the lack of attention to one or more of these basic principles at the issue. In the spirit of becoming automatic with these principles, we repeat them here:

1. Activate the student's prior knowledge

2. Link new with known information

3. Do not overload working memory

4. Manage the instructional level

5. Model the desired responses

6. Provide accurate practice

7. Develop automaticity.

SUMMARY

This chapter provided a glimpse of the history, research, and evolution of what is now termed Instructional Assessment—a history firmly grounded in the belief that assessment's foremost purpose is to guide the creation of effective learning conditions for students. We have described the importance of keeping assessment aligned with what the student knows and can do so that optimal performance and optimal instruction routinely occur. When these favorable learning conditions exist, students experience success and are motivated to learn.

Bloom (1976) astutely observed that the lack of entry skill was generally reason enough to cause difficulty for a student mastering a new task. We realize now that this observation is only partially correct. The creation of matched learning conditions is much more sophisticated than only attending to a student's lack of entry skills. As discussed in this chapter, an effective instructional match is based on the strategic interplay of seven basic learning and teaching principles that are the prerequisite building blocks for providing students with opportunities to learn at their best and for teachers to instruct at their best.

As will be seen in subsequent chapters, the IA process is focused on creating and maintaining the instructional match–first, to gather reliable and valid data, and secondly, to help students achieve manageable, incremental growth by building on what they know. When the instructional match exists, and the challenge levels are managed effectively, high rates of predictable learning are the result. Furthermore, when favorable learning conditions exist, as Bloom (1976) noted, students become increasingly similar in ability as well as motivation to learn.

Chapter 4

Essential Reading Dimensions

Anything less than a well-rounded instructional program is a form of discrimination against children who have difficulty with reading.

(Fielding & Pearson, 1994)

All students need opportunities to participate fully in the literacy process and to enjoy the benefits that accrue from reading tasks that match their prior knowledge, skills, and abilities. They need sufficient opportunities to develop efficient word-recognition, cueing, and response systems that enable them to comprehend and interact successfully with a variety of genres and content leading to life-long habits of reading enjoyment. Students who struggle with reading deserve no less. They deserve the benefits of full participation in well-rounded reading programs not just because it is the fair and humane thing to do, but because it provides them "with the best possible experiences for becoming competent and eager readers" (Graves, 1998, p. 16).

Before a well-designed reading program can be established for each student, the assessor and teacher must gain a clearer picture of how the student actually reads when assessed under instructional-level conditions—conditions essential for gaining a valid reading assessment. How the student orchestrates his or her reading skills within and across the dimensions of reading provides the assessor and teacher with a picture of the student's developing reading facility. This chapter provides a conceptual picture of the essential reading dimensions. Insights gained from this developing picture are central to creating the instructional match for the student.

READING DEFINED

Reading, simply put, is the ability to derive meaning from written text. Skilled readers actively construct meaning as they read. They draw upon their prior knowledge and experience in order to make connections and to interact indirectly with the author about what they are reading (Pennsylvania's *Reading Assessment Handbook*, 1990). Skilled reading is no longer viewed as the mastery of a series of independent enabling skills, but is seen as the interdependent and flexible application of a variety of strategies in interacting with and understanding different reading content.

This description reflects the constructive nature of reading. It is an active process where students become more adept at engaging with and interpreting written material, rather than mastering sequences of enabling skills. Implicit in this description are the actions of the teacher in helping the student recognize the variety of ways authors convey meaning (Hammerberg, 2004). While reading programs and materials contribute to the reading development of the student as a reader, these are merely resources to be strategically applied. It is how the assessor and teachers use assessment data and materials to negotiate the assessment and instructional process that accounts for the development and growth of the struggling reader.

Reading Dimensions

Figure 4.1 provides a framework for viewing seven essential reading dimensions. These dimensions coincide with the five reading elements described in the 1998 Reading Excellence Act and highlighted within the *National Reading Panel Report* (2000). The outer circle represents the overarching dimensions of comprehension and metacognition. Each contributes to, and directly results from, the effective application of the other five dimensions depicted in the form of a star. These resulting five dimensions include language and prior knowledge, word recognition and meaning, word study, fluency, and responding.

The reading framework serves as a guide for the assessor and the teacher as they explore how the student gains meaning and reading and how the student orchestrates the mechanics of reading. This visual representation of the seven reading

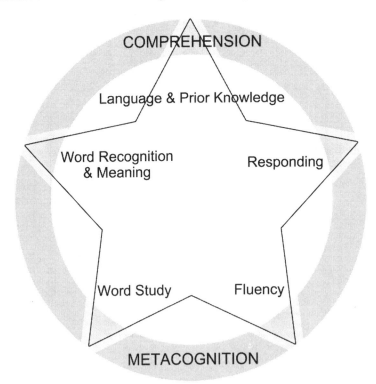

Figure 4.1 Essential reading dimensions

dimensions reflects the reciprocal and interactive nature of the reading process, giving the assessor and teacher opportunities to explore how the student applies his or her reading skill to derive meaning from various reading content.

The placement of the reading dimensions is intentional and does not suggest an ordered sequence of reading development. The way students develop and exhibit their skills and engage in reading content defies this notion. Instead, we believe that the ultimate goal of the assessor and teacher is to ensure that students have available a strong repertoire of skills across all seven dimensions.

Table 4.1 further defines each dimension and poses essential questions concerning how the student orchestrates his or her reading skill within and across each dimension. The different questions also provide a glimpse of how the student uses strength in one dimension to compensate for a lesser skill. The questions illustrate the complex nature of reading. Development of real competence requires a lengthy journey involving the integration, orchestration, and mastery of a host of literacy skills, both within and across all seven reading dimensions.

Reading Comprehension

Reading comprehension represents an ongoing constructive process where the reader uses cues supplied by the author to acquire meaning (Goodman, 2006). Grasping main ideas, recognizing sequences of events, connecting major and minor details, making judgments, and drawing conclusions are all central to good comprehension. However, comprehension is not limited to these areas of study. Different aspects of reading comprehension occur at all levels of reading development—at the phonemic, letter-sound, letter-pattern, word, phrase, sentence, paragraph, page, and text levels. Such aspects of comprehension are embedded in all reading functions and, for that matter, in all learning.

Activities supporting the development of reading comprehension begin early in life as parents, grandparents, and siblings read to children. They eagerly point to pictures and discuss what is happening in stories. They ask children questions such as, "What do you think will happen next in the story?" and, "Why do you think that will happen?" They encourage children to be inquisitive and to elaborate by asking questions on their own, such as, "Why didn't he like the girl in the story?" and, "What does pushy mean?" They engage children in conversations and let them know how much their thinking is valued. Early learning experiences such as these, along with developing a positive regard for meeting the reading requirements set forth in school, strongly influence children's desire to read for meaning and to enjoy all types of reading.

While the early experiences gained from listening and talking about a variety of stories and subjects help prepare children to read and enjoy books, it is hard to think about reading comprehension without thinking about the very nature of written language. It is the language chosen by authors to impart information and ideas that is the medium of their craft. One way of conceptualizing the importance of written language is to think of it as the author's "talk," and, as with talk, it is the interpretation of the author's talk that defines reading comprehension.

Reading Dimensions and Essential Questions

Reading Dimensions	Essential Questions
Comprehension The ability to confirm, predict, reflect upon, and retain the author's message.	Does the student grasp the meaning of what the author is conveying?
Metacognition The ability to monitor and regulate one's own learning.	Does the student use specific strategies for monitoring his or her own learning?
Language/Prior Knowledge The grammatical and broad range of experience that gives meaning to the student.	Does the student demonstrate adequate language, concepts, and experience to understand the text?
Word Recognition The ability to identify, prounounce, and know the meaning of words that are linked together in print.	Does the student possess a sufficient sight-word pool to read and comprehend the selection?
Word Study The use of organized approaches for unlocking words outside one's own sight-word vocabulary.	What strategies does the student use to unlock or figure out unknown words?
Fluency The speed of reading and the use of phrasing and expression during reading.	Can the student read with adequate speed and expression orally? How well does the student read silently?
Responding The ability to convey orally or in writing what is read or said.	Can the student retell or write about what is read accurately and effectively?

Table 4.1 Reading definitions and essential questions

These indirect conversations and interactions between the student and the author determine the level of understanding the student attaches to the author's writing. Engaging in these types of indirect conversations with an author is what capable readers do, a skill that is often learned from early family experiences. Capable readers form questions that are similar to those they formulate when engaged in direct discourse. They confirm, clarify, predict, reflect upon, and make judgments about what the author is saying.

Difficulties with comprehending arise for a variety of reasons. When reading content is unfamiliar or poorly written, the student may not be able to decipher what the author is saying. Similarly, lack of experience, limited language, or insufficient background knowledge can all disrupt understanding. Not having sufficient opportunity to read and understand a particular subject, however, is not necessarily limited to the reader's lack of language, experience, or reading ability. Being unable to understand a subject occurs even for the mature reader if the material is outside the range of the reader's preparation and experience. The following paragraph illustrates this point.

> If a cation is placed in the center of a face-centered cubic anion lattice, it is surrounded by an octahedron of anions. In addition, there are equivalent octahedral holes in the center of each of the 12 cube edges. A cation in each edge hole will have four nearest-neighbors ions of opposite charge in the same cube and two in a neighboring cube. In all common crystals with face-centered anions lattices, *all* octahedral holes are filled with cations. (Kotz & Purcell, 1987, p. 406).

This passage exemplifies how reading comprehension, even for the capable reader, is contextual. Your ability to pronounce the words and still not understand the paragraph does not imply you have poor comprehension. As a reader, in most instances, you would be able to demonstrate excellent comprehension, but in this instance understanding the passage requires more than word recognition and definitional knowledge. Not having the conceptual knowledge and language background of chemistry is what is lacking to understand the passage.

Assessors and teachers are cautioned not to draw premature conclusions when assessing reading comprehension. Schell (1988) acknowledged, "Just because readers inadequately comprehend something doesn't mean we can conclude that they have trouble in general with reading comprehension. It is quite conceivable they can adequately comprehend other material at the same reading level" (p. 13). When assessing a student's reading comprehension we would be well advised to remember that "poor comprehension may be more text specific than it is a generalized deficit. Maybe about all we can say in some instances is that a reader had trouble comprehending specific material under specific conditions" (p. 13).

Our own experience confirms that the apparent lack of reading comprehension does not mean that the student *cannot* comprehend. Many struggling students are able to survive in school because they have excellent listening comprehension skills. When comprehension appears as a concern, it is often the excessive vocabulary burden and/ or the unfamiliar concepts that specific narrative and informational texts impose that create an imbalance for the student.

Reading comprehension is certainly made easier when both the content and vocabulary are familiar to the student. As Templeton (1995) said, "The more you know about a topic you're reading about, the more you will comprehend as you read" (p. 44). Smith (1978) stated it this way, "The more you know already, the less you need to find out" (p. 15). For comprehension to remain high, prior knowledge needs to remain high. From the early work of Betts (1946) we learned that reading comprehension diminishes as the level of unknown words generally exceeds five percent. Studying the behaviors of students, Gill (1992) reconfirmed this fact through further studies. When good readers were assigned to read from grade-level basal programs, chapter books, and content area texts, good readers read fluently, read with fewer than five percent error, and maintained high comprehension levels. When poor readers were given similar material to read, their error rates routinely exceeded 15 percent, severely limiting their ability to comprehend (see also Cramer & Rosenfield, 2008). From an assessment perspective, these findings reconfirm that a valid appraisal of a student's reading comprehension cannot be obtained when an excessive vocabulary burden exists or when there is the absence of conceptual knowledge about the material being read.

Metacognition

Most of us have the skill and knowledge to accurately interpret what we read without analyzing why we are able to understand. This form of mental activity is called cognition. Metacognition, on the other hand, reflects a different level of understanding that not only encompasses the awareness of knowledge but also the ability to self-monitor and self-regulate the acquisition and retention of knowledge. As students mature, many exhibit this self-regulating quality which enables them to digest and fully comprehend what they are reading. Some students lack the self-regulating and self-monitoring facility needed to guide their understanding, and as a consequence they are not able to gain full meaning from what they are reading.

Holdaway (1979) described the difference between cognition and metacognition as the presence or absence of self-direction on the part of the learner. Routman (1991) expanded this notion, indicating that to become strategic requires the type of self-direction that enables the student to generalize and apply newly acquired skills in other contexts.

> A skill—no matter how well it has been taught—cannot be considered a strategy until the learner can use it purposefully and independently. Application of a skill to another context is far more likely to occur when the skill has been taught in a meaningful context that considers the needs of the learner (Routman, 1991, p.135).

While there are obvious benefits from directly fostering the development of self-regulating skills, unless the student is able to make appropriate generalizations within other contexts they will not fully benefit from these skills. Obtaining such strategic facility requires the execution of a number of self-directive behaviors such as:

- exploring and activating prior knowledge

- making connections between what is new and what is known

- asking relevant questions and requesting clarification

- assessing and verbalizing one's ongoing understanding

- knowing when and how to use appropriate "fix-up" strategies.

In another sense, this type of self-monitoring and self-regulating behavior could easily be referred to as self-assessment. Students who understand and experience the value of self-assessment can discern when instructional materials are too difficult or too easy, or when more knowledge is required. They take ownership of their own learning and are more reflective. They are able to ask questions such as, "What do I know?", "What do I need?", and "Why do I need it?" as a way to guide their own thinking and learning. They look for what they know, and are able to talk about what they need to know, concerning a particular topic in order to understand the topic more fully.

Using self-questioning and self-monitoring skills to solidify comprehension gives students a distinct advantage as they encounter all types of reading situations. As noted by Resnick and Klopfer (1989), all students should receive the benefits that come from instructional activities to stimulate and nourish their "own mental elaborations of knowledge and to help them grow in their capacity to monitor and guide their own learning and thinking" (p. 4). Such activities should not be confined to any particular critical period, but should be "an intrinsic part of good instruction from the beginning of school" (p. 2). This type of strategic self-monitoring and self-regulating activity is what metacognition is all about.

Language and Prior Knowledge

Prior knowledge refers to the broad range of knowledge and experiences children acquire that give meaning to their beliefs, attitudes, skills, and interests. As their language skills develop during their early years, noticeable changes occur in the development of their listening and speaking abilities. Although not yet able to read, children enjoy being read to. They comprehend a wide variety of children's literature, follow story plots, relate to different characters, and even keep pace with the sequence of events when being read to—all in preparation for learning to read (Strommen & Mates, 1997).

By the time most children enter school, they have mastered the language of their place of birth. They have the ability to engage in routine conversations using all of the grammatical forms of their native language. This accomplishment seems remarkable since it happens without conscious efforts on their part. The speaking and listening abilities acquired are implicit. Children have no real knowledge of how they obtained language. The only major factor limiting their ability to communicate is the range of their vocabulary development (Hargis, 2006).

While oral language develops without any real explicit knowledge of how it is acquired, gaining essential reading and writing skills is a different matter. To learn to read, the student must be able to comprehend spoken language as a readiness base and become aware of how the temporal and auditory forms of language are represented graphically. They must learn that the seemingly flowing speech sounds they hear are actually a number of distinct sounds used to produce discernable speech (Hargis, 2006). With phonemic awareness as a base, children must learn where letters, letter patterns, and their accompanying speech sounds are placed to form words and sentences. In addition, they must learn that words are separated from each other by spaces and that reading and writing occur from left to right and top to bottom. As this explicit knowledge is gained about how oral language is represented in print, children begin the process of learning to recognize the printed counterparts of familiar spoken words.

The relationship between oral language and its printed counterpart is illustrated in Figure 4.2. The first skills to develop are the oral language functions of listening and speaking. Unlike the attainment of oral language, which develops naturally for most children, the processing of language's printed counterparts of reading and writing are not easily acquired. Attaining these skills generally requires years of concentrated instruction and practice to reach reasonable levels of reading and writing proficiency (Hargis, 2006).

Listening and reading represent the receptive forms of language, whereas speaking and writing represent its expressive forms. These language functions are interdependent, working in unison to interpret, clarify, and construct meaning. Just as individuals engage in verbal exchanges to clarify and gain meaning, the reader engages in a mental exchange with the author to seek clarification and gain meaning.

What each student knows is defined in terms of the different mental concepts that reflect the student's knowledge about things, and about how things work. This conceptual knowledge is referred to as *schema*, meaning the mental processes the individual uses to interpret and organize one's thoughts concerning events, places, and actions (Anderson & Pearson, 1984; Miller, 2002). "This organized body of knowledge guides our expectations about what we will experience every time we encounter another instance of a particular type of event" (Templeton, 1995, p. 42).

It is the effect of cumulative experiences and conceptual knowledge students bring to each new learning task that sets the conditions for reading. Establishing the purpose for reading, tapping into the student's prior knowledge, and providing the necessary vocabulary and background information are all essential assessment components for successful reading preparation. This type of preparation goes beyond merely matching reading materials to the student's instructional level. It involves developing genuine interests in reading and constantly nurturing those interests.

It is difficult to fully appreciate reading content without acknowledging the necessity of language and prior knowledge as its readiness base. That is to say, oral language attainment is prerequisite to processing and constructing meaning from written language. Cunningham and Stanovich (1998) remind us of the qualitative differences that exist between oral language use and how it appears in print. These differences have major instructional implications involving the vocabulary and conceptual burden posed by printed material.

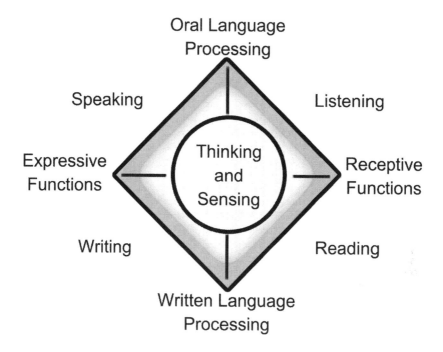

Figure 4.2 The Language Process

   We have all seen situations where the listening and oral language skills of students are vastly different from the ability to process the language contained in printed material. When a student lacks sufficient language and prior knowledge to make sense of written material, the problem is not simply a reading problem; it is also a language problem. Whenever the student lacks essential background information, comprehension suffers no matter how well or how fast the student reads. Likewise, whenever text selection fails to match the instructional level of the student, comprehension suffers no matter how fast the student may read. Each new reading text creates its own reading demand. Poor text selection can result in children pondering over obtuse wording, archaic language, and vague concepts. Even with age appropriate and well-written literature, certain children will not possess sufficient language background to understand what they are reading.

Word Recognition and Word Meaning

   The concepts of word recognition and word meaning consist of the ability to quickly identify, pronounce, and use words correctly. Singularly, each word is merely part of a mental picture, but when words are syntactically combined the mental pictures become more complete. Words and their usage are the conveyors of meaning. The ability to recognize and pronounce words quickly and correctly without connecting them to meaning is not reading, but "word calling." With students who are word callers, the difficulty does not lie with accurate word identification; instead, it involves a lack of language concepts, insufficient language background, and not knowing how words work together to form meaningful chunks of information.

At the least, a student's expanding sight-word vocabulary and language use should occur concurrently. Otherwise, a delay in the development of language concepts will hinder the student's reading and comprehension. While vocabulary development and concept development need to occur jointly, Vacca and colleagues (1991) indicate that the major focus should be on acquiring conceptual knowledge and using such knowledge correctly. They state as follows:

> Although words are labels for concepts, a single concept represents much more than the meaning of a single word. It might take thousands of words to explain a concept....The relationship of experiences to concepts and words sets the stage for an important principle of vocabulary instruction: in order to learn new or unfamiliar words it is necessary to have experiences from which concepts can be derived (p. 213).

While a large, stable, sight-word vocabulary is generally viewed as the hallmark of a successful reader (Johnston, 1998), this holds true only if the language concepts underpinning one's vocabulary development are intact (Cramer & Rosenfield, 2008). It is the growth of both of these aspects of language that frees the reader to use his or her mental energy to concentrate on and comprehend what is being read rather than expending more energy sounding out or guessing at unknown words.

In reviewing the effects of vocabulary burden on reading comprehension, we are left with two thoughts. First, although having a large, stable sight-word vocabulary does not assure the existence of good reading comprehension, it certainly helps. Secondly, without the existence of sufficient word-recognition, reading comprehension is virtually impossible. Therefore, this observation demands that the vocabulary load of printed text remains within the student's instructional and independent reading boundaries in order for the student to perform at his or her best. Preparing reading tasks to match these boundaries helps sustain the student's desire to read and gain the full meaning intended by the author.

While previously emphasized in Chapter 3, it bears repeating that students' instructional reading levels reflect reading tasks that contain appropriate margins of challenge. These margins require accuracy to remain within the 93-97% range for word recognition and meaning when reading connected text and within the 70-85% range during rehearsal and practice. Comprehension should always remain high, hovering at least at the 80% level. Providing tasks at students' instructional levels creates the best condition for optimal learning and teaching.

An independent level allows the student to read for pleasure and is often referred to as "recreational reading." Easy reading activity should remain within the 98-100% known sight-word range and within the 85-100% range for rehearsal and practice. Comprehension should hover in the 90% range. Allington (1999) went further, stressing the importance of creating independent reading level opportunities by recommending that at least 80 % of reading time for children be devoted to easy independent reading activity.

Word Study

Effective readers need an organized approach for unlocking words that are not within their sight-word vocabulary. We refer to this organized approach as word study. Word study encompasses any strategy employed by the reader to unlock and identify unknown words. It includes the use of a broad range of orthographic and contextual clueing systems. These systems involve letter-sound relationships, letter/ spelling patterns, words-within-words, base or root words, and context clues. Efficient word study systems provide a deliberate method for increasing the student's sight-word pool.

Developmental Aspects of Word Study

As young children begin formally exploring the world of reading, they begin to understand that words they hear in speech are also written in print, and that letters making up printed words reflect different sounds they hear in speech. This early recognition that spoken words are composed of small speech sounds refers to phonemic awareness. In the early stage of learning to read Adams, et al. (1998) noted that, in the early stage of learning to read, "it is awareness of phonemes that allows children to understand how the alphabet works—an understanding that is essential to learning to read and spell" (p. 4).

Once formal reading instruction begins, students start to learn about letter-sound correspondences as part of learning to read (Stahl, 1992). For instance, when primary-grade students are asked to describe what they do when encountering unknown words, they generally reply that they try to "sound them out." This response alone indicates that they have received some form of direct or indirect phonetic instruction.

With respect to the teaching of phonics, we are reminded of Stahl's admonition that the "purpose of phonics is not that children learn to sound out words." Instead, the primary purpose of phonics "is that they [students] learn to recognize words quickly and automatically so they can turn their attention to comprehension of the text" (p. 624). The mastery of phonics is merely considered an enabling skill, with the end result being automatic sight-word recognition.

Word study activities and reading comprehension are functionally bonded— one does not precede the other. Teaching word study skills often occurs as a "part to whole" process—where instruction in phonics precedes combining letter sounds into words—or as a "whole to part process"—where instruction in word study skills occurs during the natural context of reading familiar language—or as a combination of both. Support for teaching a "whole to part" process was provided by Moustafa (1997) and Dombey and Moustafa (1998). Their reviews of the literature led them to conclude that many students benefit from being taught whole-to-part strategies—teaching words first within context, then linking letter sounds to words (synthetic phonics)—rather than part-to-whole strategies (analytic phonics)—teaching letter sounds first then blending letter sounds to form words.

The discovery that children make analogies between familiar and unfamiliar print words to pronounce unfamiliar words informs us that we should begin phonics instruction by first helping children learn to recognize a lot of print words. The discovery that early readers read better in context informs us that the most effective way to help children learn to recognize a lot of print words is to help them read stories with familiar language. (Dombey & Moustafa, 1998, p.18).

Learning how to identify unknown words has expanded beyond relying on the traditional teaching of phonics rules, and for good reason. Clymer (1963) early on noted that less than one-half of the most commonly taught phonics rules are applicable three-fourths of the time. While the sounds made by consonants and blends are fairly stable, the sounds of vowels are a different matter and introduce greater variability. However, when vowels are combined with consonants to form letter clusters and rimes (e.g. ike, ick, ite, etc.), their pronunciations become more stable. Adams (1990), for example, pointed out that "of the 286 phonograms that appear in primary grade texts, 95 percent of them were pronounced the same in every word in which they appeared" (Stahl, 1992, p. 623). These findings confirm the value of recognizing the pronunciation of spelling patterns in syllables and words rather than over-relying on individual sounds.

Learning how to look for both spelling patterns and little words within bigger words has also expanded as part of the decoding process. "Even where a word as a whole is not visually familiar, fragments of its spellings almost certainly will be" (Adams & Bruck, 1995, p.12). For example, *ran, an,* and *or* are imbedded in the word *transport.* When spelling patterns and little words are embedded in bigger words and when bigger words contain base or root words, decoding and meaning-making are magnified. *Trans,* for instance, means across whereas *port* means to carry. Therefore, *transport* means to carry across—as in transportation or transporting merchandise across state lines. The use of root or base words, prefixes and suffixes, little words, and spelling patterns are all facets of word study.

Meaning, of course, is always central to the word-study process. Situations occur daily illustrating this natural bond. For example, the golden arches of McDonald's provide special meaning for young children long before the formal decoding of letters and print begins. In contrast, stringing together sequences of letters, such as b-a-l-l, has little meaning unless the child understands the concept of a ball. Meaningful experiences are essential to solidify the student's concepts of printed forms of words. Henderson (1990) described how this process emerges:

The concept of word is a benchmark on the advent of literacy. Prior to this achievement, children may have learned many things about written language. They may know what stories are and what printed text looks like. They may, and frequently do, know what letters are and learn to write them. Even so, until the word as a concrete object is conceptualized, children cannot examine words systematically, think about them, and begin to note the inner workings of their form (p. 45).

Word-study requirements increase as students' reading skills and sight-word pools increase. In addition to blending sounds to form words such as *fr-og* and *ch-ill*, they begin to respond to patterns in words such *ing* in *sing* and *single*. They also begin to look for context clues as they attempt to decipher challenging words. By the third grade, students have generally mastered sound-symbol relationships, sound blending, and recognizing patterns in high frequency words like *wanted* and *elephant*, but they need more time to master the syllabic requirements of advanced words like *recreational* and *magnesium*. By the fourth and fifth grades, the focus shifts to syllable analysis and deciphering the meaning and structure of words like *geography, anthropology, amphitheater*, and *amphibian*. The challenge for sixth-graders and beyond is to accurately apply systematic decoding skills to advance their vocabularies and to gain meaning from an even wider variety of content areas.

As children mature, they also bring meaning to words without always accurately decoding them. For example, the word "equestrian" can immediately be associated with horses, and "schizophrenia" with a psychological disorder. Likewise, how many of you have read a Ludlum or Tolstoy novel with immense interest and comprehension without accurately pronouncing the names of numerous characters and foreign locations?

Contextual Clues

Context literally means to be "connected and coherent," reinforcing comprehension's central role in literacy development. How words are used, what they mean, and how they are strung together must make sense. It is this sense-building process that enables the reader to use surrounding words to estimate and determine the meaning of the target unknown word. The semantic *(word meaning and usage)* and syntactic *(word order)* features of language help predict what the author is saying based upon the reader's prior knowledge of each of these features.

It was once thought that unskilled readers, unlike their more skilled counterparts, were less likely to make use of context clues to predict unknown words. We now know that the opposite is true. Unskilled readers rely more on the use of context clues to predict unknown words in an attempt to acquire meaning. Skilled readers, on the other hand, have well-developed sight-word vocabularies and read sufficiently well that they seldom need to rely on the use of context clues for word identification purposes. As noted by Stanovich (1993/94), "although good readers employ contextual information more fluently in the comprehension process, they are not more reliant on contextual information for word recognition" (p. 282).

While these findings are in opposition to what was traditionally thought, they reinforce the fact that unskilled readers, just like their more able-reading peers, focus on reading for meaning. The real difficulty unskilled readers face when relying on the use of context clues is that reading material is often at their frustration level, where neither context clues nor decoding skills are likely to be of much assistance. However, even under instructional-level conditions, using context clues to decipher unknown words is not all that reliable because too often it is the unknown word that conveys the sentence's meaning. This is the case regardless of whether the student is a skilled or an unskilled reader (Adams & Bruck, 1995).

Reading Fluency

Until recently, little attention was paid to fluent reading as an instructional concept (Griffith & Rasinski, 2004). Since good readers seemed to read fast and poor readers seemed to read slowly, it was assumed that reading fluency was the natural outcome of the students' reading skills. The underlying assumption held that halting, word-by-word reading robs students of the cognitive resources needed for text integration, thereby making speed and accuracy necessary conditions for good comprehension. In addition, it was observed that slow readers do not process words sufficiently to digest adequate quantities of written text (Adams & Bruck, 1995; Stanovich, 1993/94). Unfortunately, this assumption has created a narrow focus on the need to increase reading rates as the main vehicle for improving students' overall reading performance. While we understand the advantages of being able to recognize words automatically and to read effortlessly, there is danger in over-generalizing the relationship between the speed with which students read and their reading comprehension. Instead, students need to develop a pace and quality of reading that produces both efficient reading and effective comprehension.

Fluency Rate

Historically, classroom teachers could tell you what fluent reading sounded like and that it had to do with speed and accuracy. However, they had little idea of how fluent reading manifests itself at different grade levels. It was not until the work of Deno (1985) and his associates that reliable data became available regarding the rates at which students read. He and his associates wanted to develop a standard process that could easily be administered on a frequent basis using classroom reading materials. What resulted from years of study was a normative process for taking one-minute oral reading samples. This sampling process required the student to read from grade-level material while the number of words read correctly per minute was recorded. The student's reading rate was determined by subtracting the number of reading errors from the total number of words in the one-minute reading sample.

Figure 4.3 is an extrapolation of several studies (Hasbrouck & Tindal, 1992, 2006; Howe & Shinn, 2001; Marston & Magnusson, 1985) involving students' oral reading rates from mid-year to end of year for first through sixth grade. As shown, oral reading rates increase approximately 20 to 25 words-read-correctly per minute per year beyond first grade. The rates show that first-graders are mostly word-by-word readers. There is also very little difference between the oral and silent reading rates of first-and second-graders. However, by mid-third grade, rates of oral and silent reading begin to branch, with proficient readers relying more on silent reading. The silent reading rates provided in Figure 4.3 are estimates based upon the authors' experiences and observations.

Inferring too much from students' oral reading rates, though, can be misleading. Assessing the quantity of information a student is able to read via one-minute fluency sampling represents only a surface-level measure of reading. Speed and accuracy alone fail to address the fundamental issue of how well a student comprehends what is being read.

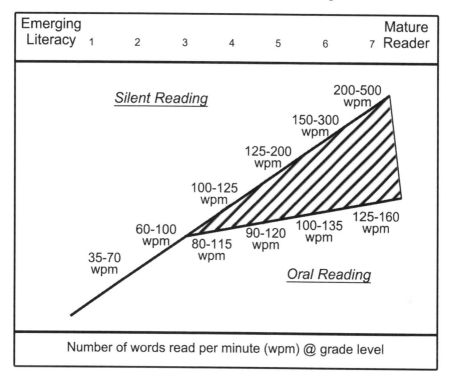

Figure 4.3 One-minute oral and silent reading rates

Fluency Flow

While speed and accuracy are key features of fluency, becoming a fluent reader requires more, as these features alone do not equate to reading comprehension. The ability to recognize how an author uses words to construct meaning is what enhances and enriches comprehension. Seeing how words are clustered together, pausing at the end of each relevant thought, and making appropriate use of tone and pitch are what truly foster expressive language and reading flow. Hudson, Lane, and Pullen (2005) describe the importance of these key features and what happens when these features are disrupted.

> Each aspect of fluency has a clear connection to text comprehension. Without accurate word reading, the reader will have no access to the author's intended meaning, and inaccurate word reading can lead to misinterpretations of the text. Poor automaticity in word reading or slow, laborious movement through the text taxes the reader's capacity to construct an ongoing interpretation of the text. Poor prosody can lead to confusion through inappropriate or meaningless grouping of words or through inappropriate applications of expression (p. 703).

Each of these features is essential for the reader to interact successfully within a variety of written texts. In addition to word selection, these elements include the prosodic features that authors use to give "voice" to their writing. How and what a reader reads needs to be interpreted through the inner "voice" that resonates throughout the author's written work (Romano, 2004). In many ways, "voice" acts as a road map for expressive reading by providing the reader with cues that inform and solidify comprehension. The goal of reading should always be one of teaching the student how to decipher the author's voice correctly and quickly. The ability to read with expression, or prosody, and to comprehend what is being read are powerful and defining features of reading flow and of reading fluency (Kuhn, 2004; Rasinski, 2002).

Instead of using the generic term "reading fluency," Flurkey (2006) makes a strong case for using "*reading flow*" as the term of choice to describe the way efficient and effective readers naturally speed up and slow down when deriving meaning from what they are reading. Figure 4.4 illustrates how oral reading rates fluctuate from sentence to sentence as part of the normal reading process. In this illustration, a seventh-grader and a third-grader were each asked to read the same 68 sentences from a folktale.

Chart 1 (in Figure 4.4) shows the sentence-by-sentence fluctuation in reading rate exhibited by the efficient seventh-grader who read at an average of 181 words per minute. Efficient reading refers to making sense of the written text while expending as little energy as possible. Chart 2 shows the sentence-by-sentence rate for the effective, but inefficient, third-grader who read an average of 44 words per minute. Effective reading refers to making sense of the written text only. Interestingly, Flurkey (2006) noted that while efficient in rate, the seventh grader made some unexpected responses, some of which were correct and some of which were not. What is gained from these two illustrations is an understanding that *both* effective and efficient readers constantly speed up and slow down "as they encounter conditions in the text that require time to think as they go about making sense" (p. 47).

The salient point in thinking about reading flow is that students who become skillful readers know how and when to adjust their reading speed to match the reading demands of different texts. They become increasingly more adept at mastering the sight-word demands imposed by authors to gain full meaning from the author's writing. Conversely, the lack of reading flow inhibits the student's reading development, which warrants serious attention as part of reading assessment and reading instruction.

Responding

Although often used interchangeably, comprehension and responding are not one and the same. Comprehension refers to understanding the meaning of what was said or read; responding, on the other hand, requires the ability to convey, either orally or in writing, one's level of understanding. The quality of a student's response depends upon the degree of understanding, the amount of prior knowledge, and the language skills displayed to create the response.

It is important for the assessor and teachers to recognize that exhibiting responding difficulties does not automatically mean a person lacks comprehension. For example, we have all heard a very humorous joke, comprehended it, laughed, and enjoyed it. However, when we attempt to retell the joke, no one laughs, because we fail to correctly deliver the punch line. Similar difficulties are often exhibited by students who understand what they read but require questioning and prompting to effectively

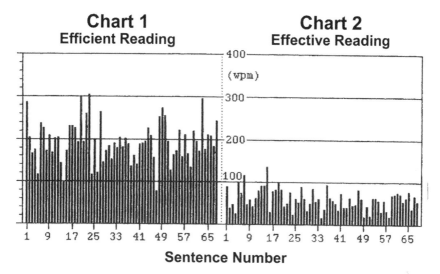

Figure 4.4 Normal fluctuations in the oral reading rates of two students

convey back the information. This can also be seen with students who can recall main ideas, but have difficulty recounting specific details or vice versa. Knowing and assessing the difference between comprehension and responding is important if teachers are to accurately support students' reading performance.

Paratore and Indrisano (1987) divided responding into two broad categories: unaided and aided. An unaided response reflects the student's skills at conveying what was read or heard when given little or very general instructions such as, "Tell me what you just read." This includes the ability to retell, summarize, and write about what they understand with little assistance. Aided responding occurs when students are prompted by guided questioning or cuing such as, "When did they discover the old mine?"

Historically, comprehension questions and the resulting responses have been divided into three levels: literal, inferential, and evaluative. Although teachers tend to rely too heavily on the literal aspect of assessing comprehension, helping students develop a literal level of understanding is still an important feature of comprehension instruction. Having students answer who, what, when, where, and why questions elicits basic yet essential information. However, it is important to remember that developing literal (or, for that matter, inferential and evaluative) understanding can be accomplished at both aided and unaided levels.

The current emphasis is on supporting students to be more reflective, to stretch their thinking, and to take more ownership of their own responding. The practice of "retelling" a story or summarizing key events are only two examples of this effort. The value of this approach is that much of the responsibility for learning is shifted from the teacher to the student. Students are directed to ask and answer their own questions rather than depending upon the teacher for guidance. Such actions encourage students to move beyond factual responses and engage in reflective and substantive thinking. The teacher is there to redirect student questions and guide them toward more involved responses as needed.

Responding extends to having students write about what they read or hear. Many states now emphasize written responding as a requirement in their standards, with some states actually evaluating reading comprehension via students' written responses. Research indicates that, under these circumstances, a student's written response will not represent a true assessment of a student's reading comprehension (Nelson, 2013). Tests that require integrating ideas from what was read into written responses often fail to recognize the number of complex structures involving meaning, memory, spelling, and fine hand-eye coordination–along with the knowledge of grammar, syntax, and style–that affect writing output. These complex language structures are already accounted for in prepared text, but they are not accounted for when the student is required to produce a well-developed, written response from what was read or said.

SUMMARY

While the construction and monitoring of meaning are the over-arching purposes of reading, these are fostered by the student's growth and development within and across the seven essential reading dimensions described in this chapter. These dimensions are central to the successful maintenance of a balanced approach to reading assessment and instruction and include the following: comprehension, metacognition, language and prior knowledge, word recognition, word study, fluency, and responding.

Rather than reflecting a linear sequence of skills, the dimensions are interwoven and interdependent. One cannot expect adequate word recognition to develop without accompanying word meaning, nor expect the student to develop fluent reading habits in the absence of good word-recognition and word-study skills. Similarly, one cannot expect meaningful responses from students without the presence of background knowledge and adequate reading mechanics. But the student's reading development does not end here. It is essential for students to gain self control (metacognition) over what they are reading if they are to become strategic readers. They need to be able to self-assess, monitor, and use "fix-up" strategies when needed to guide and regulate their own learning and thinking.

The culminating message of this chapter is that reading development is a complex endeavor for the learner and for the teacher. The student is required to skillfully navigate these interconnected dimensions to construct meaning. The teacher in turn must precisely assess how the student orchestrates his or her reading skills within and across these interconnected dimensions and then use this assessment information to ensure that appropriate instruction is provided.

Chapter 5

Reading Assessment:
Orchestrating the Dance

*Assessment should emphasize what students can do rather than
what they cannot do.*

(IRA/NCTE Joint Task Force, 1994)

Instructional Assessment (IA) is grounded in the realization that obtaining valid data can only be achieved under instructional-level conditions, and that gaining a precise picture of a student's reading progress depends upon maintaining instructional-level conditions. Such conditions enable the assessor and teacher to not only correctly identify specific reading concerns but also to effectively guide the selection, delivery, and management of appropriate reading strategies that allow the student to function successfully. By working collaboratively with the student, the assessor and teacher are able to gain insight into the student's responses, which ultimately informs and guides ongoing instruction.

While previous chapters emphasized the necessity of building upon a student's prior knowledge and entry skills as the starting point for creating optimal learning and teaching conditions, this chapter describes how to operationalize these principles to enable the student to perform at his or her best. It specifically describes the steps taken to gain an in-depth picture of how the student orchestrates his or her reading skills within and across the seven essential reading dimensions. In other words, this chapter describes how the real work is done to gain valid and reliable data to guide instruction effectively for the struggling student.

In developing effective problem-solving teams (i.e., Instructional Consultation Teams, Rosenfield & Gravois, 1996; Instructional Support Teams, Kovaleski, Tucker, & Duffy, 1995), we encourage teachers and other professionals to work "shoulder-to-shoulder" when using and applying the steps of the IA process. We have seen great benefit accrue from having one professional conduct the assessment while the teacher observes and takes notes, followed immediately by joint reflection about the student's performance. The ultimate goal, of course, is for each professional to gain the knowledge and skill of conducting student assessments that provide precise data to effectively guide instruction. Whether working collaboratively with another professional or alone, the classroom teacher follows the same assessment steps, engaging in self-talk and self-reflection concerning how to use the data to maintain optional learning conditions for the student. For writing convenience, the term "assessor" is used to describe the person conducting the assessment, whether it be a support person or the classroom teacher.

ORCHESTRATING THE DANCE

In many ways, the process of conducting an effective reading assessment is like dancing, with each partner attending to the pace and rhythm of the music. Metaphorically speaking, the assessor leads the student in the dance. However, since students do not all dance in the same manner and with the same ease, the assessor is responsible for creating the conditions that bring the music into harmony with the student's skills. The rhythm, tone, and pace of the assessment are managed strategically by the assessor in order to maintain a comfort level that allows the student to perform with ease. Only when the student is actively engaged and working under optimal conditions can the assessor accurately observe what the student knows and what the student can actually do. This is the juncture where the principles and concepts described in the previous chapters converge, allowing the assessor to gain valid authentic assessment data.

As the assessment process progresses, the assessor adjusts his or her actions to the student. Such ongoing adjustments allow the assessor to alter the approach depending upon the specific purpose of the assessment. Valencia, McGinley, and Pearson (1990) capture the rhythm, tone, and pace of the dance by stating as follows:

> At times, we enter into the assessment situation with pre-specified criteria and tasks in mind. At other times we are simply knowledgeable observers of students in their natural learning environment, we look for patterns that will enlighten our understanding and add to our assessment portfolio. And at other times, we interact with students, prompting them, guiding them, questioning them, and listening to them with the skills of a knowledgeable educator (p 127).

Just as there are basic steps to any dance, there are basic steps to conducting an IA. These steps provide structure and function as guidelines to the reading assessment process. However, unlike formal protocols that require rigid adherence, the IA steps do not restrict the assessor in addressing additional questions that naturally arise when assessing and working with the student. These questions may open new avenues of inquiry that should be pursued to gain a better understanding of where and how best to instruct the student. The metaphor of the dance is a constant reminder for the assessor to adjust to the comfort level of the student and to remain flexible in order to gain insights into the student's thinking and reading skills. Throughout the process, the assessor actively looks for clues as to how to work with the student and how to help the student become a better reader.

THE INSTRUCTIONAL ASSESSMENT SNAPSHOT

Each time an IA is conducted, the data represent a ***snapshot*** or sample of the student's reading performance. Each IA snapshot yields new data that guide the assessor's thinking and actions, data that ultimately lead to relevant and appropriate instructional decisions. Collecting a single snapshot is not sufficient to gain an accurate picture of what a student knows or what the student is capable of doing. Naturally, the number of snapshots required to make an informed instructional decision depends upon the assessor's ability to create instructional-level conditions sufficient to gain answers to the following relevant assessment questions (Gickling, 1998):

- What does the student know?
- What can the student do?
- How does the student think?
- What does the student do when unsure of the task?
- Now what do I do as the teacher?

Collecting additional reading snapshots creates an expanded picture of the student's reading skills in response to what has been taught (Gravois & Gickling, 2008).

Preparing for the Assessment

When conducting an IA snapshot, a conscious effort is always made to ensure that optimal learning conditions are present. These conditions must exist if the student is to put forth his or her best effort during the actual assessment. This is such a crucial requirement that the following statement from the *Standards for the Assessment of Reading and Writing* (IRA/NCTE, 1994) bears repeating:

> The quality of information is suspect when tasks are too difficult or too easy, when students do not understand the tasks or cannot follow the directions, or when they are too anxious to be able to do their best or even their typical work. In these situations students cannot produce their best efforts or demonstrate what they know. Requiring students to spend their time and effort on assessment tasks that do not yield high quality, useful information results in students losing valuable learning time. Such a loss does not serve their interests and is thus an invalid practice (p. 14).

Collaborating with the Teacher

The IA process begins with the assessor having a conversation with the classroom teacher and helping the teacher describe as explicitly as possible his or her perceptions concerning the reading skills and needs of the student. Initially, the conversation is centered on how the student relates to reading and their reading performance in general. As it proceeds, the conversation becomes more focused on how the student orchestrates his or her reading skills with respect to the seven essential reading dimensions introduced in Chapter 4 (see Figure 4.1). Working definitions and key questions to facilitate this conversation are presented in Table 4.1. The teacher's observations and insights concerning these dimensions help guide the direction of the initial assessment snapshot. While a single snapshot will not provide answers to every question, it does provide direction for further assessment inquiry.

Selecting Material

The IA process was designed to assist classroom teachers in planning and delivering instruction to struggling readers using the curriculum materials of the classroom (Gickling & Havertape, 1981). The starting point for the IA begins with the use of peer-expected text (material read by typical grade-level peers). If the student is assigned reading material other than grade-level material, it, too, should be accessible. Having grade-level and other material available provides the assessor with a range of material to capture the student's reading knowledge and skill related to each reading dimension. Rather than worrying about whether the material is appropriate or not, the assessor feels secure in the knowledge that, by following the assessment steps described here, student frustration will be avoided.

For young readers (e.g., kindergarten, early first grade), the assessor will want to augment the selection of material to include books that are read orally to the class. Since early reading texts (e.g., Little Books) often have few words and rely heavily on pictures, their content is not rich enough to fully assess what the emerging or beginning reader may actually know. By including oral reading of chapter books or stories that contain richer content, the assessor is able to gain a more robust picture of what the emerging reader knows and is able to do.

Building a Relationship

The assessor needs to develop rapport and build a working relationship with the student, but also needs to work efficiently. Talking with the student about the reason for working together and also explaining to the student that assessment is not a test but a way of finding out what the student knows and what the student can do helps put the student at ease. This honest description conveys to the student that the purpose of assessment is to help the student become a better reader and the teacher a better teacher of reading. We have found that even the most struggling reader wants to demonstrate what they know and what they can do. This initial discussion also serves as an opportunity to observe the language skills and prior knowledge exhibited by the student.

Establishing Optimal Conditions

Before the student is asked to read any material, three critical assessment steps are taken to ensure that the difficulty level of the material is appropriate. Specifically, these three steps help the assessor determine if the student's language and sight-word vocabulary satisfy instructional-level conditions existing within the chosen material. The steps also ensure that key principles of effective learning and teaching are accounted for—activating prior knowledge, linking new information with what is known, and honoring the limits of working memory.

Step 1: Reading to the Student

Teachers and specialists frequently assign lower level texts to struggling students with the goal of creating comfortable reading conditions, without considering the students' language and conceptual skills. This practice inadvertently deprives such students of accessing the language, concepts, and vocabulary provided in peer-expected texts. Simply placing a struggling student in a lower-level text ignores the fact that most students who struggle with reading are able to handle the thinking elements required of peer-expected texts even though they lack proficient reading skills (Ellis, 1997). Instead of perpetuating this practice, IA starts with assessing the student's ability to listen and understand the vocabulary and language concepts that are routinely presented in the classroom to the more proficient reading peers.

To gain a sense of the student's prior knowledge and listening skills, the first step of the IA process entails reading a suitable passage from peer-expected material to the student. Reading the passage aloud serves two important purposes. It encourages the student to relax and concentrate on what the assessor is reading without having to read themselves, and it eliminates potential word-recognition and/or decoding difficulties that could interfere with the assessor gaining a clear picture of the student's listening comprehension skills.

Before reading, the assessor tells the student that he or she will have a chance to "tell what the passage was about" or "summarize what was read." For younger students, the assessor may want to quickly review the title and pictures to orient the student to the story. For older readers, the assessor may want to explore the student's prior knowledge or to have the student make a prediction about the story. Of course, the content and length of each passage needs to be age appropriate. While the content and length of the passage often varies, young emerging readers are generally read a passage of 50 words of less, while older readers are generally read passages of 100 to 150 words.

Each IA snapshot allows a good deal of flexibility depending upon the questions the assessor is pursuing. For example, the student may be allowed to view the text while the assessor is reading, or at other times the student may simply listen as the assessor reads without seeing the text. Both approaches have merit depending upon the questions the assessor is attempting to answer.

Step 2: Assessing Listening Comprehension and Responding

After reading orally to the student, the assessor immediately engages the student in a dialogue about what the passage contains in order to assess the student's listening comprehension and language concepts. The dialogue begins with the use of unaided prompts and/or questions and then strategically moves to the use of aided prompts (Paratore & Indrisano, 1987). Using the reading response profile seen in Figure 5.1 as a guide, the assessor first asks the student to retell what was heard using an unaided prompt (a prompt that does not direct the student how to respond). The student is merely encouraged to "tell about what was read," "tell what happened so far," and "tell more." When given unaided prompts, even poor readers are usually able to provide some limited information. With each unaided prompt, the assessor should

Name: _____ Date: _____ Oral Response: _____ Written Response: _____

READING RESPONDING PROFILE

| | UNCUED QUESTIONS | | | | CUED QUESTIONS | | | |
| | Unaided Responses | | Aided Responses | | Forced Choice Responses | | Visual/Referent Responses | |
	General Idea	Supporting Details	General Idea	Supporting Details	General Idea	Supporting Details	General Idea	Supporting Details
Student Supplied Main Idea								
Characters								
Setting								
Beginning								
Middle								
End								
Prediction/ Inference								

Profile Analysis:

Figure 5.1 Reading Response Profile

provide time for the student to respond rather than prematurely introducing an aided prompt or asking a guided question.

Aided prompts and guided questions are then used to gain a more thorough retelling of what the student heard after the student has had ample opportunities to respond. Guided questions direct and help the student structure the responses and are generally in the form of "who, when, where, what, and why" questions. Depending upon the particular passage read, aided questions can be either specific or global. The assessor may need to provide even more structure in the form of forced-choice questions to gain more accurate or detailed response from the student. Forced-choice represents either/or questions (i.e., was it a hot or a cold day?). Finally, students may require additional support or structure in the form of visual/referent prompts. Visual prompts allow the student to look at pictures while referent prompts allow the student to reread or refer back to the text. Beyond looking for right or wrong answers, the use of aided questions and prompts allows the assessor to observe the structure and support needed by the student in order for the student to convey his or her level of understanding of the sampled passage.

As a caveat, remember there is a difference between assessing a student's reading comprehension and assessing a student's responding skills. Comprehension refers to the ability to understand what was heard or read, whereas responding refers to the ability of the student to convey understanding. Teachers often prematurely overuse aided questions to elicit students' responses, perhaps because teachers feel that good comprehension requires immediate answers or that delayed responding raises anxiety and uncertainty in students. Whatever the reason, students are often not given adequate opportunity to think, reflect, and develop their retelling and summarizing skills. Students' class experiences almost exclusively consist of expecting, practicing, and answering aided questions. As a result, they have become increasingly dependent on classroom teachers to guide their reading comprehension at the expense of learning how to guide reading comprehension on their own.

Step 3: Conducting a Word Search (Sight-Word Recognition and Meaning)

Using the passage immediately following the segment that was read orally, the assessor uses a word-search strategy to assess the student's sight-word vocabulary. Applying the research on instructional level and information processing, the assessor selectively points to words that the student has a high probability of knowing and intermittently points to a word that appears more difficult. For most students this entails pointing to 4-5 basic sight words (e.g., *it, the, when, went*) followed by pointing to a more difficult word (i.e., *a multi-syllabic word or a word with an irregular phonetic pattern*). This process of folding in known and unknown words is repeated throughout the reading passage. The repeated pointing to 4-5 known words followed by pointing to one unknown word keeps the student engaged by providing an appropriate level of challenge and at the same time allows the assessor to assess the student's word-recognition facility of the passage. It is important to end the word search by pointing to 4-5 known words.

The pace of the word search needs to remain peppy, as the primary focus is on automatic sight-word recognition and not on word-study. Pointing to individual words is done quickly by allowing the student only 2-3 seconds to say a word before moving to another word. When encountering an unknown word, the student often immediately wants to use some form of word-study to decipher the word. When this happens, the assessor simply states "we'll come back to it" and moves immediately to a word the student has a high probability of knowing and resumes the ratio of pointing to 4-5 known words followed by an unknown word. The temptation of both the student and assessor to stop and decode or use other word-study skills is avoided during this step of the assessment.

Once the assessor confirms sufficient word-recognition facility (93-97% known words), the focus of the assessment can shift to assessing word meaning. The assessor strategically points to a few key words and asks the student to describe the meaning or to use the words in a sentence. The student's responses to the listening portion of the assessment, combined with the student's capacity to convey meaning of individual words, provides the assessor with a picture of the student's instructional reading level.

Assessor Decision #1: Does the student possess the language, conceptual background, and sight-word vocabulary to read and comprehend the selection?

Prior to having a student read the word-searched passage, the assessor must be assured that the reading conditions are optimal. Based upon what is learned from the three previous steps, a positive response to this critical question is needed.

If the answer to the question is "yes," meaning the reading passage is at the student's instructional reading level, the assessor can continue with the next step of the assessment by having the student read the word-searched passage. If unsure ("maybe"), the assessor may conduct an additional word-search activity within the passage, or choose to select a new passage to conduct additional word-search activities until the student feels confident to answer "yes" to the decision question. If the answer to the decision question is "no," the assessor cannot continue until additional actions are taken to ensure the presence of instructional-level conditions. The student should not be asked to read the passage until the assessor is confident the answer to the decision question is "yes."

If the initial assessment steps fail to provide the right conditions to ensure student success, a series of options are available to create the conditions. For instance, if the sight-word vocabulary and/or prior knowledge of the student are below the student's instructional level, one option is to strategically teach a few new words and/or concepts in order to elevate the reading passage to the student's instructional reading level. An additional option is to review the preceding or following pages and to select another passage to meet the student's language and vocabulary needs. Another option is to use smaller segments of the same passage and control the vocabulary load contained in each segment. This series of options allows the the continued use of peer-expected material without having to stop and search for other appropriate material. These and other essential options will be discussed in detail in Chapter 6.

By employing these three initial steps (i.e., reading to the student, asking unaided and aided questions, and conducting a word search) two goals are accomplished. First, the steps create and maintain a comfort level enabling the student to have a positive reading experience. Secondly, attention to the steps provides the necessary information to affirm that instructional-level conditions exist for the student. By assessing the student's sight-word vocabulary and comparing the words the student knows against the vocabulary load of the passage, the assessor can determine if the passage is appropriately matched--that is, it is not too hard or too easy but within the optimal window of challenge for the student (see Figure 3.10). This level of challenge allows the student to perform under the best of conditions. As stated by a Michigan principal learning the IA process, "It is hard to make a mistake when you read to a student and find words the student knows!"

As reaffirmed in Figure 3.10, we know a well-established sight-word vocabulary (93-97% known words) creates the conditions that promote good comprehension. We also know that the amount of new information the human brain can process in working memory at any one time is age-related. By not overloading the limits of a student's working memory, the assessor is more assured that the vocabulary load of the passage is not likely to inhibit the student's comprehension when the passage is acually read.

Step 4: Sampling Content Reading (Word Study and Reading Fluency)

The fourth step of the assessment is to have the student read the instructionally-matched passage aloud. With the passage within the optimal window, the assessor can now observe the student's word-recognition, fluency, and reading flow, as well as any word-study and meta-cognitive strategies that the student may employ.

Each new snapshot provides the assessor with additional data that steer the assessment and decision-making process. At times, the assessor may merely observe the student while the student reads. For example, if the student attempts to apply a strategy to unlock a word or to make sense by rereading a particular part of the passage, the assessor may wait before providing assistance. On the other hand, the student should not be allowed to flounder. In this vein, the assessor should provide strategic assistance after a reasonable delay has occurred (e.g., 3-5 seconds), thus allowing the student to continue to maintain reading continuity.

The IA process allows flexibility when additional questions arise. For example, the assessor might be interested in the student's ability to read and comprehend during silent reading. While the preceding steps for conducting an IA snapshot remain the same, the fourth step can be augmented by having the student read the selected text silently. The assessor can monitor the student's reading rate by asking the student to point to where they are in the passage at the end of each timed interval. This allows the assessor to observe the student's silent reading rate (words read per minute) as well to assess the student's silent reading comprehension. After oral or silent reading, the assessor then moves to Step 5 of the IA process.

Step 5: Assessing Reading Comprehension and Responding

Once the student has finished reading the instructional-level passage, the assessor uses the same prompting/questioning sequence described in Step 2 to assess the student's reading comprehension. Again, unaided prompts occur first, followed by asking aided questions (who, where, when, what). Forced-choice questions and visual/referent prompts are also applied when necessary. By sampling the student's responses in this manner the assessor is able to compare and contrast the student's reading comprehension with the student's listening comprehension.

As a final caveat, if the student was told by the assessor during the word-search step that they would "come back" to certain words, they will need to return to those words before ending the assessment snapshot. This allows the assessor an opportunity to look more closely at the student's word-study skills within the context of reading. If steps 1-3 of the IA have been followed, the number of unknown words at this stage of the assessment should be confined to only four or five new words. Questions concerning what the student knows about each unknown word and how the student approaches each unknown word should guide the discussion. Studying a few unknown words in this manner and not overloading the student informs the assessor and teacher where additional word-study help may be needed.

Assessor Decision #2: How did the student perform relative to the various reading dimensions? What reading dimensions will need to be observed further and what future snapshots will be needed? What specific dimensions require immediate support?

With the student no longer present, the assessor and teacher are in a position to discuss their observations and ask and answer the next set of decision questions.

The discussion between teacher and assessor focuses on how the student responds when reading under instructional-level conditions related to each reading dimension. There is also discussion about how the instructional match was created, including what actions (i.e., options) were taken to create it. Providing a single snapshot rarely permits the assessor to choose an instructional focus. The data gathered from the first snapshot often are useful in narrowing where additional snapshots need to be focused in order to learn more about the student's actual reading skills. Each subsequent IA snapshot provides an opportunity to further define the student's prior knowledge and performance on the various reading dimensions.

Of course, having the classroom teacher present during the assessment sessions is indispensable. Trying to convey IA information second-hand is never as effective as having the teacher directly involved in the assessment sessions where both the assessor and teacher are able to immediately reflect upon what just occurred when the student read under instructional-level conditions. Naturally, each IA snapshot becomes part of a collaborative cycle between the assessor and teacher whereby direct observations of the students, discussions, and decision-making are a shared process.

As additional assessment data become available, the assessor and teacher are in an ideal position to decide which reading dimensions need immediate support and what that support should involve. By using material at the student's instructional-reading level and following the IA steps, the assessor and teacher are able to gain a clear picture of the student's reading skills. They are also in a much better position to select instructional strategies to support and improve the reading skills that are out of balance for the student.

Step 6: Matching Instruction

The logical conclusion for conducting IA snapshots is to pinpoint the precise reading needs of the student and to select specific instructional strategies that directly address the assessed needs. Conversations between the assessor and teacher are crystallized during this step. The focus of this step is on selecting appropriate reading strategies to use within the classroom and on creating and maintaining the instructional match while delivering the strategies. A more detailed review of several key strategies that have proven to produce significant student outcomes will be reviewed later in Chapter 7.

Trial Teaching

Prioritizing reading needs and matching instructional strategies to meet those needs is part of the IA itself. A well-designed IA snapshot will, at times, quickly result in clarifying what strategies to use. Teachers, for example, will often have "ah-ha" moments and exclaim, "I now know what to do." At other times, the assessor and teacher need to work closely during the IA process to identify viable strategies and to "test" whether these potential strategies will effectively address the identified area of reading concern. The concept of "trial teaching" as part of an IA snapshot has several benefits. It allows the teacher and assessor to confirm that they have correctly identified the instructional priority. Likewise, trial teaching provides an indication of how the student might respond to a particular strategy when planned as part of larger in-class instruction. Finally, trial teaching is an excellent way to model a strategy and allows for a discussion of how and when the strategy can be used by the teacher within the classroom.

Assessor Decision #3: What fine-tuning needs to occur to insure ongoing reading success?

As the teacher becomes more comfortable managing instructional-level conditions, creating the instructional match, providing the student with the appropriate feedback, and monitoring and recording the student's progress, the assessor's role begins to fade and the final decision question is addressed by the assessor and classroom teacher.

Answering this question requires critical analysis to ensure that the student achieves ongoing reading success and that incremental adjustments enable the student to manage his or her learning with little or no teacher assistance.

APPLICATION OF INSTRUCTIONAL ASSESSMENT

A better understanding of the IA steps is possible when applied to an actual reading case. The following case illustrates the difficulties facing a struggling first-grader and indicates just how quickly reading material can move beyond where the student is able to function. The case also highlights the importance of conducting the assessment with the teacher being an active participant. While the case involved a first-grader, it is important to realize that the research principles and practices that form the basis of the IA process provide a structure that enables the assessor in collaboration with the teacher to work with all students across *all* grade levels, skill levels, and curriculum content areas.

The Case of Taylor

At the end of the third marking period, the teacher described Taylor as a struggling first-grade reader. He was receiving reading instruction in the classroom and was also removed from the classroom to receive additional reading support for 30 minutes a day from a reading specialist. Taylor was described as a below grade-level reader with poor comprehension, weak decoding skills, low retention skill, and poor spelling skills. Data from quarterly reading assessments indicated very little progress since the beginning of the school year. His most recent assessment indicated he read a beginning first-grade passage with 24 correct words per minute and with 88% accuracy.

Several observations were made by the assessor and teacher as they began working together and reviewing the data. First, most of the descriptive information about Taylor involved what he did not know and could not do. There was little information offered about his existing reading skills and prior knowledge. The second observation involved how the data were presented. At no point was Taylor reading at instructional level. Most troubling was the fact that his teacher could not provide specific information about the instruction he was receiving from the reading support specialist. The lack of a cohesive instructional plan between the classroom teacher and the reading specialist is reminiscent of our own experiences and is consistent with Slavin's (2003) findings. He and others had observed that special programs are rarely integrated or connected to the instruction provided within regular classroom settings.

Selecting Material

The teacher provided the basal reader used by Taylor's grade-level peers as well as the "little books" used by Taylor in his guided reading group. The teacher also indicated she read a chapter a day from a novel as part of whole-class instruction. The assessor asked the teacher to have the chapter book available along with the other two types of material to facilitate the IA.

Building A Relationship

The assessor and teacher talked with Taylor and told him they wanted to help him become a better reader and that his teacher wanted to become a better teacher. They explained that the purpose of the assessment was to look for what he knew and what he could do. Taylor was also told that if something was too difficult or confusing not to worry because the assessor was looking for what he knew and what he could do. During the discussion, Taylor volunteered information about his hobbies. He shared that he liked to ride bikes and play and explained that he had a baby sister and an older brother. As a first-grader, he was able to provide a detailed description of how reading instruction occurred in class. He explained that his teacher would read from the chapter book each day. She would read a page, then stop and ask someone a question. During reading he worked in a small group with four other students and pointed to the little book the group was using. He also explained that when he went with his other teacher (the reading specialist) they worked on letters, letter sounds, and completing worksheets.

Step 1: Reading to the Student

The assessor chose to use the chapter book to conduct the first part of the assessment. The chapter book provided a more comprehensive story with which to observe Taylor's listening skills, unlike the little books that contained only one or two sentences per page. While the chapter book was being read, the assessor encouraged Taylor to look at the page and to follow along, giving the assessor and teacher another glimpse of his reading behaviors.

Step 2: Assessing Listening Comprehension and Responding

After reading the passage aloud, the assessor asked Taylor to summarize what he remembered from the previous chapters. He described the plot of the story, referred to the characters using pronouns *(he, she)*, and told the last thing that happened. He was able to provide names of the characters and to describe the setting when prompted with aided questions. He was also able to make a prediction when asked, "What do you think will happen in the next chapter?"

After listening to a segment from the new chapter, Taylor was able to retell about the character and events without being cued. When asked several aided questions, he provided additional details about the setting and made an inference about what the character was feeling. Since Taylor was able to provide sufficient information through both unaided and aided questions, the assessor did not employ force-choice or visual-referent questions or prompts.

Step 3: Conducting a Word Search (Word Recognition and Meaning)

Although the chapter book was considered too difficult for Taylor to read, the assessor chose to use it for two reasons. First, the word-search strategy was designed to maintain optimal learning conditions for Taylor. The assessor carefully pointed to known and unknown words using a 4-5:1 ratio to control the challenge level. Secondly, the chapter book contained substantially more words to assess Taylor's sight-word knowledge. While little books (i.e., leveled readers) often contain fewer than 25 words, the chapter book provided a large pool of words, offering a greater chance of finding words that Taylor knew.

The assessor first pointed to small structural words (e.g., *I, to, a, the*), including high frequency words (e.g., *do, go, can, that*), and then to a harder word. The ratio of at least 4-5 known words followed by one unknown word was consistently employed. Because of Taylor's limited sight-word vocabulary, the assessor had the teacher record each known word Taylor correctly identified from the chapter book. The assessor then conducted the word search in two little books using the same technique.

Interestingly, the vocabulary difficulty contained in each little book was consistently found to be at a frustration level. For example, out of a total of 15 words in the first little book, Taylor knew only 3 of the words. The second little book was somewhat better but still well within a frustration range, with only 6 out of 22 words being known. While little books often appear to be appropriate, as seen in Taylor's case, their use illustrates how quickly these seemingly highly controlled readers can become mismatched.

Conducting the word search in the different texts provided an "ah-ha" experience for his classroom teacher. She had always assumed the level of these little books to be appropriate and supportive of Taylor's reading needs. She quickly recognized as she observed the word-search procedure that each book remained well beyond the conditions that would be considered at Taylor's instructional reading level. At the end of the word search, the following 18 known words were recorded by his teacher (most coming from the chapter book):

to	had	in	I	the	at	went	a	he
we	and	she	my	on	said	book	into	look

Assessor Decision #1: Does the student possess the language, conceptual background, and sight-word vocabulary to read and comprehend the selection?

After reading to the student and conducting a word search, the assessor and teacher agreed that Taylor's language and prior knowledge were sufficient to interact with most first-grade concepts. In addition, Taylor's ability to respond orally was considered to be at or above the level of most students in the class. The teacher highlighted the fact that Taylor remembered and could retell the previous chapters and commented that many of the students would not have provided as much detail in their responses. This was one of many observations made by the teacher concerning what Taylor "could do" and represented a major shift from the teacher's initial descriptions prior to the IA.

Working together, the assessor and teacher determined that a limited sight-word vocabulary was preventing Taylor from successfully reading any of the available texts. Considering how mismatched the chapter book and the little books were compared to Taylor's limited sight-word vocabulary, it was fruitless for the assessor to continue attempting to find the "just right" book for Taylor to read. At this point, the assessor and teacher reviewed the various assessment options (see Chapter 6). The option of teaching him 2-3 new words (his working-memory range) was not sufficient to elevate any of the available texts to his instructional level. A better choice was to use the known words the teacher had recorded during the word-search to create teacher-made stories that would conform to his instructional reading level.

Step 4: Sampling Content Reading (Word study and Reading Fluency)

Taylor was asked to return to his class while the assessor and teacher developed a story that would allow for the reading assessment to continue (see Option 5, Chapter 6). The following story was written in less than ten minutes and met instruction-level conditions. While clearly not a Pulitzer Prize winner, the story used Taylor's known words along with three unknown words to achieve an accuracy rate of approximately 95% known words. The three unknown words are underlined.

Look! Look at my book.

"Look at my book," said Taylor.

"I <u>see</u> the book," said <u>Mom</u>.

"My book is <u>big</u>," said Taylor.

"I <u>see</u> the <u>big</u> book," said <u>Mom</u>.

<u>Mom</u> and I look at my <u>big</u> book.

"Look in my book," said Taylor.

"I <u>see</u> in the book," said <u>Mom</u>.

<u>Mom</u> and I look into my <u>big</u> book.

Upon returning, Taylor was told that his teacher and the assessor had written a story just for him and that the story was special since it contained many words that he already knew. Although initially apprehensive, he began reading the story aloud. He read with expression and even provided emphasis when encountering punctuation (exclamation mark, quotes). His voice also showed inflection when reading the story. When Taylor encountered two of the three new words, he used decoding to correctly read "big" and said "mother" for "mom," but used context to quickly self-correct. He read the story with no errors in 45 seconds, which converted to 78 words read correctly per minute.

Step 5: Assessing Reading Comprehension and Responding

The assessor then asked Taylor to retell what he read. He was able to retell the entire story with no prompting and with ease. When asked what title he might give the story, he responded, "Taylor's Book."

Assessor Decision #2: How did the student perform relative to the various reading dimensions? What specific reading dimensions require immediate support? What reading dimensions will need to be observed further, and what further snapshots will be needed?

After Taylor returned to his class, the assessor and teacher discussed what they saw as a result of the first reading snapshot. Before conducting the reading assessment, Taylor's teacher had described him as being a poor reader with few reading skills. After creating instructional-level conditions and gaining a valid snapshot of Taylor as a reader, her perception of his reading skills changed. She observed that when Taylor performed under optimal conditions, comprehension and responding during listening and reading were both at high levels. She also observed that he demonstrated good fluency (both rate and flow) and that he applied several word-study strategies (decoding and using context clues). A joint decision was reached to collect additional snapshots with an emphasis on further assessing Taylor's sight-word vocabulary (word recognition).

Three additional snapshots were conducted using teacher-made stories as the assessment option. This choice was derived based upon the first decision question—does the student have the sight-word vocabulary to read and understand the selection? In each instance, Taylor continued to read each teacher-made story without error while consistently employing effective word-study strategies to unlock each new unknown word. His fluency remained in the 65-85 correct-words-per-minute range throughout each snapshot. During the final two snapshots, Taylor was taught how to do his own word search. He was told to scan ("look, but don't read") the page and to put his finger on each word he knew and could pronounce. With practice, he was able to quickly look at a page and identify words he could pronounce and knew what they meant. This process resulted in a growing sight-word vocabulary of 55 known words by the end of the final snapshot.

Step 6: Matching Instruction

Results of the IA snapshots highlighted word recognition as the focus for continued strategic instructional support. Taylor was taught how to conduct his own word search and to identify words that he knows. This trial teaching period informed the teacher of possible classroom strategies. Using known words from Taylor's word search, the teacher was able to strategically design and deliver instruction effectively to him. She had an understanding of his sight vocabulary (word-recognition skill) and understood how many new words could be effectively introduced for practice purposes (working memory). Most of all, she now knew how to manage the reading content so that a range of 93-97% known words were maintained (instructional reading level) prior to having Taylor read.

Follow-up to Taylor

The teacher used the IA experience to design and deliver instruction not only for Taylor but also for other students in his small reading group. The group's instruction over the next several weeks used teacher-made stories written at instructional level. At first, the teacher had Taylor and his peers conduct their own word searches in targeted books. Using the known words from these books, the teacher strategically created teacher-made stories written at the students' instructional reading levels (93-97% known). She strategically selected new words that appeared in targeted published text, and incorporated these into her teacher-made stories. She also applied drill and practice activities (i.e., drill sandwiches with 7 known words and 3 new words) to further each student's sight-word development. As the students made progress, each student was gradually moved away from relying on teacher-made stories to working in published text. After two weeks of using teacher-made stories and related practice activities, Taylor was able to join the rest of the class in successfully reading the next published story. Teacher-made stories and related practices were repeated two more times, after which Taylor and his reading group were fully integrated back into using the published texts used in class.

SUMMARY

Instructional assessment demonstrates that effective assessment instructs and that effective instruction assesses. It reinforces the reality that learning and teaching are never complete and are ever-changing (Valencia, 1990). It capitalizes on using the content of the classroom so that the assessor and teacher can "observe and interact with students as they read authentic texts for genuine purposes" (Valencia & Pearson, 1987, p. 28), and it ensures that the content used during each reading assessment is appropriately matched and managed to enable students to perform at optimal levels.

While IA is a structured process, it does not follow a script nor is it a collection of tools and techniques. Instead, the steps and structure act as guidelines, allowing the assessor and teacher to pursue additional areas of inquiry that naturally arise when working with students. These steps ensure that instructional-level conditions are managed appropriately and that the assessor and teacher are able to gain clear pictures of how each student orchestrates his or her skills within and across the essential dimensions of reading. Each snapshot offers clues on how best to instruct each student, and enables the assessor and teacher to detect both subtle and obvious improvements in the reading skills of each student.

Although this chapter highlights its application to the area of reading, the underlying principles of IA apply to all curricular areas. Using the basic steps of the IA process, the assessor, working in collaboration with the teacher, is able to select material used in the classroom, assess the student's performance under instructional-level conditions, identify what the student knows and what the student can do, and isolate the dimensions of reading that require additional support. The data collected from ongoing assessment snapshots enable the teacher and assessor to design, implement, and evaluate the effectiveness of using targeted strategies to improve the student's academic areas of need.

In reflecting upon the value of the IA process and its direct application to reading, it is important to remember that the process is based upon sound learning and teaching principles. The process provides a path that ensures the implementation of sound instructional strategies proven to produce positive growth in the reading achievement of struggling readers.

An outline of the steps used in assessing a student's reading performance has been attached for easy reference in Appendix A. Also included are two examples of summary forms that have been used to document the student's performance during each step of the reading assessment process.

Chapter 6

Options for Assessing Students with Limited Reading Skills

The quality of information is suspect
when tasks are too easy or too difficult.

(IRA/NCTE Joint Task Force, 1994)

Chapter Five described the steps for conducting an IA snapshot and stressed the importance of assessing students' reading and comprehension skills under instructional-level conditions. A key feature of the IA process is that students only read when the assessor is assured that instructional-level conditions are present (i.e., Assessor Decision #1). When these conditions are not present, the assessor is responsible for creating them, ensuring the challenge level is within the students' optimal window—where reading tasks are not too difficult or too easy. This chapter describes a series of options available to the assessor for creating optimal conditions for students who are struggling readers.

For students exhibiting few or fragmented reading skills to perform well, it is essential that the assecor use appropriate options to create instructional-level conditions for the IA. The alternative is unacceptable. When struggling readers are assessed using material that is too hard, the data simply confirms what everyone already knows–that they perform poorly. Asking poor readers to read material that is too hard not only perpetuates frustration, but also invalidates the results of the assessment. Furthermore, information collected under conditions of frustration fails to provide assessment data useful to guide the planning and delivery of effective reading instruction.

Unfortunately, the practice of narrowly focusing on acquiring baseline data or monitoring grade-level progress ignores or actively bypasses the creation of instructional-level conditions. Furthermore, these practices perpetuate a normal curve mentality, a mentality that merely focuses on "weighing the lambs." The overreliance on the use of universal screening and formal progress monitoring procedures provides little assurance that such practices accurately portray students' reading skills or correctly identify what students truly know and need (Altwerger, Jordan & Shelton, 2007; Goodman, 2006; Howard, 2009). Disappointing assessment results will continue to plague education as long as screening and progress monitoring are emphasized at the expense of assessment that creates instructional-level conditions. Such instructional-level conditions are essential to obtain valid data to inform and guide instruction.

Assessment practices that mirror the optimal window guideline depicted in Figure 3.10 provide an accurate picture of what readers, poor or otherwise, are capable of doing when the content matches their instructional and conceptual reading levels. Establishing learning and teaching conditions that conform to these guidelines provides the best opportunity for meeting and improving the literacy skills of the truly struggling reader.

USING OPTIONS TO ESTABLISH OPTIMAL CONDITIONS

The first three steps of the IA snapshot described in Chapter 5 ensure that the difficulty level of the passage to be read does not inhibit the student from doing his or her best. By reading orally to the student, assessing the student's listening comprehension, and conducting the word search, the assessor can gauge the student's language and sight-word vocabulary with respect to the reading demands of the passage and can answer the first decision question: ***Does the student possess the language, conceptual background, and sight-word vocabulary to read and comprehend the selection?***

Figure 6.1 displays the three possible choices an assessor will have when considering this decision question. A "yes" means the word-searched passage is at the student's instructional-reading level, allowing the assessment process to proceed by having the student read the passage. If the answer is "maybe," the assessor may elect to conduct a more thorough word search on the existing passage or continue to read aloud from subsequent passages, selecting a new passage and conducting a new word search

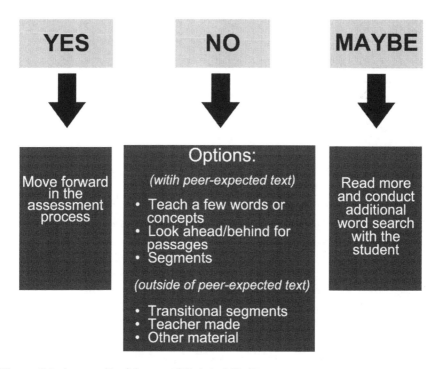

Figure 6.1 Assesor Decisions and Related Options

in order to arrive at either a solid "yes" or "no" decision. If the assessor concludes that the answer is "no" and that the conditions are outside the student's instructional-reading level due to excessive vocabulary demands and/or difficult language concepts, the student is not asked to read until the conditions are made optimal.

It is intuitive in reading instruction to avoid giving students books they are unable to read. Once a teacher or specialist sees that grade-level material is too difficult for the struggling reader, the knee-jerk response is to assign easier material. However, when conducting an IA snapshot, the practice of assigning lower-level material is purposely delayed and, at times, actively avoided for two important reasons.

First, the goal of the IA process is to observe the student's highest level of conceptual knowledge and skill when reading under instructional-level conditions. IA carefully incorporates the research of Betts (1946), which found that struggling readers often have the ability to listen, discuss, and interact with the reading content of their peers even though their reading skills may not be at the level of their peers. The use of options allows the assessor to manage the assessment conditions to create the best reading and conceptual match for the students.

The second reason for not immediately rushing to lower-level material and for maintaining the assessment at the student's highest level of conceptual knowledge is how it benefits the teacher. The introduction of options during the assessment might be the first time the teacher actually observes how the student reads using grade-level material and how appropriate reading conditions are established. Classroom teachers already have limited choices, especially when content reading material is used (e.g., science, social studies). The assessor's use of options to create instructional-level conditions within grade-level content provides a model for how to manage text variability, a model the teacher can ultimately generalize for classroom use.

Gone are the days of the simplistic belief that there are "just right" reading materials to be used during highly-structured, guided reading as a means to compensate for hours and hours of non-reading during the remainder of the school day. A certain way for struggling readers to fall further and further behind their peers is to confine them daily to 30-45 minutes of matched instruction and 4-5 hours of non-profitable reading experiences not delivered at instructional level. Teachers need options to manage the variability found in students' texts, and students need teachers skilled in using appropriate options to match and accelerate their reading development.

ASSESSMENT AND TEACHING OPTIONS

At first, the use of peer-expected text when assessing struggling readers will seem counterintuitive and improbable, but as the assessor becomes more experienced with conducting IA snapshots the choice of lower-level material will be a necessity less frequently. The choices presented in Figure 6.1 consist of using peer-expected and non peer-expected materials--with three options available in each area. Mastering the first three options using peer-expected texts can quickly prove valuable to the assessor for practical reasons. It is generally more efficient to use peer-expected texts to create optimal conditions rather than searching endlessly for the "just right" reader. Likewise, when considering alternative material it is often more efficient to actually create transitional segments or teacher-made stories as opposed to hunting for supposed easier material to ensure that instructional-level reading conditions exist. While the use of lower-level material is still available, many experienced IA assessors find this practice to be a last and infrequent choice.

Options Within Peer-Expected Text

Option 1—Teach a Few Words or Concepts

If the student's sight-word vocabulary and conceptual knowledge are only slightly below what is required to read peer-expected text and the student is able to understand the text when read aloud, the assessor's focus is on strategically teaching a few unknown words and/or concepts to create an instructional-level passage for the student to read within the peer-expected text. Consideration must be given to the number of new words and/or concepts that need to be taught. Specifically, teaching a few new words should result in a reading passage that is within the optimal window (93-97% known words) while the number of words taught should not violate the limits of the student's working memory.

Option 1 Illustration. Reading tasks that are too difficult produce frustration. When this repeatedly happens, students experience what would aptly be called "misery reading."

The Blimblat

Once when I was a child my tomly and I were standing in line to buy motts for the Blimblat. Finally, there was only one plam between us and the mott counter. This plam made a big impression on me. There were eight utzs, all probably under the age of 12. You could tell tures did not have a lot of willen. Their clothes were not yanker, but tures were clean. The utzs were well-behaved, all of them standing in line, two-by-two behind their potents holding zibits. Tures were excitedly talking about the plums, fonts, and other acts tures would see that night. (80 percent known)

Attempting to make sense of the above passage when 20% of the words are unknown is futile. By pre-teaching a few words, though, it is possible to create optimal learning conditions. For example, the assessor could pre-teach the following words:

Blimblat = circus   *tomly = father*

plam = family   *tures = they*

By pre-teaching only these four words, more favorable conditions are created, enabling the reader to apply his or her prior knowledge effectively to read and understand the passage.

The Circus

Once when I was a child my father and I were standing in line to buy motts for the circus. Finally, there was only one family between us and the mott counter. This family made a big impression on me. There were eight utzs, all probably under the age of 12. You could tell they did not have a lot of willen. Their clothes were not yanker, but they were clean. The utzs were well-behaved, all of them standing in line, two-by-two behind their potents holding zibits. They were excitedly talking about the plums, fonts, and other acts they would see that night. (93 percent known)

While several contrived words remain, it is much easier to decipher and retain the meaning of the remaining words since context clues are strengthened and working memory is not overloaded. Instructional-level conditions—meaning an appropriate margin of challenge—now exist.

Option 1 Skill Practice. The following passage contains 145 words, of which 14 are contrived (unknown). Take a moment to read and reflect upon your ability to comprehend the passage.

Long raidans were forming when Matthew arrived. He tried to phindate the amount of time it would take to get to the cornvorster. Vort it would be too long, plast he would miss the game. He varaxted for a moment until the raidans became even longer. He decided that he would ordrul in the raidan opet see vort it would start moving more expeditiously. No sooner had he started fleedjuul, when it began mostulalag quite hard. Matthew became disgusted, zipped up his ornaforger, then walked back to his car. He drove home ov the mostul. By the time he put the car in the garage, the mostul was droim, and the faedos was out. Matthew was doubly disgusted now. Suddenly, he went inside opet watch the game. He turned on the television set but nothing happened. Matthew said to himself, "What a lousy frol." (Hargis, 1987, p. 33)

Did the excessive number of unknown words adversely affect the flow of reading and your ability to comprehend the passage? Did you slow down to phonetically attack the unknown words? Did you reread the passage in an attempt to understand it? Did the use of context clues help create meaning? Were you able to use your prior knowledge?

Teachers often consider the text unworkable when there are so many unknown words and begin a search for easier material. However, in this example, and in many cases for struggling readers, if only a few words are strategically substituted, instructional-level conditions can be created. Below are the contrived words and their meanings. Cover the list of words and reveal them one at a time.   After each substitution, read the passage and see if it makes sense without needing additional instruction.

Contrived Words	Meanings
raidens	lines
cornvorster	ticket office
ordrul	stand
mostulalag	raining
opet	to
phindate	estimate
fleedjuul	going
vort	if
ornaforger	jacket
plast	maybe
droim	over
varaxted	waited
faedos	sun
frol	day

How many contrived words did you need to replace so the passage approached an instructional-reading level?   Which words provided the best opportunity to understand the passage?   Remember, an instructional level requires an appropriate margin of challenge—not too hard and not too easy.

In summary, when the student is faced with a limited number of unknown words or concepts, strategically pre-teaching a few words and/or concepts is often an effective and efficient way to create instructional-level conditions that allow the student to perform well. However, this option requires knowing what the student knows relative to the vocabulary demands of the passage and highlights the importance of the word-search procedure during the initial assessment steps. With this information, the assessor is in a strategic position to manage and monitor the difficulty level of the reading passage at the student's instructional level. The option of pre-teaching selected unknown words or concepts will likely remain even if another option is to be applied.

Option 2—Look Ahead or Look Behind

If there are too many unknown words or concepts in steps 2 and 3 of the IA, or if teaching a few words or concepts using a passage from a peer-expected text does not achieve instructional-level conditions, the next available option is to look ahead or behind in the same text for a more suitable passage to assess the student. Because the vocabulary and conceptual demands of texts vary greatly from page to page and even from paragraph to paragraph, the assessor will often find occasions where one passage of a story is beyond the student's optimal window while the very next passage may be suitable.

<u>Option 2 Illustration.</u> Books that are rich and engaging will vary a great deal in their vocabulary and concept development. This is not a criticism of any particular author or publisher; it is merely a fact, especially when text selection moves beyond predictable or patterned books. The following story written by Mary Pope Osborn (2002), entitled "*Revolutionary War on Wednesday*," provides a good example of how the difficulty level of a text varies from page to page in rich and engaging stories.

Revolutionary War on Wednesday

(Page 29)

Even at a distance, Jack thought the commander-in-chief looked familiar. But he couldn't figure out why.

"A dangerous mission lies before you all," the man shouted above the wind. "But I want you to have courage. You must remember the words of Thomas Paine." The commander-in-chief held up a piece of paper. He read to his men.

(Page 30)

"These are the times that try men's souls. The summer soldier and the sunshine patriot will, in this crisis, shrink from the service of their country. But he that stands it now deserves the love and thanks of man and woman..."

"Wow, that's great," whispered Annie. Listening to the powerful words, Jack felt his spirits rise, too.

"The harder the conflict, the more glorious the triumph," the commander-in chief read on. "What we obtain too cheap, we esteem too lightly. It is dearness only that gives everything its value." There was a silence, as if everyone were thinking about the words the man had read. Then the soldiers started cheering and clapping. They didn't seem tired at all anymore.

(Page 32)

..."I know who the commander-in-chief is!" he exclaimed. "He's George Washington!" "George Washington? Really?" said Annie.

"Wait—don't go far," said Jack. "I just want to make sure. "Yeah, I think he is!" said Jack.

"Wow! Where'd he go?" said Annie. "I want to see him again! Come on!" She started toward the river, "It's him."

He opened the Revolutionary War book. He found a picture of the riverbank. He read...

This exemplifies how typical reading material fluctuates, sometimes even on the same page. In perusing the three pages of text, it is immediately clear that pages 29 and 30 are more difficult than page 32, and that page 30 especially requires a higher level of conceptual understanding than the other pages. The difficulty of these pages ranges from easy first-grade reading (page 32) to challenging middle-school-level concepts (page 30).

This example also illustrates how looking ahead or behind is a viable option to establish instructional-level conditions rather than stopping the IA process and searching for other suitable material. By recognizing the inherent variability in reading content, the assessor can efficiently move the assessment process forward while remaining within the same peer-expected text. Employing this second option provides an opportunity for the assessor and teacher to discuss how to manage and maintain optimal learning conditions for the student when using another passage.

This second option requires the assessor to orally read portions of the text that are too difficult for the student and then to allow the student to read those passages that have been assessed to be within his or her instructional level. For example, if page 32 reflected the student's instructional-reading level and would be used to assess the student's reading skills, then pages 29 and 30 would be read aloud to, and discussed with, the student before asking the student to read page 32. Strategically selecting passages (Option 2) may also require the assessor to incorporate pre-teaching (Option 1). Teaching a few unknown words is often needed because of how words and concepts constantly change within most printed texts.

Option 2 Skill Practice. As you turn the pages of almost any text you will find passages or consecutive lines of text that contain more complex language and vocabulary difficult for the struggling reader. This fact is illustrated in the delightful primary-level book written by Mike Thaler entitled *The Teacher from the Black Lagoon* (1989).

Think about a struggling reader who has only beginning reading skills. Read the story and decide which passages or lines of text would be suitable for meeting instructional-level conditions for the student.

It's the first day of school.

I wonder who my teacher is.

I hear Mr. Smith has dandruff and warts,

and Mrs. Jones has a whip and a wig.

But Mrs. Green is supposed to be a real monster!

Oh my, I have her!

Mrs. Green...room 109. What a bummer!

I sit at a desk,

I fold my hands.

I close my eyes.

I'm too young to die.

Suddenly a shadow covers the door.

It opens. In slithers Mrs.

Green. She's really green!

She has a tail.

She scratches her name on the blackboard with her claws.

Freddy Jones throws a spitball.

She curls her lips and breathes fire at him.

Freddy's gone.

There is just a pile of ashes on his desk.

"Talk about bad breath," giggles Eric Porter.

She slithers over and unscrews his head,

and puts it on the globe stand.

The variability from paragraph to paragraph and from line to line should be apparent. If you chose the passage, *"I sit at a desk, I fold my hands. I close my eyes. I'm too young to die,"* it was a good choice as these few lines of text contain the least amount of challenge compared to the other paragraphs. This allows the assessor to feel more comfortable about creating instructional-level conditions.

Rather than abandoning the story, the assessor can look ahead or behind and use these lines strategically as the option of choice for having the student read aloud. Since the four lines appear only once in the original story, the assessor can also incorporate the next option involving content segments to help the student achieve mastery of the four lines while enjoying the story in its entirety. For example, the assessor can write these four lines on a card or "sticky" note and then orally read the story. At strategic points, the assessor can stop and have the student read the four lines of text.

(Assessor)	It's the first day of school.
	I wonder who my teacher is.
	I hear Mr. Smith has dandruff and warts,
	and Mrs. Jones has a whip and a wig.
	But Mrs. Green is supposed to be a
	real monster!
	Oh my, I have her!
	Mrs. Green...room 109. What a bummer!
(Student)	I sit at a desk,
	I fold my hands.
	I close my eyes.
	I'm too young to die.
(Assessor)	Suddenly a shadow covers the door.
	It opens. In slithers Mrs.
	Green. She's really green!
	She has a tail.
(Student)	I sit at a desk,
	I fold my hands.
	I close my eyes.
	I'm too young to die.
(Assessor)	She scratches her name on the

blackboard with her claws.

Freddy Jones throws a spitball.

She curls her lips and breathes fire at him.

Freddy's gone.

There is just a pile of ashes on his desk.

(Student)   I sit at a desk,

I fold my hands.

I close my eyes.

I'm too young to die.

(Assessor)   "Talk about bad breath,"

giggles Eric Porter.

She slithers over and unscrews his head,

and puts it on the globe stand.

(Student)   I sit at a desk,

I fold my hands.

I close my eyes.

I'm too young to die.

Focusing on mastering lines of text in this manner enables the assessor to maintain instructional-level conditions while providing extra repetition. It also permits the luxury of focusing on learning a few new words and/or practicing certain word-study skills needed by the student without overwhelming the student with extensive content.

Option 3—Content Segments

According to Cole (1998), literature used to teach children to read has become more complex than what was used years ago. Using peer-expected literature of today to assess the skills of the poor reader often requires an even more restricted option than teaching a few new words or looking ahead or behind to find a more suitable passage. The use of content segments calls for the assessor to scaffold text into even smaller frames to maintain instructional-level conditions.

Instead of relying on the use of multiple sentences as shown in the previous option, the assessor may need to be even more strategic, working line by line to gain an appropriate fit or comfort zone for the student. The assessor provides support by orally reading the intervening text and scaffolding instruction throughout the assessment while the student reads at the phrase, sentence, or short paragraph level.

Option 3 Illustration. After the teacher read *Rosie's Walk* (1968) by Pat Hutchins to her class, the assessor sat down to talk with Claire, a struggling student, about the story and to assess her sight-word vocabulary. While Claire was able to listen and respond to stories when read to orally, a word search of *Rosie's Walk* indicated that "fox" was her only known sight-word.

The assessor recognized Claire's responding skills as her strength and wanted to capitalize on both context and repetition to facilitate vocabulary growth (Hargis, 1987). Seeing that the story contained her one known word in the phrase "No, fox, no!" the assessor introduced and taught the unknown word "no." However, since the phrase appeared only once in the story, the assessor wrote the phrase on a "sticky" note. The assessor then orally read the page and purposefully moved the sticky note to the bottom of each page for the student to read, capitalizing on both context and repetition to facilitate her vocabulary development. By reading in context and providing extra repetition at the phrase level, Claire was able to learn and retain the word "no," adding it to her limited sight-word vocabulary. As shown in Figure 6.2, the original story is on the left and the example using segments is on the right.

Option 3 Skill Practice. The following passage from *Miss Nelson is Missing!* by Harry Allard and James Marshal (1977) was not at instructional level for the third-grader. Out of 94 words, 78 were known and 16 (underlined) words were unknown. Instead of the passage containing 3-7% challenge, it contained a frustration rate of 17%.

Review the passage and then use the option of content segments so that each segment contains an appropriate level of challenge. How much text would you use for each reading segment? How many unknown words would be appropriate within each segment?

The next morning Miss Nelson did not come

to school.

"Wow!" yelled the kids. "Now we can really act up!"

They began to make more spitballs and paper planes.

"Today let's be just terrible!" they said.

"Not so fast!" hissed an unpleasant voice.

A woman in an ugly black dress stood before them.

"I am your new teacher. Miss Viola Swamp."

And she rapped the desk with her ruler.

"Where is Miss Nelson?" <u>asked</u> the kids.

<u>Never mind</u> that!" <u>snapped</u> Miss Swamp.

"Open those <u>Arithmetic</u> books!"

Miss Nelson's kids did as they were told.

(pp. 8-10)

Maybe you decided to divide the passage into three segments, creating instructional-level conditions for each segment. You would then be in a position to assess the student's reading skill by having the student read the first segment.

Rosie the hen went for a walk across the yard. **No, fox, no!** around the pond over the haystack past the mill through the fence under the beehive and got back in time for dinner. Watch out Rosie! There's a fox right behind you.	Rosie the hen went for a walk across the yard. **No, fox, no!** around the pond **No, fox, no!** over the haystack **No, fox, no!** past the mill **No, fox, no!** through the fence **No, fox, no!** under the beehive **No, fox, no!** and got back in time for dinner. Watch out Rosie! There's a fox right behind you. **No, fox, no!**

Figure 6.2 Use of Strategic Segment with repetition (Option 3)

(Student)	The next morning Miss Nelson did not come to school.
	"Wow!" <u>yelled</u> the kids. "Now we can really act up!"
	They <u>began</u> to make more <u>spitballs</u> and paper planes.
	"Today let's be just terrible!" they said.

By limiting the amount of challenge to only four unknown words, it would be easy to observe any word study strategies used by the student for each unknown word identified during the earlier word search. With only four unknown words, maintaining the student's interest in word study becomes easier and is a more pleasant activity. Likewise, with only four unknown words, the assessor can comfortably recall and discuss the meaning of each with the student.

(Student) yelled	began	spitballs	terrible

Can the student identify any parts of words, words within words, or patterns within words, or did he or she merely attempt to sound out words? When studying the words, how well and how quickly did the student acquire them?

After re-reading the first segment and thinking about the student's performance, do you feel comfortable introducing the next segment to gather additional data?

(Student)	"Not so fast!" hissed an unpleasant voice.
	A woman in an ugly black dress stood before them.
	I am your teacher. Miss Viola Swamp."

What insights were gained from having the student engage the second segment? Did the student make use of information from the previous student/assessor exchanges? Did you confirm any word-study patterns? How well did he or she read the combined segments? Is this a good place to end the student's reading and for the assessor to orally read the remaining segment?

(Assessor)	"Where is Miss Nelson?" <u>asked</u> the kids.
	"Never mind that!" snapped Miss Swamp. "Open those Arithmetic books!"
	Miss Nelson's kids did as they were told.

Incorporating the use of a card or note containing the following sentence could also provide extra repetition while bringing closure to this assessment snapshot.

(Assessor and Student)   **And she <u>rapped</u> the desk with her ruler.**

Combining Options Within Peer-Expected Text

While each of the previous options were presented as independent actions to create instructional-level conditions, it is more typical to combine more than one option to successfully manage the assessment process using peer-expected text. Many times the assessor can remain in a peer-expected text by looking ahead or behind, using appropriate segments, and pre-teaching key vocabulary.

Combining Options: Skill Practice. While participating in the last practice task, did you notice most of the student's difficulty involved decoding multi-syllabic words and using common endings? The underlined words reflected these error patterns. Knowing what the student knows and that certain error patterns exist can help you analyze and segment the following text. See if you can anticipate the difficult words and identify what words you would pre-teach to maintain instructional-level conditions. Also determine how you could use different segments of the passage to address some of the student's word-study needs.

They could see that Miss Swamp was a real witch.

She meant business.

Right away she put them to work.

And she loaded them down with homework.

"We'll have no story hour today," said Miss Swamp.

"Keep your mouths shut," said Miss Swamp.

"Sit perfectly still," said Miss Swamp.

"And if you misbehave, you'll be sorry," said Miss

Swamp.

The kids in Room 207 had never worked so hard.

Days went by and there was no sign of Miss Nelson.

The kids missed Miss Nelson!

"Maybe we should try to find her," they said.

Some of them went to the police.

Detective McSmogg was assigned to the case.

He listened to their story.

He scratched his chin.

"Hummmm," he said. "Hummmm."

"I think Miss Nelson is missing."

Detective McSmogg would not be much help.

Options Outside of Peer-expected Text

When the assessor is unable to establish instructional-level conditions using peer-expected text, other options should be considered to move the assessment process forward. However, it has been our experience when replacing one text with an easier text that such replacements seldom provide struggling readers with a consistent instructional match.

Option 4—Transitional Passages

The option of creating (writing) transitional material is one that bridges between peer and alternative texts. The purpose of transitional passages is to prepare students to return and read originally assigned text successfully. The assessor uses the student's known sight-words while keeping the key concepts and content of the published material intact. By retaining the main ideas, settings, characters, and events of the original material, the assessor manages the vocabulary load to create material written at the student's instructional level (Gickling & Havertape, 1981). This option allows for a smooth transition from one area of text to another and from one story to another.

Option 4 Illustration. Writing transitional passages or stories is a sentimental favorite since it was the approach we used more than 30 years ago with our first case. We had just realized that assessment's most important function was to determine precisely what a student knows in order to consistently manage instructional-level conditions and we were eager to apply that knowledge. The opportunity came when meeting a beginning third-grader, Rick. Rick's school records indicated he had average intelligence and possessed good oral language skills, but he lagged substantially behind in his expected reading development. He was referred to a diagnostic learning center for reading and related behavioral concerns that included disturbing other students and task avoidance.

During our first encounter, we learned Rick was assigned to read *Jim Forest and the Bandits* by John and Nancy Rambeau (1967). The book was selected from a category of high-interest, low-vocabulary material supposedly to match his first-grade reading skill. A record detailing his performance while reading the first paragraph showed unknown words (underlined) and hesitant words (parentheses).

THE RED (TRUCK)

There is a forest far up in the <u>mountains</u>. It is <u>called</u> Big <u>Pines</u>. There is a (little) (store) <u>there</u>. <u>There</u> is a <u>ranger</u> <u>station</u> <u>there</u> (too). It is <u>called</u> Big <u>Pines</u> <u>Ranger</u> <u>Station</u>.

Rick read 27 words correctly out of a total of 37, for an accuracy rate of 73%. He took 87 seconds to read the passage containing only 10 known words. (Table 6.1 summarizes Rick's known, unknown, and hesitant words). Observing how taxing it was for Rick to read the first paragraph we knew better than to ask him to read the second and third paragraphs, since they offered no reprieve from frustration. The second and third paragraphs of the story would be used later, however, and are as follows:

Jim lives at the ranger station. He lives with his uncle Don. Jim's uncle is a forest ranger. A ranger's job is a big one. He looks out for all the forest. He looks out for all the things that live in Big Pines. One day Jim and the ranger went into the forest. They took their horses. Star is the ranger's horse. Big Boy is Jim's horse.

Jim and Ranger Don were away all morning. At last they started back. As they came down the mountain, Jim said, "Look! You can see the ranger station from here." Ranger Don looked out over the trees. "Yes, I can see it. I can see the barn, too," said Ranger Don. Then the ranger looked again. "Did you close the barn door, Jim?" "Oh yes, Uncle Don. You said to close it, and I know I did," Jim said.

The option to create transitional stories was selected, continuing to use *The Red Truck* as the assessment and instructional text. However, this represented a formidable task of scaffolding the material to create instructional-level conditions since 102 words remained unknown. Using the word list in the back of the book, Rick was assessed to know an additional 17 words, for a total of 27. By selecting from his known word pool, a number of transitional passages were developed one at a time. The first four transitional passages or stories appear in Figure 6.3. Again, unknown words are underlined.

Prior to reading, the unknown words in each story were placed on index cards and sandwiched between known words for practice and repetition. Five unknown words were in the first story, four in the second story, and so forth. As words became known they were used in subsequent stories to offer repetition and provide content continuity.

The level of challenge of each subsequent story was controlled in this manner to provide sufficient practice for Rick to achieve mastery. After pre-reading practice in which unknown words were always sandwiched between known words, Rick was given the transition story to read. Following each story, he was asked to answer basic comprehension questions (comprehension was never a problem).

Known Words	Unknown Words	Hesitant Words
a	called	little
Big	mountain	store
Far	Pines	too
Forest	Ranger	truck
in	Station	
it	there	
Red		
The		
up		

Table 6.1 Rick's Known, Unknown, and Hesitant Words

This process of using pre-reading word practice followed by reading transition stories was repeated for approximately two weeks starting in late January. On February 5th, Rick was asked to read the original published text while continuing to be provided pre-reading practice. By February 8th he consistently read at an instructional-reading level and by February 15th he read at an independent level. A record of his sight-word development over the three-week period is seen in Figure 6.4.

Within three weeks, not only had Rick's sight-word vocabulary rapidly improved, reading fluency increased from 19 to 80 correct words read per minute (CWPM). As his sight-word pool increased, his attempts at decoding difficult words emerged--a skill that initially appeared absent. Only eight transitional stories were needed to raise his sight vocabulary to a point where he was comfortable reading the entire published book independently.

While creating transitional stories eventually enabled Rick to master the reading requirement of a first-grade level book, significant work remained to close the third-grade reading gap. However, this initial experience demonstrates the power that strategic actions displayed by assessors and teachers can have on struggling readers. In only three weeks, by the process of creating and maintaining instructional-level conditions and successfully managing the vocabulary of reading material, Rick was able to master reading an entire text for the first time. Moreover, the gradual and strategic introduction of a few words placed in transitional stories made the greatest difference.

Story 1

"Uncle Don"

Uncle Don took Jim to the mountains. Uncle Don is a Forest Ranger there. He lives on top of the mountain. He lives in the trees on top of the mountain. He took Jim to look at all the trees in the forest. Jim looked far into the forest at all the big trees.

Uncle Don took Jim to the

_____.

Did Uncle Don live on top of the mountain?

_____

He took Jim to see the _____.
Is Uncle Don a Forest Ranger?

Story 2

"Big Pines"

There is a forest far up in the mountains. The forest is called Big Pines. There is a little store on top of the mountain. A ranger lives on the mountain. He lives in a ranger station. The station is called Big Pines Ranger Station. Jim lives at the ranger station. Jim lives with his Uncle Don. Uncle Don is a Forest Ranger.

The forest is called _____.
There is a little _____ on top the mountain.
The ranger lives in a _____.
The ranger station is called _____

_____.

Jim lives with his _____.

Story 3

"A Ranger's Job"

Jim lives by a little store. He lives at Big Pines Ranger Station with his Uncle Don. Jim's uncle is a forest ranger. A ranger's job is a big one. He looks out for all the things that live in the forest. He looks out for all the animals and trees in the forest. He took Jim up the mountain to see the animals and trees.

Jim's uncle is a forest _____.
Jim lives in _____ forest.
Uncle Don lives with _____.
Uncle Don took Jim to see

_____.

Story 4

"Up The Mountain"

Uncle Don's job is to look out for all the things that live in Big Pines. He is to look out for all the trees and animals there. One day he took Jim and went into the forest. Uncle Don and Jim took horses. Star is Uncle Don's horse. Big Boy is Jim's horse. The ranger and Jim went up the mountain on Star and Big Boy.

Did the ranger look out for the trees?

_____

Jim and the ranger took_____.
The ranger's horse is called _____.
Jim's horse is called _____.

Figure 6.3 Rick's Transitional Stories

Option 5—Teacher-made Stories

A fifth option available to the assessor is to create stories using the student's known sight vocabulary without fully incorporating any of the content and key concepts found in published material as done when using transitional stories. Creating teacher-made stories is similar to developing transitional stories in many respects. Both options recognize that published materials, no matter how primary, do not always provide an appropriate instructional match. However, there are students who have such limited sight-word vocabularies and so few reading skills that even using transitional stories is not a viable option.

For these students to experience any real success, reading material needs to be created for them. In such cases, developing teacher-made stories is the preferred option since it allows the assessor to construct stories using the student's prior knowledge and sight-word vocabulary. By combining the student's sight words with a limited number of challenge words, the assessor is assured that the material is at the student's instructional-reading level, which provides an accurate sampling of the student's true reading skills.

This form of writing capitalizes on students' interests similar to creating language experience stories (Hargis, 2006). Unlike language experience stories, which are scripted from what the student dictates, in teacher-made stories the difficulty level is controlled using known words selected directly from the student's sight-word pool and a strategic number of unknown words so as not to violate the limits of the student's working memory. After the teacher-made story is developed, a practice sequence is provided to ensure successful vocabulary development, followed by reading of the story.

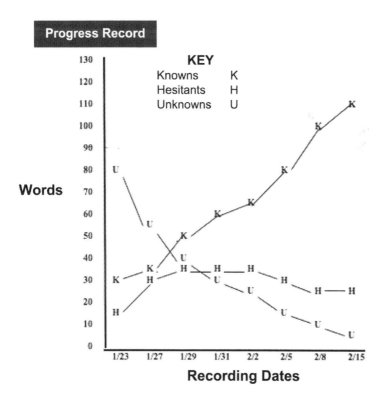

Figure 6.4 Rick's Word Development Progress

Option 5 Illustration. The following case illustrates how quickly major gaps develop due to the limited reading skills of the student and the ever expanding word-recognition demands of grade-level material. As a first-grader, Alan was referred to the school's Child Study Committee in mid-March for consideration for placement in special education. The information reported to the committee focused entirely on what he did not know, citing poor decoding skills, guessing at words, exhibiting low retention of information, and poor comprehension. Figure 6.5 depicts the summary data, including a spelling assessment presented to the committee.

As seen in Figure 6.5, data involving an initial reading showed that he knew only 26% of the words in *I Wish I Could Fly*. Although his word recognition increased as a function of repeated reading, instructional-level conditions were never achieved during any of the repeated reading episodes. Upon listening to the committee's discussion, it became apparent that they had little data concerning what Alan knew or what he could do. Realizing each literacy activity was at a frustration level, the assessor asked for permission to work with Alan during the lunch hour to better assess what he actually knew and could do.

In initial conversation with Alan it was learned he lived on a farm with his grandparents, liked to work on the farm, and liked riding on the tractor with his grandfather. After becoming acquainted, the assessor conducted a word search using the first-grade basal reader to identify his sight-word vocabulary. After making a list of Alan's known sight words, the assessor asked the two teachers observing the assessment to write a teacher-made story. The story contained several known words and four new words. Figure 6.6 depicts the list of known words, new words, and the teacher-made story.

Alan was pre-taught the four new words. After a limited amount of review and practice on both the known and new words, he was given the story, "The Tractor" to read. He read it with ease and good comprehension. He even read it with some expression. At the end of the school day, without any further review or practice, he remembered three of the four new words and was still able to read the story accurately and effectively.

While it was obvious that the committee continued to favor special education placement, the assessor could not help but wonder what the outcome would have been if meaningful support had been provided in the classroom prior to the referral. More importantly, if the teacher had been provided support, would a referral to special education even have been considered?

Alan's capacity to learn and retain three out of four new words per day without any review would have informed the teacher and committee that he could acquire new information at a rate considered average for most first-graders, provided he were taught under instructional-level conditions. Further, comparing Alan's success when taught under instructional-level conditions with the dismal 20 words learned during the first six months of school raises more questions about the appropriateness of instruction than about his ability to learn. His progress using teacher-made stories also challenged the faulty premise that letter sounds and decoding were necessary prerequisites to sight-word attainment and comprehension (Altwerger, et al., 2007; Dombey & Moustafa, 1998; Goodman, 2006; Herron, 2008). The committee's focus

Descriptive Data

First grade
Physically large for his age
Poor listening comprehension
Guesses at words
Low retention rate
Weak decoding skills
Trouble recognizing sounds
Reading & writing weaknesses
Recommend testing for LD

Reading Assessment Data

Instructed in grade level 1-2
I Wish I Could Fly reader
First reading ---26% Words
                    Read Correct (WRC)
Repeated readings
        Mar. 4th   46/61 WRC
        Mar. 5th   48/61 WRC
        Mar. 7th   45/61 WRC
        Mar. 8th   55/61 WRC

Spelling Assessment

path	*Pay*	camp	*Kom*
lap	*lam*	drop	*stq*
top	*Taq*	rip	*Taq*
cut	*Kat*	this	*sos*
bird	*drb*	fish	*fas*
crib	*KrB*		

In spite of displaying spelling difficulties, additional obervations indicated Alan:
- made use of initial consonants p, k, l, t, r, f
- made use of final consonants t, b, p (but reversed p)
- confused dr for j, (not unusual for children who have difficulty blending sounds)
- had vowel presence but used them incorrectly in most cases
- was developing letter/sound correspondence
- was perhaps asked to spell words not in his sight-word
  vocabulary.

Figure 6.5 Alan's Child Study Team Referral Data

needed to be on building immediately on what Alan knew and what he could do.

A second illustration of using teacher-made stories is that of an eight year-
old inner-city student labeled a "non-reader." Although Trae had been placed in the
simplest of books, he achieved very little success. The material he was assigned to
read is on the left of Figure 6.7 and shows the unknown words underlined.

Known Words	New Words	Teacher-made Story
a	can	"The Tractor"
at	Papa	
come	ride	Look at the tractor.
I	tractor	Run to the tractor.
in		Can the tractor run?
look		The tractor can run.
no		Can I run the tractor? No!
of		Papa can run the tractor.
run		I can ride the tractor.
see		Papa can run the tractor.
the		You and I can ride the tractor.
to		
you		
he		
and		
book		

Figure 6.6 Alan's Teacher-made Story Using Known and New Words (Option 9)

A brief word search indicated only 4 of the 11 words were known *(to, can, go, see)* in the story. Using other sources (i.e., other stories, word lists), the assessor found that Trae also knew the pronoun "I" and his own name. These 6 words represented the entire sight-word pool of this 8 year-old!

Using a combination of his known words and adding 3 new words *(and, school,* and *stop),* a teacher-made story was written for Trae to read. The story is depicted on the right of Figure 6.7, again with unknown words underlined. On the surface, there does not appear to be a great deal of difference between the original assigned text and the teacher-made story. Both have high repetition, but needing only to learn 3 words honored Trae's working memory and was much easier than having to learn 7 new words.

Maintaining the ratio of known to unknown words at instructional level and folding in both known and unknown words for practice, Trae quickly learned the new words. He was then given the story to read. When asked after reading the story what he would like to title the story, he replied, "Trae Can Read."

Alan and Trae's cases illustrate how quickly students can lag behind when the reading materials and accompanying instruction outstrip students' limited reading skills. These cases also demonstrate why assessment and instruction must focus on what the student knows to be successful. Students in the primary grades obviously are not the only ones who can profit from teacher-made materials. While there are fewer older students who similarly struggle, this option is occasionally required to start older students successfully on the road to reading connected text.

Class-assigned Reading	Teacher-made Story
Read and Jump	
Nan likes to read. Nan likes to read to Don. Don likes to read. Don can read to Nan. Nan likes to read and jump. Don likes to read and jump. *Written by Virginia Arnold.* *Taken from "Close to Home,"* *McMillan, 1987 Red Book.*	Trae can go. Trae can go to school. See Trae go. Can Trae go? Can Trae go to school? See Trae go to school. Trae, stop and go to school.

Figure 6.7 Comparison of Trae's Class-assigned Story and Teacher-made Story (Option 5)

Because teacher-made stories are written on the spot, they do not always represent the best literature.   But they do serve one important purpose, which is to create content students can read, first for the purpose of assessing and then, if appropriate, for instruction. Constructing teacher-made stories starts with the assessor developing rapport with the student by talking about things that are important to the student, including what the student enjoys doing. In developing rapport, do not be afraid to orally read to the student using content the student enjoys and to use it also for word search purposes.

Option 5--Skill Practice. Jean is a struggling third-grade reader. Your task is to study her list of known words and to create a teacher-made story for her. Consider the number of new words that could be added. As you create the story, do not be afraid to build in repetition. Most importantly, ensure that your teacher-made story conforms to instructional-level conditions.

Known Words:				Possible New Words:		
a	five	four	get	?	?	?
I	if	is	it	?	?	
Jean	little	me	one			
put	that	this	who			
will	yes	your				

How creative were you? Were you able to write several lines of text that flowed smoothly and provided substantial repetition involving the new words? By following the scaffolding process of using Jean's known words and incorporating three to five new words in each teacher-made story, were you able to provide ample repetition while creating favorable learning conditions to support real reading progress? Keeping the number of known words high and unknown words low, and providing plenty of repetition and practice, students' sight-word pools can quickly expand, eventually making it possible to transition struggling readers back into published texts, which is the ultimate goal of creating teacher-made stories.

When conducting a word search with students with limited word-recognition skills, it is often best to have them conduct their own word searches, looking just for words they know. For instance, with young readers tell them to place a finger on a word they know and to say the word. Have them do this even with words they have already identified. The assessor can also select books from different reading levels in order to have them identify as many known words as possible.

Extended Use of Teacher-made Stories. Teacher-made stories are developed around a student's sight-word pool and are typically created independent of one another. A variation of this concept can be to extend it to create a series of stories that strategically introduce a limited number of high-utility words in context, along with sufficient repetition to help the struggling reader gain a basic sight-word vocabulary. In the following example, each little story adds a few new words to stretch the content of the previous story (see Figure 6.8).

These little stories are reminiscent of the humorous and witty stories of Theodore Geisel (Dr. Seuss), who developed his first stories following a challenge from a friend to create a story using the fewest number of words possible (e.g., "The Cat in the Hat"). However, unlike the Dr. Seuss stories, these stories are created using decodable words, many containing initial consonants and short-vowel sounds recommended for teaching beginning readers (Adams, et al., 1998).

The reasons for creating pre-written stories are, first, to ensure that the vocabulary demand does not overwhelm the emerging reader and, secondly, to maintain the continuity of the story. In contrast, the stories in many commercially printed little books are unrelated. Their content varies tremendously, with limited word overlap from story to story and limited frequency of word use within stories. Johnston (1998) found, for example, that words used in predictable little books appeared only once 52 percent of the time, and that the average number of repetitions was only 3.3 per word. These findings can be seen in many predictable and decodable little books as illustrated in Figure 6.9.

According to Hargis (1987), "The need for repetition is un-remittent.... The fact that a word is decodable because its letter-sound associations are accurate does not lessen the required number of repetitions it needs for mastery" (p. 36-37). The lack of sufficient repetition, the volume of new words being introduced, and the lack of word overlap from book to book collide with the limited reading skills of poor readers, resulting in learning fragmentation. Remember, selecting little books because they appear to be written at beginning reading levels offers no guarantee they represent an appropriate instructional match for the struggling reader.

Word Introduction and Repetition Rate in "My Words" (Set 1)

Get Up
Get up! Get up!
Get up now.
Yes! Get up.
Get up now.
Get up! Get up!
Yes! Get up.
Get up now.
Get up! Get up!
Get up now.
Yes! Get up now.

It Is Time
It is time.
It is time now.
It is time to get up.
It is get up time now.
Yes! It is time now.
It is time to get up.
Time to get up now.
Get up! Get up!
It is time to get up.
It is get up time now.

Get Out of Bed
Get out of bed.
Get up! Get up!
Yes! It is time now
to get out of bed.
It is get up time.
Time to get out of bed.
Get up! Get up
and get out of bed.
It is time to get up now
and to get out of bed.

A Good Day
It is a good day now
to get out of bed.
Yes! It is a good day
to get up and get out.
It is get up time.
Time to get up now
and to get out of bed.
It is a good day.
Now get up! Get up
and get out of bed.

Come On Out
Come on! Come on
and get out of bed.
It is a good day now
to come out and play.
Come on! Come on
and get out of bed.
It is get up time now.
It is time to play.
Yes! It is a good day
to come out and play now.

Get Up	It is Time	Get Out of Bed	A Good Day	Come On Out	Total # of Repetitions
up	up	up	up	up	33
get	get	get	get	get	46
now	now	now	now	now	17
yes	yes	yes	yes	yes	7
	is	is	is	is	19
	it	it	it	it	20
	time	time	time	time	17
	to	to	to	to	14
		and	and	and	8
		bed	bed	bed	12
		of	of	of	11
		out	out	out	15
			a	a	6
			good	good	6
			day	day	6
				come	7
				on	5
				play	3

Figure 6.8 Related Content of Teacher-made Stories (Option 5)

Even when these little books focus on providing instruction in letter-sound relationships, we are reminded how meaningful the learning/teaching principle of working from the concrete to the abstract is for the struggling reader. Stahl (1992) cautioned, "good phonics instruction should help make sense of patterns noticed within words.... However, for the child with little or no exposure, phonics instruction would be an abstract and artificial task until the child has additional meaningful encounters with print" (p. 620). Reflecting on these thoughts, the following actions are worth considering when working with struggling readers:

- Actively engage them in pre-reading activities.

- Stay concrete initially by teaching basic sight words.

- Create little stories using the few sight words the student knows.

    while gradually sandwiching in one to three new words at a time.

- Connect words into phrases and sentences.

- Start the student's writing activities using the same words.

- Develop an initial sight-word pool of 25-50 words.

- Link letters/sounds to known sight words (see Dombey &

    Moustafa, 1998).

- Study word patterns in words.

- Provide plenty of reading and writing practice.

- Make smooth transitions into other printed texts.

Option 6—Other Published Material

Classroom teachers frequently select easier books for struggling readers, feeling this is the *only* option available. However, as we have shown, there are other options available to create instructional-level conditions prior to abandoning peer-expected text. Likewise, we have shown that creating reading passages may be a more efficient (i.e., quicker) way to move the assessment process forward. When alternative reading materials are used for assessment purposes, the IA process advises the assessor to proceed with caution. This is not to insinuate that using other materials is not an option. There are times when the use of easier published material is needed to continue the reading assessment. However, when this is the option of choice, the assessor must still ensure that the reading material conforms to instructional-level conditions and that all steps of the IA process are repeated, starting with orally reading to the student and conducting a word search prior to having the student read the material.

Assessors should never assume that lower-level material equates to instructionally-matched conditions, nor should they assume that lower-level material is always an appropriate source for teaching struggling readers to read. As Cole (1998) lamented, today's textbooks containing so-called "real literature" are not written

Words Used in Level A–Sunshine Books

Baby Gets Dressed	Huggles Breakfast	Huggles Can Juggle	The Birthday Cake
The pants	A carrot	An orange	A red cake
The shirt	A cake	An apple	A yellow cake
The petticoat	A fish	An umbrella	A blue cake
The dress	A bone	An elephant	A pink cake
The socks	A banana	An ice cream	A brown cake
The shoes	A sausage	An accident	A green cake
The rain	A telephone		Happy birthday to you
The mess			

Words Used in the first decodable mini-books of Open Court (1995)

The Baby	Nan's Family	Nat the Crab	In the Pond	Amanda's Sax	
are	a	a	and	am	of
baby	am	and	bat	Amanda	panda
cake	and	at	cats	and	pop
in	can	bat	dogs	are	sax
on	cat	bit	five	band	says
shirt	dad	cab	four	can	sobs
the	Dan	can	hippo	can't	spot
	family	can't	hopped	cat	stand
	I	cap	hot	damp	stop
	is	crab	in	drips	the
	on	crib	is	drop	this
	mat	have	it	Fans	Tom
	Nan	here	not	hands	tops
	Pan(s)	I	one	has	yes
	Pat	in	pigs	have	you
	sad	it	pond	here	
	scat	map	said	his	
	Taps	Nap	the	I	
	the	Nat's	three	in	
		sit	too	Max	
		snap	two	mop	
		spin		mom	
		Taps		no	
		trip		on	
		the			

Figure 6.9 Illustration of limited word repetition in published little books

specifically to teach children to read but are written mostly to convey information and to foster reading enjoyment. Much of the literature written today often presents problems for the student who is at a stage in his or her own reading development where carefully selected language and vocabulary usage would provide the student better opportunities to overcome his or her own reading gaps and master the essential reading skills needed to be an effective reader.

There is another caution to be made when selecting other published material, namely, a student's self-conciousness as a struggling reader. Occasionally, the placement of students in easier books can result in student resistance, which occurs when struggling readers want to read books they cannot read and do not want to read books they can read (Forbes & Roller, 1991). When this happens, Fielding and Roller (1992) suggest that practitioners should find ways "to enable them to read some of the books they want to read, and then find ways to make them want to read the books they can read" (p. 680). The previously reviewed options presented in this chapter certainly provide ways of accomplishing both tasks when used strategically and creatively.

When the student is resistant to reading an easier book, we have learned that it is best to talk to the student about achieving different reading purposes and goals. Often, the goal of reading easier books is not about appreciating the content but about recognizing words quickly and becoming a more fluent and effective reader. What matters most is for the student to understand the important goals of increasing word recognition, understanding what is read, and reading with voice and expression. Directly talking with students about these goals gives meaning and value to the practice students receive when reading easier books.

Allington (2001) stresses that instead of focusing on how students read poorly and on how they lack motivation, "we need to worry more about putting enticing, just-right books in children's hands and less about schemes that attempt to bribe children into taking home an uninteresting book that is too difficult" (p. 9). But putting interesting "just-right books" into the hands of struggling readers is not as easy as it sounds. As has been previously discussed, the shifting vocabulary burden and linguistic complexity that comprises most commercially-printed literature make book selection haphazard. The fact that there are students who feel "dumbed down" when given supposedly just-right books must also be addressed more intelligently than merely telling students the books are at their "reading level."

We agree that finding enticing books which peak the interest of struggling readers is important, but finding just-right books does not start with book selection. The process starts by first ensuring that instructional-level conditions are present, enabling the student to read at his or her best and enabling the assessor to determine precisely what the student knows and can actually do. Achieving these conditions often requires the judicious selection and application of one of the assessment options to make sure the reading material works and is right for the student.

SUMMARY

A key characteristic of IA is having options to create and manage the instructional-level conditions for struggling students during the assessment process. This chapter presented a range of options available to the assessor for use with students who possess a diminishing range of reading skills. While the focus of each option involves managing the assessment task to create optimal conditions and avoid jeopardizing or invalidating the reading performance of the student, in many cases the use of different options also becomes the very tool used to effectively support and manage the ongoing instruction for students. The fact that different students benefit from different approaches at different times demonstrates why different assessment and instructional options are needed. This requires selecting reading materials, making content adjustments, and managing the instructional conditions to make it possible for the student to perform at an optimal level.

Instead of abandoning peer-expected text too quickly when the material is not appropriately matched, the first three options (teaching words and concepts, looking ahead or behind, and segmenting the content) provide avenues for effectively creating instructional-level conditions that allow assessment and instruction to continue. When the match cannot be achieved within peer-expected text, the assessor will have to rely upon their own knowledge and skill in creating instructionally-matched passages to gain a valid reading assessment (transitional and teacher-made stories). These two options allow the assessor to construct reading passages that conform to instructional-level conditions as a precondition for conducting an assessment. When the option is to use other published materials, the assessor does so with caution in order to maintain the integrity of the IA snapshot and to ensure that the instructional match occurs.

We want to stress again that the IA process requires more than one snapshot. This means the assessor is likely to use one or more of these options during the second and subsequent assessment snapshots. In each instance, comfortable conditions are assured that allow students to demonstrate what they know and what they can do. The teacher also benefits by observing concrete ways to manage and create favorable reading conditions using a variety of material and strategies.

Chapter 7

Matching Reading Strategies to Assessment Data: Becoming Aware, Accurate, and Automatic

"If students are taught the importance of using specific strategies, if they understand how to use those strategies, and if they understand what they do well and what they need to work on, they will be empowered to improve."

(Brookhard, Moss, & Long, 2008, p. 54)

Throughout the previous chapters we have repeatedly emphasized the importance of creating conditions that enable struggling readers to learn and perform at optimum levels. Such conditions are essential if these students are to demonstrate what they know and what they can do and if assessors and teachers are to gain accurate data that reflect these students' best efforts. We have also repeatedly emphasized the importance of taking several assessment snapshots with each snapshot representing an appropriate fit, meaning the student should be asked to do only what he or she is ready and able to do (Tomlinson, 2008).

If the student lacks sufficient prior knowledge, or if there are too many unknown words or concepts to make sense of the reading content, the assessment will convey a distorted and invalid picture of the student's actual reading skills. Popham (2008) said it another way—"Students who don't understand something really can't own it" (p. 80). Conversely, when the focus of assessment is only on comparing the performances of students and identifying their deficiencies, then assessment really has no ownership for ensuring that students perform at their best. When optimal conditions are lacking, struggling readers simply continue to be struggling readers. To counter these adverse effects, the challenge level during each IA snapshot should conform to the guidelines displayed in the optimal learning window (see Figure 3.10). Each snapshot should match the student's prior knowledge and instructional reading level sufficient to enable the student to read and understand the material.

The purpose of IA snapshots is first to gain an accurate picture of how the student orchestrates his or her skills within and across the seven reading dimensions and then to identify precisely what will help the student become a better reader. Each snapshot needs to provide a clearer picture of the student's reading skills, how the student interacts with the material, and what reading dimensions require strategic support to move the student to higher levels of performance. Each snapshot also provides an opportunity to view how instructional-level conditions actually influence the student's reading.

While being assessed under instructional-level conditions certainly promotes students doing well, the conditions have their limitations. As Chapter 3 notes, the instructional-level concept is not precise enough to inform teachers about what should be taught or how it should be taught, nor can it ensure that struggling readers have sufficient word recognition and language usage skill to comprehend what is read (Cramer & Rosenfield, 2008). Likewise, using the instructional-level concept to teach discrete skills does not ensure application and generalization (Burns, M.K., 2004). As beneficial as the instructional-level concept is, it is but one essential component for creating the instructional match and managing effective instruction.

The instructional match is a fluid and complex concept. It constantly changes as the assessor and teacher build upon the student's improving reading skills. The matching process begins by skillfully crafting instruction to ensure student engagement and understanding. Ensuring sound engagement means matching what the student knows while considering the real reading concerns of the student, and at the same time providing the student a comfortable level of challenge to assist with reading development and comprehension. As the matching process evolves, it is essential to guard against thinking that most of the hard work of assessment is over once instruction takes hold. In fact, most of the hard work of assessment remains ahead, requiring IA's long-term support to narrow and close the achievement gap.

As the daily work of teaching commences, the assessor and teacher "use ongoing assessment to understand what a student needs next, and they adjust their teaching in response to what they discover" (Tomlinson, 2008, p. 29). They consistently adjust their teaching techniques and strategies to match the subtle changes occurring in the student's reading, and they make each strategy visible through explicit instruction and practice to fully benefit the student. They describe, teach, and model how different strategies are fundamental to certain reading dimensions, and they describe, teach, and model how other strategies provide the necessary scaffolding to build more sophisticated reading habits. They appreciate the contextual nature of reading and consistently tailor and embed the teaching of reading strategies within the natural context of real reading.

Frequent conversations are used to clarify any questions or misunderstandings the student may have concerning the purposes of specific reading strategies, how and when they are to be applied, and the best techniques to build upon and connect them. As the student learns, internalizes, and successfully applies different strategies in different contexts, responsibility for creating and sustaining the instructional match is methodically transferred to the student. While adult support is still provided when needed, the student takes ownership of creating the match to guide his or her own learning. When faced with new unfamiliar content, the student is challenged to be self-aware, to self-assess, to problem-solve by applying effective fix-up strategies when needed, and to continually seek to enlarge his or her knowledge and understanding as a reader.

These are some of the long-term assessment and instructional objectives sought in the Common Core State Standards. While the assessor and teacher endeavor to deliver high-quality instruction, it is not enough just for them to take charge. Real sustained reading progress actually occurs when students demonstrate ownership by applying the strategies they have acquired to efficiently and effectively direct their own learning. This chapter brings the matching process full circle where ongoing assessment decisions direct the actual selection and delivery of specific reading strategies, first by the assessor and teacher, and eventually by the student. As a personal challenge, as you study the strategy sections in this chapter and ponder the long-term objectives, let your mind wonder about what specific reading strategies you would definitely want students to acquire and about how you would facilitate the acquisition and transfer to enable students to take charge of their own literacy development.

READING STRATEGIES MATRIX

Assessors and teachers do not want to lose sight of the long-term objectives of having self-assessing and self-directed learners, nor lose perspective about the limited entry points of struggling readers. All of us know that reading strategies need to be carefully selected and skillfully taught to match the targeted reading dimensions identified as major concerns, and that targeted areas change as different reading skills develop. The matrix seen in Figure 7.1 is designed to facilitate this initial matching and selection process. The matrix illustrates how different strategies serve different reading purposes at different levels of reading development. No attempt was made to list every reading strategy. Instead, the matrix provides a healthy sampling of carefully selected strategies proven to be effective during our decades of work with teachers, assessors, and students. We chose these particular strategies because they clearly embody the research principles of learning that have been emphasized throughout the previous chapters. Most of the strategies are designed for students to take ownership.

It has been our experience that different strategies positively impact multiple dimensions and levels of reading. As such, it was not our intention to infer that a particular strategy should be applied only with reference to where it appears on the matrix. The matrix is merely a visual tool that provides a starting point to carefully select an appropriate reading strategy.

Stages of Learning

Determining where initial reading support should begin is the first step in the selection of a strategy. The second step is skillfully matching that strategy to the needs of the student and to the student's stage of learning. The rows of the matrix reflect three stages of learning encountered by students in becoming efficient and effective readers. The stages illustrate that learning begins with a general awareness of essential skills and concepts, proceeds with the development of accuracy and understanding, and culminates in the automatic retrieval and application of essential skills and concepts. The various reading strategies assigned to these stages exemplify this progression.

	Word Development *Recognition-Meaning-Study*	Fluency Development	Comprehension/ Reading in Narrative Text	Comprehension/ Reading in Informational Text
Awareness	• Word Search	• Chunking • Visualization	• Activating Prior Knowledge • Forming Questions • Fat and Skinny Questions	• Activating Prior Knowledge • Pre-reading Plan • I Wonder/ You're The Teacher • Forming Questions
Accuracy	• Pocket Words • Drill Sandwich • Incremental Rehearsal • Phonemic Awareness • Rainbow Words • Spot & Dot • Rime Clusters • Word Sorts	• Model Reading • Echo Reading • Impress Reading	• Forming Questions (connecting Questions to Text) • Question Matrix • Retelling • Graphic Organizers • Someone, Wants, But, So	• Forming Questions (Summarizing Strategies) • Graphic Organizers • Magnet/Key Words • Free and Cued Retelling
Automaticity	• Multiple Meaning • Word Maps • Who Has, I Have • Ticket to Leave • Word Sort	• Repeated Reading • Six Inch Voices • Drop Word Reading	• Free and Cued Retelling • Question Cubes • Fat and Skinny Questions • Trio/Quad Reading	• Free and Cued Retelling • Question Cubes • Fat and Skinny Questions • Trio/Quad Reading

Figure 7.1 Strategy Matrix: Awareness, Accuracy, Automaticity

Awareness strategies provide opportunities for teachers to introduce new approaches and for students to engage in self-assessment activity.

Accuracy strategies provide students with opportunities to practice and receive confirming and corrective feedback. Automatic implementation is fostered with embedding strategies that ensure accurate responses.

Automatic strategies provide students with opportunities to receive added practice to become proficient in the application and generalization of skills and concepts that have become accurate. The concept of automaticity allows students quick retrieval of skills and concepts to be applied to increasingly complex learning tasks.

Once an appropriate strategy has been selected, its use has a two-fold purpose. It must be modeled effectively, followed by students receiving immediate and sufficient practice to gain facility over its use. Secondly, as students gain facility over its use, they need to take ownership of the strategy by demonstrating their ability to apply it effectively both as a self-assessment and as an instructional tool across multiple settings. Accomplishing these joint purposes requires the assessor and teacher to attend to several key factors.

Reading dimension. Which reading dimension (i.e., word recognition, fluency, etc.) is central to the identified reading needs of the student? Strategy selection is based on the specific dimension selected as a result of the problem solving and assessment process.

Learning stage. Strategy selection should match the student's point of entry—awareness, accuracy, or automaticity.

Goal Attainment. What level of attainment do you want the student to achieve? Should the skill be left at the awareness level or does it need to be taken to a higher level to integrate the skill into chosen content? For example, it is developmentally appropriate in the earlier grades to introduce inferential skills at an awareness level. Likewise, acquiring an accurate and automatic sight-word pool is paramount for first graders. Obtaining sight-word automaticity provides an essential foothold for refocusing the cognitive energy to be able to gather information and is also essential for developing efficient and effective reading behavior.

Working memory. Does the strategy conform to the principles governing working memory and effective instruction? Is the strategy appropriately matched for the student's entry skills and is it delivered appropriately to fit the student's reading needs?

A word of caution: selecting a research-based strategy while failing to maintain the appropriateness of the instructional match is a clear violation of the research principles of effective learning and teaching. Whether the strategy remains research-based or not, the violation jeopardizes the value of the strategy and even calls into question the results of its use as an intervention (Gravois, Gickling, & Rosenfield, 2011).

MATCHING READING STRATEGIES TO STUDENTS' READING NEEDS

Although the reading strategies and management structures addressed in this chapter are not exhaustive, they do reflect a core of instructional practice that has been proven instrumental in meeting both the needs of struggling readers and the reading goals of their teachers. Not only is the careful selection of appropriate strategies vital, how and when they are applied is just as vital if the student is to improve and achieve.

WORD DEVELOPMENT

It is common knowledge that all students either formally or informally receive some form of phonemic or phonics instruction when learning to read. While this form of instruction involves the development of enabling skills, we share Stahl's (1992) view that the real purpose of this area of instruction is not that children learn to sound out words but that they learn to recognize words quickly and automatically so attention can focus on comprehension. We also share Johnston's (1998) view that the hallmark of a successful reader is a highly developed sight-word vocabulary. The focus of this section is on developing word consciousness (helping students become aware of words spoken and written around them, how they are used, and what they mean (Graves & Watts-Taffe, 2008)). The various strategies presented in this section reflect these points of view.

Strategies to Develop Word Recognition

Word recognition is the ability to pronounce words quickly and accurately in the context of authentic reading. As reading content becomes more enriching and demanding, acquiring a large sight-word vocabulary is essential if the student is to become an effective and proficient reader. The following strategies have proven to be particularly useful in improving and increasing the sight-word vocabularies of struggling readers.

Word Search

Description. The word search strategy quickly and accurately assesses a student's sight-word vocabulary in existing course content. It includes word recognition (the ability to pronounce each word quickly and correctly within 3 seconds) and word meaning (the ability to give a correct response when asked what a word means). A major feature of the word search is that it is conducted in a manner that maintains a high ratio of known to unknown words so as not to frustrate the student.

Procedures (Assessor/Teacher-Directed). From a chosen passage, the assessor selectively points to 4-5 words the student has a high probability of knowing (starting with smaller words) then intermittently points to a larger word. This process is repeated again and again to help the assessor gauge whether or not the passage is at the student's instructional-reading level. The word search is first used to determine the range of the student's sight-word vocabulary, which requires the assessor to focus solely on word recognition. After gauging the strength of the student's sight-word vocabulary, key words can be selected to check for word meaning, enabling the assessor to gauge the strength of the student's background knowledge. This can be achieved by asking the student to either describe what the word means or to use it in a sentence. By determining the range of the student's sight-word vocabulary, and by pointing and asking for the meaning of key words, the assessor is in a position to decide whether the passage can be used to continue the reading assessment process.

Procedures (Student-Directed). Once students are aware of the purpose of the word-search strategy, it can be taught directly to the students to engage in their own word search procedures prior to reading. Teachers discuss the meaning of known and unknown words with students and the importance of knowing how many words are needed to read and understand text. Using a chart, teachers can have students identify or "search" for three types of words:

- words that the student cannot pronounce
- words that the student can pronounce but are not sure of what they mean
- words that the student is proud of, which are large or more difficult words, or words that have more that one meaning depending upon the text.

Initially, students are often reluctant to identify or write down words they do not know. Sometimes it helps to encourage them to look for "tricky" words—words that trick them or might "trick" someone else. They soon learn that it is important to be totally honest with themselves about what words they know and what words they need. Based upon their word search, students should self-assess their comfort level with the selected passage. They should think about the number of words they identified, and their comfort level in reading the passage to decide:

- YES I am comfortable that the assessed passage is at my instructional reading level and that I have sufficient word recognition and word meaning to read and understand the passage.
- NO The passage has too many unknown words or unknown word meanings for me to read the passage without being frustrated.
- MAYBE I need to conduct a more thorough word search before determining if the passage is at my instructional-reading level.

The teacher provides blank cards for each unknown word (see Figure 7.2, pocket cards). Students write only one word per card. While students are searching for unknown or proud words, the teacher assists by conducting word searches with targeted students using the procedure noted above. This targeted checking provides feedback to increase accuracy for students. When the teacher's word search results in a word that the student has not identified the teacher should say, "This might be a good word to practice," or "This might be a good word to know the meaning of before reading," and should encourage the student to write it on a card. The number of cards should conform to the developmental limits of working memory.

After identifying their words, students work in cooperative groups to help each other pronounce the different words and learn their meanings. They work in cooperative groups taking turns "flashing" their word cards to each other and asking each other to say each word. On every third or fourth word they can ask a student to define the meaning of a particular word or to use it correctly in a sentence. Throughout, the teacher moves about the class listening to and monitoring the students' practice. The teacher also uses this activity to assess the general word-recognition needs of the entire class using commonly searched words for purposes of whole-class instruction when needed.

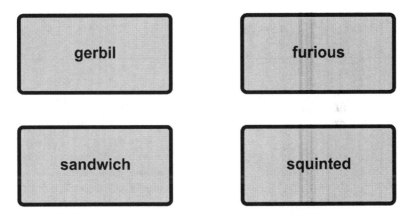

Figure 7.2 Pocket Cards

Pocket Words

Description.   Pocket Words provide students opportunities to develop accuracy and automaticity while honoring the limits of working memory. The strategy involves cutting 3-by-5 inch cards into four equal parts, as shown in Figure 7.2. Each pocket word is selected from the content the student is reading and is placed on a separate card for practice. The cards are small enough to be placed in the student's pocket to be reviewed and practiced at a number of convenient times. Pocket cards can be made for any discrete skill the student is practicing (e.g., letter recognition, math facts, spelling words).

Procedures.   The word search procedure is an effective source for selecting words for pocket cards. The teacher can either direct students to do a word search or teach them to conduct their own word searches and create their own pocket cards. By cutting 3-by-5 inch index card into sets of four, writing one new word on each card, and reviewing the words on each set of four cards, the limits of working memory are not violated.

The student then puts the words in his or her pocket. As the student carries the cards with him or her throughout the day, another person, such as a teacher, teacher's aide, fellow student, parent volunteer, or member of the staff, periodically can ask the student to review his or her pocket cards, thus providing the repetition and spaced practice needed by the student to master each new word. The practice should be quick and conducted in a variety of settings such as during seatwork, at break time, in the hall, or whenever a little extra review time seems beneficial. The amount of repetition needed to achieve mastery will vary from student to student. Some will need fewer repetitions while others may need as many as 50 repetitions.

Teaching parents to use this technique helps them learn not to overload the child with too many unknown words at one time. This process also helps in developing a more relaxed atmosphere for the parent to help the child.

Maximizing and Extending Pocket Words.   Some schools have created buttons for students to wear that state: "Ask me about my pocket cards." For younger students, wearing these buttons prompts adults and older students throughout the school building and throughout the day to provide additional practice and repetition for targeted students.

Drill Sandwich

Description. The drill sandwich, also referred to as a folding-in technique, provides opportunities for developing word accuracy and automaticity. This strategy is built upon the learning principle of keeping practice ratios within the 70-85% known to 15-30% unknown range when mastering discrete skills (e.g., word recognition, math facts, letter sounds).   Research on the drill sandwich technique (Coulter & Coulter, 1991; Gickling & Thompson, 1985; MacQuarrie, et al., 2002; Roberts, Turco, & Shapiro, 1991) found that the strategic introduction of known and unknown words during discrete word recognition practice enhanced students' success and motivation. The strategy can be used with words from narrative or informational text, and is easily generalized to practice in other subjects (e.g., math facts, letters, letter sounds, state capitals).

Procedures. The drill sandwich technique makes use of flashcards (typically 10) practiced in a specific order. After identifying the student's known and unknown words using the word search procedure, the teacher–and, ultimately, the student–constructs a practice set of words by selecting seven known words and three unknown (new) words as they appear in the story or text. The order for arranging the practice of new words is K K K **N** K K **N** K K **N,** with K representing known words and N representing unknown words.

The teacher has the student practice identifying all ten words in the recommended order until each new word is known by sight. This can be done by using flashcards or by pointing directly to the words in the text in the order described above. As an unknown word becomes known, it is maintained within the practice set by removing an originally known word. Removing an originally-known word and replacing it with the newly-learned word (previously unknown word) gives additional practice to the student. The teacher should always end the practice session by returning to the text from which words were selected.

Learning is accelerated once the teacher recognizes when an unknown word becomes known and efficiently reorganizes the practice set as described above. To aid in·keeping track of a student's progress, various teachers have adopted a coding system that assists in monitoring students' learning of words. For example, as a student practices the drill sandwich, the teacher can monitor learning by marking the back of the card for each correct practice of an unknown word:

First correct response to practice = ╲

Second correct response to practice = ✕

Third correct response to practice = ⊗

Incremental Rehearsal

Description. Incremental rehearsal (Tucker, 1989) encourages accuracy and automaticity in word development by providing high rates of repetition of a *single* newly introduced word (unknown) interspersed among five known words. Research by MacQuarrie, et al. (2002) suggests a specific pattern for organizing each practice set so the single new word is strategically practiced between an incrementally increasing

	Flashcard Ratio		Presentation
1	**The New Word**	**(N1)**	1st Presentation
2	1st known word	(K1)	
3	**The New Word**	**(N1)**	2nd Presentation
4	1st known word	(K1)	
5	2nd known word	(K2)	
6	**The New Word**	**(N1)**	3rd Presentation
7	1st known word	(K1)	
8	2nd known word	(K2)	
9	3rd known word	(K3)	
10	**The New Word**	**(N1)**	4th Presentation
11	1st known word	(K1)	
12	2nd known word	(K2)	
13	3rd known word	(K3)	
14	4th known word	(K4)	
15	**The New Word**	**(N1)**	5th Presentation
16	1st known word	(K1)	
17	2nd known word	(K2)	
18	3rd known word	(K3)	
19	4th known word	(K4)	
20	5th known word	(K5)	

Figure 7.3 Incremental Rehearsal Presentation Schedule

number of repetitions of known words.

Procedures. The incremental rehearsal technique makes use of six flashcards. An unknown word is written on one card while known words are written on each one of the remaining five cards. Known and unknown words should be selected from the student's current reading text (see word search procedure). The teacher folds in the new word (N) with the known vocabulary words (Ks) following the presentation schedule in Figure 7.3.

When the unknown word becomes known by the student, it becomes the first known word (K1) in the next learning set. The previous final known word (K5) is removed from the entire set, keeping the total number of flashcards at six. A second new word then becomes the new word (N1) and the incremental rehearsal process is repeated.

Using High-Frequency Word Lists

High-frequency word lists identify words most commonly used in print which, when used appropriately, can be an effective means to support the development of students' word recognition. A common feature of high-frequency words is how often they appear in print. Another common feature of many high-frequency words is that they are of low imagery. For example, unlike the word "*table,*" which is easily visualized, it is difficult to visualize "*the*" or "*that.*" Some literature refers to these types of low-imagery words as glue words because they are used to hold sentences together. Because of their low imagery, they generally require multiple repetitions for students to learn and use them effectively.

Word lists are not strategies per se, but the words they contain should be selected and applied strategically as with previously presented strategies (e.g., pocket words, drill sandwich, and incremental rehearsal). Teachers should avoid drilling students simply because certain words are on certain lists. At the same time, they need to be aware of words that are developmentally appropriate to include within well-designed practice experiences. Hillerich (1978) provided one such list where the 100 words were found to account for approximately 60% of the words elementary students commonly use when writing (Figure 7.4).

Strategies to Develop Word Meaning

Word meaning is the ability to know and understand the intended meaning that words convey within the current context of reading, listening, speaking, and writing. Part of developing word consciousness is realizing that words are taught and acquired best when used differently in different contexts. Some words, for example, are spelled the same but have different meanings and even have different pronunciations depending upon how they are used. Words and how they are phrased together can also have hidden meaning, as often occurs in slang, clichés, and regional speech.

I	do	man	then
and	don't	me	there
the	down	mother	they
a	for	my	thing
to	from	no	think
about	get	not	this
after	go	now	time
all	got	of	too
an	had	on	two
am	have	one	up
are	he	or	us
around	her	over	very
as	him	our	was
at	his	out	we
back	home	people	well
be	house	put	went
because	if	said	were
but	in	saw	what
by	into	school	when
came	is	see	who
can	it	she	will
could	just	so	with
day	know	some	would
did	like	that	you
didn't	little	them	your

Figure 7.4 Hillerich's 100 High Frequency Words Students Use in Writing

Multiple Meanings

Description. Word choices not only rely on accessing a large sight-word vocabulary, but also require an understanding of how reading context affects word choices. This includes knowing that even though certain words are spelled the same they are often pronounced differently and have different meanings depending upon the context in which they appear. This activity helps students recognize there are words that have multiple meanings and/or pronunciations depending upon how they are used

Primary Words	Stems	Intermediate Words	Stems
Mad	As in angry As in love As in crazy	Sand	As in earth As in being bold As in ages
Bat	As in a game As in a flying animal As in a cranky person	Notice	As in an ad As in seeing As in a warning
Up	As in a direction As in ready for a task As in a happy mood	Solid	As in frozen As in a stone As in dependable
Cool	As in temperature As in near As in calm down	Light	As in weight As in time of day As in a response
Play	As in having fun As in a performance As in a game	Private	As in confidence As in soldier As in a place
Super	As in great As in quantity As in the boss	Pilot	As in an airplane As in a project As in a stove
Clear	As in water As in an idea As in to erase	Court	As in tennis As in the law As in love

Figure 7.5 Multiple Meaning Words

within text.

Procedures. Teachers can introduce how words and vocabulary differ depending upon the context in which the words are used. Using words such as those listed in Figure 7.5, teachers and students work to create stems demonstrating the multiple meanings of certain words. Once the students understand that the stems provide the context for how the words are to be used, they are to create sentences consistent with the multiple meanings of the various stems.

Word Mapping

Description. Word maps are graphic representations of word features used to reinforce word meaning. They allow students to experience word associations and figurative language, and to explore multiple meaning. Figure 7.6 provides examples of common word maps.

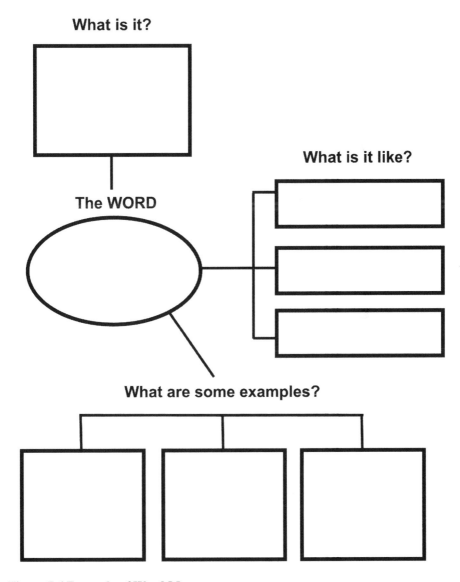

Figure 7.6 Example of Word Maps

Who Has? I Have!

Description. The purpose of *"Who Has? I Have!"* is to develop automatic comprehension of vocabulary words. The strategy is applied after students have developed accuracy for words and their definitions. It represents an effective and focused group activity for students. Student-directed word searches are a great way to identify vocabulary words for this activity. Once students search for words, they can work in cooperative groups to create word maps or to generate accurate definitions for the words. On each index card, the teacher writes one vocabulary word on the front and a non-corresponding definition on the back. Figure 7.7 illustrates a quick way to organize cards so that the definitions and vocabulary words come out evenly.

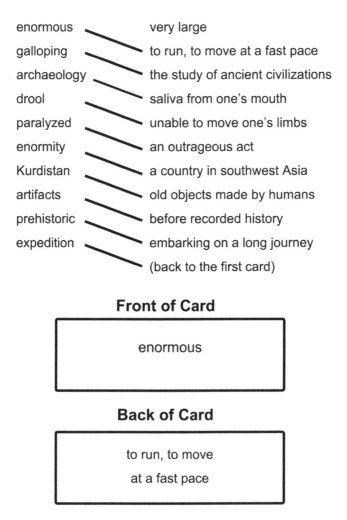

Front of Card

enormous

Back of Card

to run, to move
at a fast pace

Figure 7.7 Who has? I have! Organization

Procedures. For cooperative group activities, the cards are shuffled among 3 or 4 players, with the players placing the definitions face up. One player begins by picking up a card and asks "Who has…(stating only the word on the back of the card)?" The other players search the definitions and the one with the correct definition says, "I have"… repeats the word and reads the definition on the front of the card. That person then turns over the card and reads the next word and asks "Who Has?" The activity continues until all the words have been defined. The order is reversed on the next round by starting with the definitions face down.

Maximizing, Extending Who has?/I have! For large group activity, the *Who has? I have!* cards are shuffled, with each student receiving one card. The students form a circle. The teacher randomly taps one student, who starts the activity by saying, "Who has?" (stating the word on the front of the card). The student who has the appropriate definition states, "I have," and reads the definition. The activity continues until all the words have been defined. During the activity, students are timed to see how quickly the group can accurately identify all the words and their definitions. Timing the activity increases the students' focus on becoming automatic and proficient in quickly recognizing word meaning.

"Snowball Fight" is a variation and can extend the *Who has? I have!* activity. Students work in pairs writing a word on the upper half of a piece of paper and the definition on the lower half. Students tear the paper in half with the word on one half and definition on the other. They then crumple each half to form a snowball. Students then form a circle and on the teacher's signal the students have a "snowball fight" (they are not to throw at each others' face). When the teacher calls, "Freeze!" everyone stops and picks up the nearest piece of paper. The teacher taps one student to start by saying "Who has…?" and the student who has the corresponding word or definition states, "I have," and reads it. That person then taps another student to continue the practice.

Ticket to Leave

Description. Ticket to leave is an ideal activity to focus students' attention on key learning elements of a lesson. A question, statement, or objective is posed by the teacher that will be needed for students to exit the class. The activity creates the expectation that there are important things to learn and remember, therefore extending students' literacy skills.

Procedures. At the beginning of the lesson the teacher writes the objective for the class on the board as a statement or question, such as, "By the end of the day, student should:

- be able to provide the definition of your word
- be able to answer this question and defend your answer
- be able to give me three reasons why
- be able to determine which form of word (e.g., there, their, they're) to use in a given sentence."

The teacher calls students' attention to the objective and lets them know what the ticket to leave will be for the day. Each student must briefly provide the teacher with an acceptable response that serves as their ticket to leave during a designated time.

Maximizing and Extending Ticket to Leave. Teachers have found ways to combine this strategy with other strategies, saving time in the process. For example, teachers can place "Pocket cards" or "Who Has? I Have!" cards in a box or jar by the door. Each student randomly selects a card before exiting the room, provides a suitable definition, uses the word in a sentence, or applies any other practice task that fits the activity as their ticket to leave. Likewise, teachers can vary the strategy and use the technique as a ticket to enter in the morning, as well as when students return from lunch or recess.

Strategies to Develop Word Study

Word Study is the ability to use a variety of organized approaches to unlock unknown words. Skills in this area are facilitated by the understanding of letter-sound relationships, letter patterns, syllable development, and the strategic use of contextual clues. Instruction and practice in these areas leads to automaticity as well as the rapid expansion of the student's sight-word vocabulary.

Phonemic Awareness

Description. Phonemic awareness involves distinguishing the smallest units of speech sounds.

Procedures. Figure 7.8 can be used as an assessment activity to determine the phonemic awareness of young children. These same activities when applied strategically in small doses can also be used to enhance students' phonemic awareness capabilities, giving them an advantage in learning to read.

Rainbow Words

Description. The rainbow words strategy helps young students accurately apply phonics when learning words. As with all word study, the ultimate purpose is the development of automatic word recognition. To achieve this purpose, students need to follow word study activities with sufficient repetition at the word recognition level for each word to become a sight word.

Procedures. The teacher provides a demonstration of what a rainbow word represents. Each student chooses five of the brightest colored crayons or markers. Students copy the teacher's model of the target word on buff-colored paper. Each student's copy should be in tall, thin letters to fit the paper. It is helpful to print the letters in light pencil first if a student has difficulty with initial copying. Rather than tracing the word, students should rewrite by shadowing the letters. As they rewrite the original word in another color, they should name each letter as they print it, tracking under the word while saying each letter aloud as they move their finger.

Assessments   Examples

Assessments	Examples
Phonemic deletions	What word would be left if the sound /k/ were taken away from the word /cat/?
Word-to-word matching	Do pen and pipe begin with same sound?
Blending	What word would you have if you put these sounds together: /s/a/t/?
Sound Isolation	What is the first sound in /rose/?
Phoneme segmentation	What sounds do you hear in the word /hot/?
Delete phoneme	What sound do you hear in /meat/ that is missing in /eat/?
Odd word out	What word starts with a different sound: /bag/nine/beach/bike/?
Sound-to-word matching	Is there a /k/ in /bike/?

Figure 7.8 Phonemic Awareness

After using three colors and naming the letters each time, the student should continue shadowing the letters and saying the sound each letter makes with the last two colors. Caution is advised. For example, in the word "sight" the child should make the sound for the "s," "i," and "t" phonemes only, since the "g" and "h" are silent.

As the students repeat the above steps, the teacher can explain that learning involves practice. Each time students shadow the letters, they are practicing forming letters, identifying letters, and learning sounds that letters make. In addition, writing in very large, colorful letters helps create a stronger visual image.

Maximizing and Extending Rainbow Words. After finishing with colors, the teacher has the students trace over the colored letters with a finger while saying each sound again. Then the teacher tracks under the word and says the whole word again. Finally, using a rubber band, students look at the word and s-t-r-e-t-c-h out the rubber band as they s-t-r-e-t-c-h out the sounds making up the word. They then snap the rubber band back as they rapidly repeat the whole word.

Spot and Dot

Description. The Spot and Dot strategy is designed to help students understand the importance of vowel placement in polysyllabic words and to apply the strategy to accurately decode and pronounce large, complex words. Development of the "Spot and Dot" strategy is attributed to Dr. Judith Cohen, Florida International University.

Procedures. The teacher has students identify words they have difficulty pronouncing or recognizing (i.e., word search procedures) and discusses various strategies used by students to "unlock" unknown words. Students are reminded that any strategy that helps them unlock difficult words is good, some being more efficient than others. The teacher introduces Spot and Dot as a strategy that can be especially helpful when decoding large unknown words. A mini-lesson on vowel and syllable presence in words is often helpful when introducing this strategy to students. Specifically, teachers should remind students that each syllable must have at least one vowel. This will help students make the connection between the number of vowels in a word and the number of syllables. The following steps provide the foundation of the lesson for students:

The first step is for students to "spot" the vowels in words and to "dot" them:

    • •   • •
    winter   hotel

Then determine the number of consonants between the vowels. If there are two consonants, break between the two:

    • •
    win/ter   (vc /cv)

However, if there is only one consonant, break after the first vowel:

    • •
    ho/tel   (v /cv)

The student should pronounce the word; if it doesn't sound right, move the break over one letter:

    • •   • •
    le/mon   lem /on

Some additional hints are:

When the word has "twin" consonants, divide between the double consonant:

bot/tle   hap/py   car/rot   zip/per   run/ning

Further, when a consonant is between two vowels or vowel combinations, the consonant often goes with the second vowel:

be/gin   re/new   ca/nine   do/nut   au/burn

But again, students should pronounce the word and it if does not sound right move the break over one letter:

rel/a/tive   tel/a/phone   neg/a/tive

This "rule" is the least consistent, so students should try dividing the word before the consonant. If the word does not sound right, try dividing the word after the consonant.

When two consonants are between vowels, students should divide between the consonants, but never separate blends (bl, cl, dr, fl, fr) or diagraphs (sh, ch, th, wh, ph):

sil/ver   for/get   whis/per   car/ton

teach/er   pa/tron   reach/es   hard/ly

jump/ers

Likewise, students should not separate "next door neighbor" vowels and should use only one dot for vowel combinations such as ee, ea, oa, oy, oi, oo, ou.

Students should be instructed that prefixes and suffixes form separate syllables:

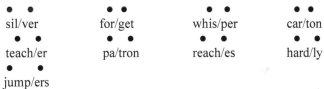

dis/close   pre/pare   in/side   re/miss

ac/tion   draw/ing   fin/est   tru/ism

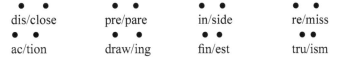

Look for common endings before you spot and dot:

ate   ing   ous   ed   s   es

Maximizing and Extending Spot and Dot. Prior to working with unknown words, it is helpful for students to begin the practice of spot and dot with multi-syllable words they know and can pronounce. This provides self-correction opportunities as well as reinforces what is already known. Teachers have found many ways to combine this strategy with other strategies, saving time in the process. For example, after developing pocket words, students can engage in their own *"personal word study"* using the spot and dot technique.

Using Rime Cluster Lists

Description. Use of rime clusters refers to the combination of letters beginning with a vowel (onset) to create consistent predictable sounds (rime). Knowledge and automatic use of rime clusters improves students' accuracy in decoding words. Efficiency is increased as students realize that particular groups of letters consistently work as units within written text (see Ehri, 1992). As depicted in Figure 7.9, a significant number of words can be derived from the relatively few rime

ale	all	ell	ill	idle
in	ing	ink	ice	ip
ir	ine	ite	ike	ight
am	ap	at	ay	aw
ame	ank	ake	ash	ack
ent	est	en	ern	op
or	ore	ock	oke	ug
uck	unk	ul		

Figure 7.9 Common Rime Clusters

clusters presented.

As with the high-frequency word lists, the list of rime clusters is not a strategy in and of itself. However, rime clusters can be used within previously presented strategies (e.g., pocket words, drill sandwich, incremental rehearsal) to promote accuracy and automaticity.

Procedures. It is important for teachers to discuss how rime clusters are consistent in their pronunciations, often comprising the ends of words. However, rime clusters can also be found at the beginning and in the middle of words. In creating awareness of rime clusters, teachers can guide students as follows:

- *Whole-to-Part Procedures.* A student-directed word search in an instructional-level text is a great way to identify words for rime cluster activities. For example, by the teacher first pointing to words the students know (e.g., thanks), students can search for similar words that fit that same rime cluster pattern while working in cooperative groups (e.g., sank, bank, hankering, etc.).

As a caution, avoid words that are rare and not useful in supporting comprehension. For example, it is not recommended that a young student learn the word *pram* or *tam*–both of which have unusual meanings–when looking at the word *Sam.*

- *Part-to-Whole Procedures.* The teacher can assess a student's known and unknown rime clusters to establish a baseline. Building upon what the student knows, the teacher can strategically introduce new rime clusters. Pocket Cards and drill sandwich activities can be used to keep the known ratios high as students increase their knowledge of other rime clusters. Selected rime clusters can be incorporated into other activities, such as extending word families, allowing students to explore more imposing words that incorporate selected rime clusters.

Extending Word Families

Description. Extending word families provides varied and multiple opportunities for students to become accurate and automatic in using rime clusters and in extending their thinking about word usage. The focus helps students to identify and practice the use of rime clusters within base words and also to see how rime clusters are present in more and more complex words.

Procedures. The teacher first discusses strategies students use to "unlock" unknown words and reminds them that as they get older certain strategies are more useful than others. The teacher then discusses how certain rime clusters are pronounced in a consistent manner and are used to both develop and create extensions of words.

Teachers begin with a text that uses a particular rime cluster. Students conduct a word search to identify the various words associated with that rime cluster. The teacher has students create a web, adding words to the family (Figure 7.10). The web starts with the basic rime and spreads out to both common and complex words, as illustrated.

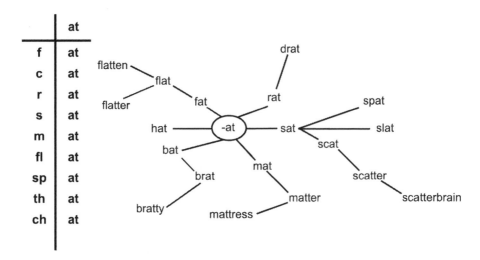

	at
f	at
c	at
r	at
s	at
m	at
fl	at
sp	at
th	at
ch	at

Figure 7.10 Extending Word Families

Word Sorts

Description. Word sort activities allow students to examine word relationships and develop accuracy in word study through varied and flexible activities. A *closed sort* requires students to sort words using predetermined categories. An *open sort* allows students the freedom to sort words in ways of their own choosing.

Procedures. The teacher should establish routines for students to practice word sort activities using a variety of texts that contain sufficient examples to examine word relationships more closely. Texts that are beyond students' comprehension levels should be avoided. Words can be sorted for a variety of instructional purposes. For example, the teacher may select words that have a useful pattern or structure (e.g., vowel-consonant patterns) or that fit a specific need (e.g., descriptive words). Bear and colleagues (2008) suggest *concept sorts* to reinforce a particular concept (e.g., geographical features, states, currency). Whatever the choice for sorting, keep the categories, examples, and complexity within the students' comfort zones. Examples of *closed, open, and concept sort* activities are shown in Figure 7.11.

Maximizing and Extending Word Sorts. Use a word notebook, journal, planner, or log to keep a record of the pattern, set of words, or concepts to be reviewed as needed. Allow students ample opportunity to form generalizations by hunting for other words that follow the same features, patterns, and/or concepts in different areas of the text. Encourage students to work in pairs or small groups to combine their efforts in identifying words and in determining how they wish to categorize their words.

READING FLUENCY DEVELOPMENT

Reading fluency could easily be seen as a direct extension of the author's voice. Word choices, intonation, and inflection are all used to accurately reflect the author's intent. To understand the intent of what an author has written, the reader "continually speeds up and slows down, monitoring their understanding, as they make sense of what they're reading" (Flurkey, 2006, p. 41). Flurkey continues by describing this form of flexible reading as "reading flow," which represents a more apt description of what occurs when a person thinks about what he or she is actually reading. Reaffirming this message, Pearson (2006) notes that "human beings alike in their capacity to perform a given task with accuracy and integrity will vary dramatically in the speed or fluency with which they perform it" (p. xiii).

Closed Sort:

Sort these words according to the different vowel patterns.

CVC CVCe CVVC CV

Joan	had	box
paint	sat	rug
said	here	get
go	find	place
to	so	table

Open Sort:

Sort these words using your own categories.

next	beside	over
funny	nervous	soon
bored	behind	outside
after	angry	later
calm	now	between
last	under	first

Describe your categories and what you found.

Concept Sort:

New Mexico	prairie	moon
Texas	canyons	earth
Pennsylvania	crater	atmosphere
Louisiana	panhandle	universe
(States)	*(Landscapes)*	*(Space)*

Figure 7.11 Examples of Closed, Open, and Concept Sorts

So much energy has gone into recording the number of words read correctly per minute that too often speed is viewed as the prominent measure of good reading, at the expense of reading for meaning. While good readers often read fast, speed does not always result in good reading. The primary goal of all reading is to gain the full meaning of what is being read. This is no less the goal for reading fluency. The strategies you see in this section are designed with this fact in mind. Being able to read quickly is certainly an asset, but this is a secondary goal prompted by the increasing volume of reading material that students face as they progress throughout the grades.

Chunking (Phrasing)

Description. A "phrase" is defined as two or more grammatically related words forming a unit of thought. We prefer the term "chunking" as opposed to phrasing to convey that when words are syntactically strung together they provide meaningful chunks of information. The purpose is to develop comprehension and reading flow. Chunking also helps develop metacognition as students see how words are combined to form units of thought and how different thoughts are combined to form sentences, passages, and complete text.

Procedure. Begin by placing a vague word (e.g., "It") on the board and ask students the question, "What is an 'it'?" Add a second word (e.g.., "It was") and ask them, "What is 'It was'? Do the two words make sense yet?" Add a third word (e.g., "It was daylight") and ask, "Now, do the three words make sense? Why?" Ask the students to visualize the "chunk" of information. Discuss how a writer uses a few words to create a thought (e.g., "It was daylight") and how using different words creates different thoughts.

Next, place a complete sentence on the board (e.g., "It was daylight when he got dressed and went outside."). Discuss the different thoughts expressed in the sentence and where one might pause when reading the sentence. Note for the students that the only punctuation provided is a period ending the sentence. Have a volunteer student read the sentence as if it had two thoughts. Have another student read the sentence as if it had three thoughts. Using various sentences in this manner helps students recognize that an author may not always indicate how many thoughts are in a sentence, but instead lets the student decide as he or she reads.

Another option in introducing the chunking strategy is to write a complete sentence on the board, "It was daylight when he got dressed and went outside." Have students volunteer to read the sentence, listening for where they naturally pause as they read. Some will read the sentence with no pause, while others will read it with pauses. Discuss with the class why they think people read the sentence the way they did. Using the sentence, discuss how words are combined to convey thoughts. Ask for a volunteer to read the sentence as if it were one thought. Have another volunteer read it as if it were two thoughts, and so forth.

Write another sentence on the board, "Looking around, Mike thought his bike, which he just got as a present for his birthday, had been stolen." Have students read this sentence and discuss how many thoughts are found. Compare the two sentences. Discuss how sometimes authors use punctuation to convey or emphasize certain thoughts, while at other times the reader has to decide where the author would probably pause in a sentence as if he or she were talking. Have students look for different sentences, finding different "chunks of information" in their texts. Provide added practice by having them "pair and share" as to where they think the author would pause during the reading of sentences.

This strategy also helps students gain a better understanding of punctuation in their own writing (i.e., too many thoughts in one sentence might lead to a run-on sentence and too few thoughts might lead to "boring" or incomplete sentences). The strategy can also help young readers form mental pictures of what they are reading. Have students fold papers into four sections, then provide them with a written sentence (i.e., "He got up got dressed and went outside to ride his bike."). Instruct them to draw a picture of each separate thought or idea contained in the sentence. Next, have them write down each thought below the respective picture. Finally, have students read the entire sentence, pausing between each individual thought to strengthen their comprehension and expression or flow of reading. Another method of making thought units concrete was suggested by Rasinski (2003). A single slash-mark is placed at the end of a thought unit where no punctuation is provided, while two slash-marks are placed at the end of a punctuated thought (i.e., He got up/ got dressed/ and went outside/ to ride his bike//.).

Maximizing and Extending Chunking. Continue modeling the chunking strategy for students and provide opportunities for practice within the class. As students become automatic in reading for thoughts, shift to helping students read the different thoughts with expression and flow. Working in pairs or small groups, instruct students to read desired passages. Have them consciously read for thoughts, emphasizing where one thought ends and the next one begins. As a buddy reads a sentence, the listener identifies the number of thoughts read. Teachers often follow-up by incorporating *chunking* with other strategies such as *echo reading*, *impress reading*, *six-inch voices*, *drop-word reading*, *repeated reading,* and *timing and charting*.

Strategies for Accurate and Automatic Fluency

Once students become aware of the concepts of reading fluency, a variety of strategies are available to develop fluid reading. Some strategies assist in developing reading for accuracy and others assist in developing automaticity. In either case, the primary focus involves recognizing "chunks of information" to facilitate reading for meaning. Each strategy requires the teacher to strategically select material at an appropriate level of difficulty. For most students, this means selecting materials at an independent reading level (97% or more known words), which allows students to focus on developing reading fluency while minimizing the amount of word study needed.

Read Aloud/Model Reading

Once students grasp how chunks of information are formed, listening to the teacher read aloud and model good reading behavior is more relevant. Not only is the teacher able to model how oral language is expressed in its written form, he or she is able to model how pause, intonation, and reading flow bring greater meaning to the material.

The teacher simply says, "Let me read this next part!" The students are invited to follow along as the teacher reads. Used at the beginning of instruction, this sets the stage for fluent reading. In the case of difficult text, the teacher intentionally reads the material to prevent key words, phrases, or concepts from being lost. To maximize the strategy, the teacher should occasionally model dysfluent reading and read in an illogical manner or hesitate and pause after each word, allowing students to discuss the differences.

Echo Reading

Echo reading reinforces reading meaningful chunks of text. The teacher purposefully chooses a paragraph or portion of text for the student to repeat after hearing the reading. The length of the text is dependent on the success level of the student.

After introducing the concept of chunking or phrasing and reviewing the passage to insure the presence of instructional-level conditions, the teacher, volunteer, parent, or peer reads the text to the student, modeling how the author has chosen to pause at the end of each unit of thought or phrase. The student re-reads or echoes the same phrase or sentence, attempting to approximate the reading style of the reader. The teacher should partner less and more fluent readers.

Reverse Echo Reading

Reverse echo reading reinforces how units of text sound as read by the student. While effective readers review and reread sections of text as needed, struggling readers often forgo these essential self-management elements. In reverse echo reading, the teacher mimics how the student read the sentence. For example, after hearing the student, the teacher indicates, "Let me reread that part," or "The sentence you just read sounded this way...." The teacher then rereads the sentence exactly as the student read it. The teacher can follow up by reading the sentence correctly, allowing the student to echo the appropriately-modeled sentence to gain added practice reading with expression.

Impress Reading

Impress is a simultaneous reading activity that models appropriate flow and intonation. It generally involves the teacher and a student, but can also be used effectively with small groups of students. It was first described by Heckelman (1966, 1969) and reinforced by Hollingsworth (1970, 1978). Recently, Flood, Lapp, and Fisher (2005) applied this strategy with struggling readers.

The teacher sits slightly in front of or beside the student and, using a finger, points to the words as they are read while having the student say the words as he or she follows along. Reading directly into the student's ear, the teacher reads slightly faster or slightly ahead of the student, avoiding *word-by-word* reading. The goal is to have the teacher reading at a pace just ahead of the student's current fluency level, forcing the student to increase his or her pace to keep up with the teacher. Working in short periods of 5-15 minute sessions has been shown to enhance students' reading fluency.

Repeated Reading

Repeated reading is a popular fluency strategy with widespread research, starting with the work of Samuels (1979). The strategy is used to build accuracy, fluency, and comprehension at the student level, small group level, and with a whole class. Again, the strategy is most effective when used in conjunction with other fluency strategies (i.e., chunking and echo reading) under independent reading-level conditions.

Teachers select passages ranging from 50 to 100 words, depending on the age of the students. Students are told they will be reading the passage at least three times so they can read it better each time. Students work with partners, with each student having a passage to read. The teacher has the first student read their passage aloud and has the partner (listener) mark any incorrect or missed word read in the passage. The listener helps pronounce any unknown word after at least a three-second delay. Either the teacher times the reader or the listener times the reader. Each reader rereads any missed words marked by their listening partner correctly.

After the student reads the passage a second time, the listener tells the reader how he or she improved. They do the same after the third reading. When the first reader is finished, the second reader reads his or her passage and the process repeats itself.

Six-Inch Voices

This is a paired activity where students read aloud to each other using six-inch voices. The purpose of this activity is to give students added opportunity to become fluid readers. Each student selects a partner or the teacher may assign partners. Partners either sit side-by-side or face in opposite directions. This allows them to hear each other's reading using their soft voices. Students can use six-inch voices to read alternating paragraphs or even alternate reading phrases as in echo reading.

Drop-Word/Phrase Reading

Using six-inch voices, the reader deliberately pauses, allowing the partner to supply the next word or phrase, and continues to read the paragraph from that point on. This exchange should occur at a minimum of at least once during paragraph reading. Partners continue alternating paragraphs to complete reading of the passage.

Stop and Go

The listener signals the reader when it is time to stop reading and time for the listener to become the reader. Partners take turns reading in this fashion until they have read the entire passage. Stop and go can include a signal for reading together where, within each pair, students read the same passage aloud at the same time (i.e., unison reading).

Timing and Charting

The recording and graphing of student progress not only establishes accountability but also serves as motivation for students. Currently, the most common recording and graphing practices involve reading fluency measures—practices that require assessing the number of correct words a student can read per minute. The number of words read correctly is subtracted from the total number of words covered in the interval to establish the student reading fluency rate.

Timed readings using unfamiliar (cold) and familiar (practiced) content are of particular benefit. With unfamiliar content the assessor can gain a picture of the student's general reading fluency. With familiar content the assessor can gain a picture of the student's potential for proficient reading. Figures 7.12 and 7.13 provide a sample recording of cold and warm (practiced) reading and the graphic display of data. More specifically, the materials indicate the number of correct words read per minute (CWPM), the number of unknown words, and the accuracy rate percentages.

COMPREHENSION DEVELOPMENT

Understanding the message authors wish to convey is not confined to a literal level where basic facts and events are recalled and regurgitated with little connection to life's experience. Thoughtful comprehension is much more deeply rooted in the human mind and is the "ability to link the text with one's existing knowledge to arrive at a considered and logical response" (Applegate, et al., 2009, p. 372). The ability to connect new information to one's knowledge and experience is central to gaining meaning. Gaining substance from reading is not void of experience but is shaped by and integral to personal knowledge and experience. Without this ability, the student will face major obstacles in attempting to integrate ideas, develop concepts, make inferences, evaluate content, and draw conclusions. Given this perspective, activating prior knowledge is fundamental to all comprehension strategies.

Although much is known about skilled readers' abilities to comprehend (calling upon one's experiences, visualizing events, capitalizing on text features, answering questions as they read, summarizing, making inferences, and drawing conclusions), these skills are not always accessible to poor readers. In fact, many find reading comprehension a mystery. Some students struggle with even the most basic concepts, having little or no understanding of how to locate information or how to extract information once it is read.

This section provides a number of useful strategies for developing readers' comprehension skills. While certain strategies are more appropriate for certain ages, many of the strategies described in this section can be applied to all age groups. It is merely the instructional techniques that vary in their application.

Fluency Summary Form

Name _____

Date Mo. Day	Passage	CW PM Cold / Practiced	Unkown Words Cold / Practiced	Accuracy % Rate Cold / Practiced	Comp	Notes
/	Caterpillar	20 / 68	2 / 1	91 / 98		
/	Paw Prints	33 / 51	1 / 2	97 / 96		
/	Homer	35 / 66	2 / 1	94 / 98		
/	Red Riding Hood	21 / 54	6 / 1	75 / 98		
/	Family Pies	19 / 39	7 / 3	73 / 90		
/	Big Pumpkin	28 / 44	6 / 3	82 / 93		
/	Jack & the Beanstalk	43 / 64	2 / 1	93 / 98		
/	Little Red Hen	52 / 74	2 / 1	96 / 98		
/	Katy/ Big Snow	39 / 58	2 / 5	95 / 92		
/	Gingerbread Man	61 / 93	2 / 0	97 / 100		
/	Tiger/ Plum	53 / 69	3 / 0	96 / 100		
/	Hare/ Tortoise	50 / 74	1 / 0	98 / 100		

Comprehension Key: **Comments:**

0 Unable to respond to passage events.
1 Guided questions provide only isolated facts.
2 Requires guided questions to aid overall recall.
3 Provides main idea/general description but limited detail.
4 Important concepts and events are detailed.

Figure 7.12 Fluency Recording Form (Cold/Practiced Reading)

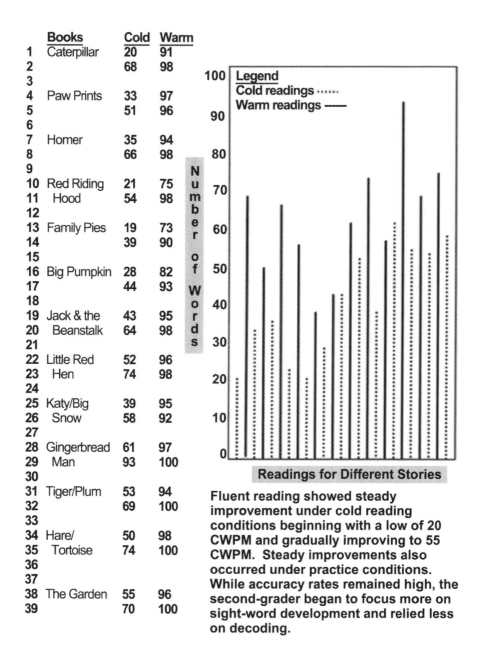

	Books	Cold	Warm
1	Caterpillar	20	91
2		68	98
3			
4	Paw Prints	33	97
5		51	96
6			
7	Homer	35	94
8		66	98
9			
10	Red Riding	21	75
11	Hood	54	98
12			
13	Family Pies	19	73
14		39	90
15			
16	Big Pumpkin	28	82
17		44	93
18			
19	Jack & the	43	95
20	Beanstalk	64	98
21			
22	Little Red	52	96
23	Hen	74	98
24			
25	Katy/Big	39	95
26	Snow	58	92
27			
28	Gingerbread	61	97
29	Man	93	100
30			
31	Tiger/Plum	53	94
32		69	100
33			
34	Hare/	50	98
35	Tortoise	74	100
36			
37			
38	The Garden	55	96
39		70	100

Legend
Cold readings ······
Warm readings ——

Number of Words

Readings for Different Stories

Fluent reading showed steady improvement under cold reading conditions beginning with a low of 20 CWPM and gradually improving to 55 CWPM. Steady improvements also occurred under practice conditions. While accuracy rates remained high, the second-grader began to focus more on sight-word development and relied less on decoding.

Figure 7.13 Graphing of Cold and Practiced Fluency Reading

Brainstorming

Of the various strategies for activating and building background knowledge, the practice of brainstorming may be the most commonly known and yet most underused strategy for activating prior knowledge. In brainstorming, as delineated by Johns, Lenski, and Elish-Piper (2004), the teacher selects a key word from the material to be read by a group of students. *Ocean,* for example, might be the key word. The teacher states that brainstorming is a great way to "get ready" to learn more about oceans, then explains the concept of brainstorming and asks the students to share all the things that come to mind upon hearing the word ocean. All responses from the students are welcomed and webbed, as depicted in Figure 7.14. Some ideas may be covered by the material and students will gain new information from the material as they read.

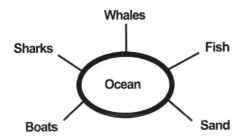

Figure 7.14 Brainstorming Web

PreREading Plan (PREP)

The purpose of Langer's (1984) PreREading Plan (PREP) is to have students draw upon their knowledge about a topic, reflect upon the thoroughness of their knowledge, and assess whether or not they need more information before the topic is assigned. The PREP strategy is used during class-wide discussion generally to introduce informational material. The teacher selects a concept central to understanding the information to be learned and engages students by eliciting initial associations using the statement: "Tell me anything that comes to your mind when you think of..." (all responses are accepted and written down on the board). As students generate reflections, the teacher asks, "What made you think of...?" to help students become aware of what they know and whether or not the information is relevant to what they will be learning. Students' responses are refined by asking, "Based on our discussion, have you any new ideas about...?" At the end of the discussion, the students are better oriented to understand the content.

Evaluating the quality of the students' responses enables the teacher to determine the extent of their prior knowledge and when and where to begin instruction. When students are able to provide definitions or analogies for concepts and are able to link various concepts, it suggests their knowledge is fairly well organized and that they will require minimal guidance when receiving new information. When students describe attributes of the concept, give examples, or define aspects of the concept only, their knowledge is less organized, indicating a need for some additional instructional assistance. When students make superficial remarks, or when they recall experiences that may be only remotely related to the topic, their knowledge is minimal, suggesting the need for considerable topic development and student assistance.

I Wonder and You're the Teacher

The purpose of this two-step strategy is to create awareness that informational text often has a well defined structure that authors use to organize the content. As students gain an increased understanding of informational text structure, they become more strategic in managing their own learning, generating more focused and specific questions to guide their reading.

Teachers should provide direct instruction about informational text features, showing how textbooks are organized and how the authors have planned how each chapter and section is structured. Building upon students' prior knowledge and experience, the teacher can engage students in thinking about how they typically approach reading informational text. For example, they may ask, *"When assigned a chapter, what do you do? What is your plan or strategy?"* As students share their approach, the teacher can begin to ask "I Wonder" questions. *"Do you think the authors had a plan when they wrote this chapter? Can you figure out the author's plan? Does the chapter give you clues to the author's plan?"* As the students offer their responses, the teacher assesses the degree to which students identify and recognize text features (e.g., section headings, subheadings, italicized words, color-coded words, boxed figures, pictures).

As students gain a better understanding of how informational texts are organized, teachers can help students gain accuracy in approaching informational text by prompting the following questions: *"If you were the teacher, what questions do you think you might ask about the main section? What questions do you think the author may answer?"* The teacher should avoid guiding students to particular sections or locations. Instead, they should use student-generated questions to explore how an informational text is organized and structured. *"In which section are you likely to find the answer to...(restate a student's question)? Why do you think the answer will be in ...(restate a student's response)? What could you do if you're not sure about...(restate a student's response)?"*

Developing Responding

Description. While comprehension is always the primary goal of reading, responding represents something slightly different. Responding refers to how well a student is able to convey his or her understanding verbally or in writing of what was read. It exists on a continuum from independent (uncued/unaided) to dependent (cued/ aided). By assessing the student's level of responding and strategically instructing the student, the teacher assists the student in becoming more independent at gleaning and sharing reading information.

Name:_____   Oral Response:_____

Date:_____   Written Response:_____

	UNCUED QUESTIONS		CUED QUESTIONS					
	Unaided Responses		Aided Responses		Forced Choice Responses		Visual / Referent Responses	
Student Supplied	General Idea	Supporting Details	General Idea	Supporting Details	General Idea	Supporting Details	General Idea	Supporting Details
Main Idea								
Characters								
Setting								
Beginning								
Middle								
End								
Prediction/ Inference								

Profile Analysis/ Notes/ Observations:

Figure 7.15 Reading Responding Profile (Narrative Text)

The reading response profile is used to assess a student's current ability to respond as well as to guide instruction in improving the student's responding skills. The rows in Figure 7.15 identify different retelling features of narrative text while the columns reflect the type of external support required for the student to convey his or her understanding. For informational text, the columns remain the same but the wording of the rows changes to conform to the features of the text and instructional objectives (Figure 7.16).

Mature readers understand story elements and can retell stories without assistance. They are not only able to supply the main ideas but are skilled at providing supporting details. Uncued questions or prompts allow the assessor to assess how well students are able to provide main ideas and supporting details on their own. These prompts are open-ended, requiring self-direction on the part of the student. Two examples are: "Can you tell me what you remember about the story?" and "Tell me more."

Cued questions allow the assessor to guide the student's responses in specific directions. Different types of cued questions used to prompt a student's responses include:

- *Aided responses.* Most students can tell about the different elements of a story when provided with aided questions. Questions such as who, what, when, where, why, and how typically evoke appropriate responses.

- *Forced-choice responses.* Forced-choice responses represent either/or types of questions. They provide additional guidance, allowing the student to convey his or her understanding by choosing from two or more teacher-provided options. For example: "Was the real leader the younger or the older boy?"

- *Visual/Referent Responses.* Occasionally, students rely entirely on finding the correct answer by visually searching a story for the exact sentence, word, or picture to convey their comprehension. Looking back is a helpful tool, but not if it is relied upon excessively.

READING RESPONDING PROFILE

Name:_____   Oral Response:_____

Date:_____   Written Response:_____

| | UNCUED QUESTIONS | | CUED QUESTIONS | | | | | |
| | Unaided Responses | | Aided Responses | | Forced Choice Responses | | Visual / Referent Responses | |
Student Supplied	General	Specific	General	Specific	General	Specific	General	Specific
Main Idea								
Fact/Detail								
Fact/Detail								
Fact/Detail								
Conclusion								
Inference								

Profile Analysis/ Notes/ Observations:

Figure 7.16 Reading Responding Profile (Informational Text)

Procedures. The responding profile is not used for testing or grading purposes but it is used instructionally to help the student become more self-directed in applying the elements of retelling to narrative and informational text. Student responses are recorded by placing "checkmarks" in the appropriate "cells." When completed, the checkmarks create a visual profile of the student's pattern of responding. Analysis of student profiles may reflect individual and class-wide needs. These profiles not only serve to establish responding/retelling goals, but also facilitate communication between teachers, students, and parents concerning students who definitely demonstrate strength and weakness in areas of retelling and responding.

Some teachers prefer to assign a numeric value to each cell. Using one of these systems, or a system of the teacher's own choice, allows the teacher to monitor the progress of an individual student by recording and graphing the scores the student has obtained on the profile over time. Examples of such coding systems include:

Coding System A	Coding System B
Unaided responses = 4	Always = 4
Aided responses = 3	Usually = 3
Forced Choice responses = 2	Sometimes =2
Visual/Referent responses = 1	Rarely/Never = 1

Forming Questions

Description. Smith (1978) defined comprehension as the reader's ability to ask and answer one's own questions. While the skill comes naturally for most students, some students wait passively to answer teacher-generated questions and, for other students, knowing where questions come from and how they relate to text remains a mystery. Forming questions* is a metacognitive strategy that helps students develop an understanding of how information can be extracted from text while reading.

Procedures. The first instructional step is to help students understand how questions are formed and how questions are derived from contextual material. It helps to activate students' prior knowledge about questioning by asking them to recall questions they ask of each other (i.e., who, what, when, where, how). The teacher lists the question words on the board, asks the students to tell what each question word refers to or represents, and records their responses. Graphics can be used to accentuate the question words (see Figure 7.17).

The teacher then writes a sentence from a story on the board and models how question words connect with the sentence. After modeling the process, the teacher selects a short passage from a classroom text and writes the passage on the board. The passage should contain sentences that have several concrete representations of characters, settings, reasons, and events. The teacher then has students look for a

---

* We are indebted to Brian Cooley at Apple Pie Ridge Elementary in Winchester, Virginia, for sharing this strategy with us.

Questions	Refer to
Who?	*person(s) or character(s)*
When?	*time*
Where?	*place(s), location(s) or setting(s)*
What?	*thing(s), event(s), or problem(s)*
Why?	*reason, plot, or purpose*
How?	*a plan or way of doing*

blue

red underline

green

purple

[bracket]

triple underline

Mr. Putter loved toys. [He was old,] and

he knew that he wasn't supposed to love

toys anymore. But he did. On Saturday,

when Mr. Putter and his cat, Tabby, drove

into town, they always stopped at the

toy store.

Figure 7.17 Forming Questions

person or character in the first sentence within the passage and places a blue square around the person or character.

Next, the teacher models for students how to form a *"Who?"* question so that the answer will be the person or character within the blue square, e.g., *"Who loved toys?"* The teacher reads the next sentence and looks for a person or character and, again, places a blue square around the person or character. This time, however, the teacher has students turn to a buddy and ask a "Who?" question so that the answer will be the character within the blue square. The teacher continues going through the passage working on "Who?" questions until students begin locating and making the connection between "Who?" questions and the text. Pronouns can be addressed in conjunction with or separate from proper nouns based upon the teacher's assessment of student skills.

After students demonstrate accuracy in identifying "who" words, and forming who questions, the teacher goes back to the beginning of the text and reads to find a "where" place or location. The teacher draws a green circle around the place or location and asks students to develop a *"Where?"* question that would have as its answer the place in the green circle, e.g. *"Where did Mr. Putter and Tabby go?"* Continue practicing until students make the correct connections between the different question words and text, e.g., *"When did Mr. Putter go into town? What did Mr. Putter love? Why shouldn't Mr. Putter love toys?"*

It is helpful to provide students the opportunity to become accurate with concrete question words, such as *who, where,* and *when,* before introducing question words that are more abstract and/or open to interpretation, such as *why.* After students have made the connections with question words and text, the teacher can discuss whether a particular sentence was a good who, when, or where sentence.

Fat and Skinny Questions

Description. Once students are able to form questions, the focus can then turn the differences in the quality of questions. One way questions differ, for example, is in the type of answers that result. *Fat questions* often require longer answers, may have multiple possibilities, and may require additional explanations to convey the person's thinking. *Skinny questions,* on the other hand, often require brief responses, may have only one possible answer, and can be found directly in the text.

Procedures. Teachers first have students read or listen to a passage of text. Working in pairs, students then write questions about the text. The teacher divides the chalkboard into two sections and writes "Fat" on one side and "Skinny" on the other side. The first student is then asked to read their question. Rather than the teacher deciding, the class is asked to categorize the question as either fat or skinny and the presenting student places their question under the heading directed by the majority of the class. The process of reading and categorizing continues until several questions are categorized under both headings. After enough questions are categorized, the teacher has the students discuss in small groups how and why certain questions are fat or skinny. The key of this sorting activity is not to give the answer, but to have students reflect on their own decisions as a way to promote metacognition.

The teacher facilitates students' thinking and discussion to create an accurate understanding of what constitutes fat or skinny questions. The teacher then returns to the board and, with the class, reexamines each question individually and re-categorizes questions as needed. As an extension, the teacher can have students review a recent quiz or test and categorize the types of questions found there. These activities increase students' self-assessment skills regarding the types of questions and answers being generated.

Strategies for Accurate and Automatic Questioning

Once students demonstrate accuracy in forming their own questions, the teacher should provide practice to enable students to become automatic in forming questions. Several activities can be used alone or in combination to provide opportunities to develop accuracy and automaticity.

THE QUESTION MATRIX

	Event	Situation	Choice	Person	Reason	Means
Imagination (HIGHER LEVEL)	31. What might?	32. Where/When might?	33. Which might?	34. Who might?	35. Why might?	36. How might?
Prediction	25. What will?	26. Where/When will?	27. Which will?	28. Who will?	29. Why will?	30. How will?
Probability	19. What would?	20. Where/When would?	21. Which would?	22. Who would?	23. Why would?	24. How would?
Possibility	13. What can?	14. Where/When can?	15. Which can?	16. Who can?	17. Why can?	18. How can?
Past	7. What did?	8. Where/When did?	9. Which did?	10. Who did?	11. Why did?	12. How did?
Present (LOWER LEVEL)	1. What is?	2. Where/When is?	3. Which is?	4. Who is?	5. Why is?	6. How is?

Figure 7.18 Question Matrix

Question Matrix

The question matrix (Figure 7.18) provides a series of question words arranged from lower to higher order thinking. The matrix reflects both story elements and questioning complexity. Teachers have used it for both direct instruction as well as in cooperative learning where students are required to accurately and automatically create lower and higher level questions.

Question Cubes

Question cubes (Figure 7.19) are great cooperative group activities once students have an awareness of questions and how questions relate to comprehension. Use one cube when wanting to have students practice and become automatic with literal/fact-based questions (Who? What? When? How?, etc.) and use both cubes together when students are ready to develop higher order questions (Who might? What would?, etc.).

Summarizing and Responding

Teachers use several instructional strategies, structures, and techniques to develop skills of summarizing and retelling. Effective strategies are those that support students' thinking about how to comprehend and concisely retell what they have read. Once developed, summarizing can become a key component of reciprocal teaching (Palincsar & Brown, 1984).

Graphic Organizers

Graphic organizers help students recall and organize central elements of what they have read. They can be specific to critical aspects of text (e.g, detailing character traits, as in Figure 7.20) or can assist students in retelling or summarizing plots or events, as in Figure 7.21. Graphic organizers can be independently completed and/ or used as part of cooperative group activities. For example, once students complete their Who am I? organizer, students can be grouped by similar or different character traits in order to compare and contrast their notes. Regrouping can also be used to draw comparisons and contrasts between different characters and their character traits within a story.

Magnet Words

The concept of magnet or key words represents a core strategy for teaching summarizing skills. "Just as magnets attract metal to them, magnet words attract information to them" (Buel, 2001, p. 80). The strategy not only helps students organize information around central concepts but also helps them distinguish important from unimportant information. Just as keys open locks, key words unlock important information related to the text. Students read or listen to text and identify and write a magnet or key word. They then surround that word with relevant details that are germane to the word (Figure 7.22).

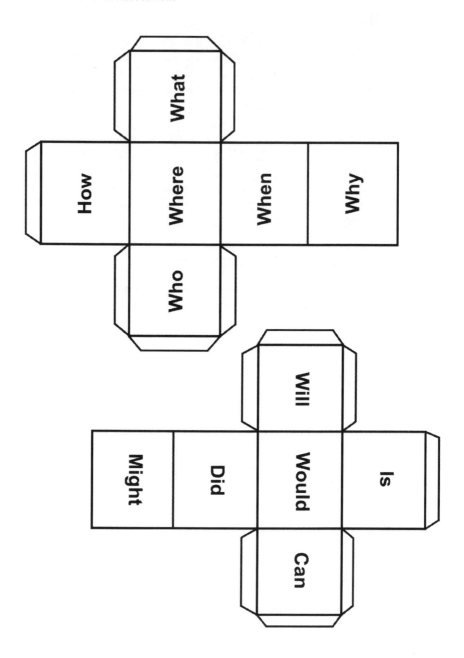

Figure 7.19 Question Cubes

Who Am I?

How the character acts:	How the character feels:
1. _____	1. _____
2. _____	2. _____
3. _____	3. _____
4. _____	4. _____

Character's Name

_____

How the character looks:	What the character says:
1. _____	1. _____
2. _____	2. _____
3. _____	3. _____
4. _____	4. _____

Figure 7.20 Graphic Organizers (Characters)

Creating a Story Frame

The story takes place _____
_____ .
_____ is a character in the story
who _____
_____ .

A problem occurs when _____
_____ .

After that _____
_____ .

Next _____
_____ .

The problem is solved when _____
_____ .

The story ends _____
_____ .

Figure 7.21 Graphic Organizers (Story Summary)

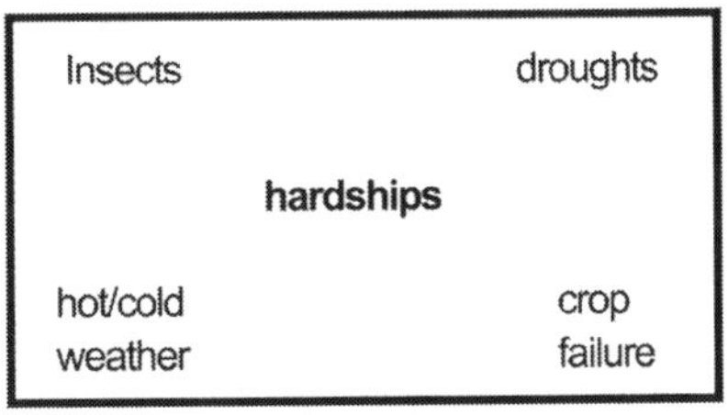

```
┌─────────────────────────────────────┐
│  Insects                   droughts │
│                                     │
│            hardships                │
│                                     │
│  hot/cold                  crop     │
│  weather                   failure  │
└─────────────────────────────────────┘
```

"In the Great Plains, people
had hardships with the very hot and
very cold weather, and their crops
failed due to drought and insects."

Figure 7.22 Magnet/Key Cards

Teachers create an awareness of the magnet or key word concept by directing students to listen to a passage and to call out to the teacher what they think is the key word of the passage. The teacher writes down their responses, which often results in disagreement among students as to which word is most central. The teacher has the students listen to the same passage again, but this time students are to think about which of the words written on the board is most central to the passage—which word do all the other words connect to or are "attracted to?" The teacher should provide practice either for the class or in small groups to identify magnet words and to develop greater skills in differentiating key words from supporting details. If students continue to have difficulty identifying key or magnet words, the teacher can try reversing the directions by having students listen for the details, avoiding magnet or key words. Likewise, the teacher can divide the class in half and have one half listen for a key word in a passage and the other half listen for the details.

Once students demonstrate accuracy and can differentiate key words from details, they can create various magnet summary cards. Working in small groups (i.e., jigsaw), students read a selection and create their cards. They then share and discuss their cards with other groups, giving summaries based upon what is on their cards.

Free and Cued Retelling

The teacher instructs students on the difference between guided responding (i.e., cued) and independent responding (i.e., uncued). After students understand the difference between cued and uncued questions and can use them accurately, the teacher provides additional opportunities for students to practice both types of questions or prompts to improve retelling skills. Students work as partners (e.g., A and B partners) to read the story. Partner A asks Partner B to retell everything about the story that they can remember. Partner A records each event or idea mentioned by Partner B (the storyteller), placing a check mark in the "free retelling" column for each event or idea told, using the chart in Figure 7.23. After Partner B has told everything he or she remembers about the story, Partner A provides aided questions to evoke a more complete retelling. The storyteller is encouraged to tell as much as possible about each

Partner A _____ Partner B _____		
Listener & cue giver Storyteller		
EVENTS OF THE STORY	FREE RETELLING	CUED RETELLING

Figure 7.23 Free/Cued Recall Recording

cued question. Each idea or event is recorded and a check mark is placed in the cued retelling column.

Someone... Wants... But... So

Helping students summarize according to typical plot sequence supports their thinking and understanding about how authors organize stories. Often, stories involve characters confronted by obstacles where they must take action. This strategy (Figure 7.24) allows students to summarize and retell according to the plot sequence that many stories follow. As students read or listen to the story, they capture and record the elements under the appropriate column. Students are then encouraged to orally

Someone...	Wants...	But...	So...

Figure 7.24 Someone...Wants...But...So

summarize the story with a partner and/or write a synopsis using their notes.

SUMMARY

A strategy is only strategic if it is selected for the correct purpose and focus. More importantly, a strategy will only be effective if taught and practiced under optimal (i.e., matched) learning conditions. When it comes to selecting and using various reading strategies, there is no doubt that some are used more often than others and that teachers definitely have their favorites. This chapter reviewed and described a representation of reading strategies found to help develop and maintain a successful instructional match and alter the halting and awkward performance of poor readers.

The importance of creating and maintaining optimal learning conditions as part of the reciprocal nature of assessment and instruction cannot be overstated. Students will not receive the full benefits of the strategy unless the instructional match is in place. Likewise, without the match, teachers may mistakenly give up on a very good strategy because they do not see the benefits. Whenever optimal learning conditions are sacrificed and frustration and failure set in, both teacher and student suffer and every instructional tool and strategy becomes tenuous.

The strategy matrix introduced provides a representation of a variety of strategies that serve different purposes (i.e., awareness, accuracy, and automaticity). Its use helps in the development of vocabulary, fluency, and reading comprehension for students, especially struggling readers. As assessors and teachers become more proficient with the different uses and specific techniques, their ultimate goal then is to teach and empower students to skillfully apply them as part of their own self-directed learning.

Chapter 8

Supporting Group and Class Instruction Using Instructional Assessment

Does the past not always seem safer, more secure than the present and far more sure than the future?

(Thunderstick, Coldsmith, 1993)

Early in her teaching career, Tomlinson (2007/2008) realized that students' knowledge and skills emerge along different time continuums at different depths of attainment. To meet their literacy needs, she would have to attend to the individual needs of students as well to the needs of student groups. Her resolve to address both individual and group needs illustrates the constant challenge facing classroom teachers and also illustrates just how central assessment's role is in guiding both individual and group instruction.

This chapter extends the practice of creating the instructional match and of maintaining optimal learning conditions on a large scale to enable struggling students to participate more fully in the daily learning experiences of the classroom. While individual assessment is useful, it is impractical for group and class purposes. Believing that assessment is a labor-intense, one-on-one event discounts the importance of ensuring that optimal learning conditions always exist during assessing and teaching, regardless of the number of students involved. To realize and appreciate the learning and teaching benefits that accrue from Instruction Assessment (IA), classroom teachers need to incorporate it into their classroom instruction.

NATURAL EXPANSION OF ASSESSMENT'S ROLE

IA provides a natural bridge for addressing the individual needs of students working in group and whole class settings. Figure 8.1 depicts the transition that occurs as assessment widens in scope. The learning triangle on the left depicts how assessment is routinely applied to create and maintain instructional-matched conditions for the individual student. Individual assessment is focused on creating optimal learning conditions by aligning instructional objectives and demands of the learning task with the knowledge and entry skills of the student. Knowing how to use assessment to create instructional-matched conditions for individual students is invaluable, but it is not a practical approach to use with a class of students.

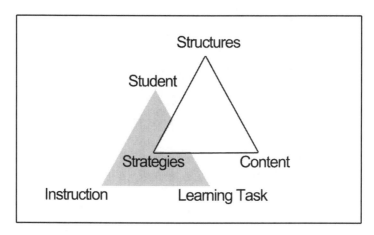

Figure 8.1 Key variables to meet the broader concerns of the classroom

In contrast, the triangle on the right illustrates how the structure of the classroom and appropriate reading strategies assume increasing importance in assessing and delivering instructional content in group and whole class settings. The constant blending of assessment and instruction allows assessment to assume an expanded role in support of the learning needs of every student in the classroom. The sequential goals of assessment remain: (1) creating optimal learning conditions to ensure that the learning content is matched to the entry skills of students; (2) providing timely, confirming, and corrective feedback; and (3) systematically monitoring students' progress. Although the management of group and whole class assessment activity adds complexity to the assessment process, there are rewarding outcomes as student participation increases and reading improves.

Strategies Versus Structures

For our purposes, a strategy refers to a set of teaching procedures or techniques that provides a plan of action designed to help students learn and grow continuously. As described in Chapter 7, assessors and teachers use instructional assessment to pinpoint the strengths and needs of students, then present specific reading strategies to complement those strengths and needs. When judiciously applied, strategies help students become aware of their own learning, increase learning efficiency, and ultimately assist in regulating their current and future learning.

Structures, on the other hand, help teachers arrange, organize, and facilitate the delivery of strategies germane to the individual needs of students and to the needs of groups of students. Structures can, for example, be very basic, allowing teachers to employ a single strategy with an entire class or they can be comprehensive, involving the scaffolding of multiple strategies for multiple students. Efficient management of classrooms and effectiveness of instructional delivery depend to a large extent on the structures teachers employ.

Building Automatic Strategy Use

The IA process, when group and whole class involvement is initiated, typically focuses on teaching first to create an awareness of and rationale behind the strategy. Then the teacher proceeds to demonstrate its use, allowing students sufficient opportunities to practice and receive feedback concerning its application. For students needing more guidance, additional instruction and practice are provided in order to gain adequate facility in using the strategy. When a strategy is taught in this manner, observations are conducted to assess how the group or class reacts to the use of the strategy–a practice referred to as "strategies as assessment." Observing student's responses to the introduction of a strategy serves an important assessment purpose in these instances. It can help teachers better define a concern or differentiate which and how many students have a particular need.

Whenever a strategy is taught and modeled, the assessor or teacher should keep the demands for student attention to short bursts of no longer than the age of students in minutes (Goldman, in O'Neil, 1996). After a particular strategy is demonstrated, students should be given sufficient time to process what was heard or to practice employing the particular strategy. Cooperative learning and other management structures help develop automatic strategy use (Rohrbeck, Ginsburg-Black, Frantuzzo, & Miller, 2003). Such structures capitalize on the fact that students learn best when instruction is relevant, when they know what they are to do, when they have the prerequisite skills, and when they are able to share their understanding with others. Part of IA's task is to help assessors and teachers create learning environments that allow students to be actively engaged while keeping the pace of learning moving steadily forward (Slavin, Chamberlain, & Daniels, 2007).

STRUCTURES FOR MANAGING LEARNING

Applying IA beyond individual students requires managing the learning of multiple students using appropriate strategies at appropriate times. This is where management structures help facilitate learning. Just as individual strategies have to be taught, practiced, and brought to automaticity, students also require direct instruction and practice in applying classroom structures routinely.

A rich literature exists describing the use of classroom management structures and research showing positive impacts on student learning outcomes (e.g., cooperative learning, Kagan, 1994). However, instead of reviewing the literature, our purpose here is to share a few management structures that have been useful in facilitating group and whole class learning with IA. From our experience, too many students have not received well-structured learning opportunities and, conversely, too many teachers are unaware of how management structures can be used to support ongoing assessment and the creation of instructional-level conditions for groups and whole class instruction.

Clock Partners

The clock concept is a convenient structure for pairing students when tasks or activities call for working with a partner. At the start of the school year the teacher gives each student a clock graphic (Figure 8.2) to complete and directs them to circulate, asking different students to be one of their twelve "clock" partners. For example, if one student asks another student to be his or her three o'clock partner, both students

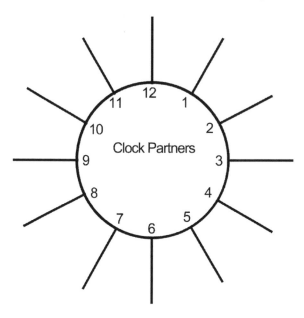

Figure 8.2 Clock Partners

sign each other's three o'clock space. Students circulate until their entire clock partner charts are filled. Any fine-tuning of "clock partners" that may be required is done by the teacher. Once the charts are complete, the teacher simply instructs the students to, as examples, "Get with your three o'clock partner," or "Get with your ten o'clock partner" whenever the teacher wants students to work in pairs.

Flexible Groups

The use of flexible groups is an effective way to organize, group, and regroup students. By using colors, symbols, and numbers, students can be pre-assigned to multiple groups. Figure 8.3 illustrates how students are organized into different working groups depending upon the particular lesson or practice activity. A red, blue, green, or yellow index card is taped to the upper right-hand corner of each student's desk. A symbol of a triangle, circle, or square is place in the center of each card. In the example the color of the card represents the student's assigned math group, while the symbols in the center of the card designate large-group activity. One of six numbers appears on the upper left hand corner of each card, numbers that designate small group activity. One of four letters appears in the upper right-hand corner, letters that designate reading and writing group activity.

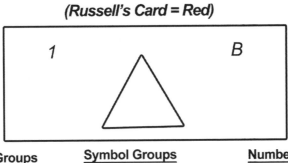

(Russell's Card = Red)

Math Color Groups	
(Red)	**(Green)**
Jason	Charley
Amanda	Nicole
Chris	Deanna
Shawna	Tobby
Russell	Jack
Tabitha	
(Blue)	**(Yellow)**
Mary	Rachel
Gary	Erin
Robie	Brian
Sarah	Melissa
Steven	Matthew

Symbol Groups

△	○	□
Nicole	Jason	Gary
Deanna	Steven	Melissa
Chris	Sarah	Rachel
Jack	Mary	Erin
Robie	Brian	Shawna
Charley	Amanda	Tobby
Russell	Tabitha	Matthew

Number Groups

(1)	**(2)**
Russell	Charley
Gary	Melissa
Mary	Steven
	Brian

(3)	**(4)**
Robie	Tabitha
Sarah	Matthew
Erin	Nicole

(5)	**(6)**
Jason	Rachel
Deanna	Shawna
Brian	
Jack	
Amanda	
Chris	

Letter Reading & Writing Groups

(A)	**(B)**	**(C)**	**(D)**
Tobby	Nicole	Steven	Rachel
Charley	Sarah	Melissa	Matthew
Robie	Brian	Shawna	Mary
Tabitha	Deanna	Erin	Jack
Jason	Russell	Gary	Chris
Amanda			

Figure 8.3 Flexible Groups

Expert and Heterogeneous Groups

A variation of flexible grouping consists of expert and heterogeneous groups. This management structure enables students to move smoothly from learning a targeted set of knowledge and skills in expert groups to working in heterogeneous groups to share added knowledge and skill (e.g., jigsaw). Expert groups are arranged based upon students' knowledge and skill, whereas heterogeneous groups are made up of students from each expert group. Figure 8.4 is an illustration of a fifth-grade teacher's use of

Color Groups (Expert)

Red (High expert) — Present unusual facts about the skeletal system (e.g., babies have 270 bones and adults have 206)

Blue (Medium expert) — Place bold words on cards and create definitions (e.g., marrow, cartilage, ligaments, etc.)

Green (Medium expert) — Construct a backbone out of various materials and describe the function of the backbone to the groups

Yellow (Lower expert) — Identify, illustrate, and demonstrate the types of joints in the skeleton (e.g., gliding, ball and socket, hinge, pivot, and fixed joints)

Shape Groups (Heterogeneous)

Square		Circle		Triangle		Oval		Rectangle	
R	Y	R	Y	R	Y	R	Y	R	Y
B	G	B	G	B	G	B	G	B	G

Figure 8.4 Expert and Heterogeneous Groups

these two grouping arrangements during a one-hour science lesson.

In this example, each grouping arrangement consisted of four to five students, with each adhering to cooperative learning principles. Students were instructed to get into their assigned groups depending upon the nature of their written assignments. Students within their color groups were given directions to become "experts" on specific content related to the skeletal system. Once achieved, the teacher instructed them to return to their shape groups (i.e., heterogeneous groups) to share, teach, and support their group membership in learning the content they had mastered in their color groups.

Trio/Quad Reading

This cooperative learning strategy encourages active participation and risk-taking in reading, summarizing, and forming questions while working at students' reading and listening levels. After introducing and practicing forming questions (see Chapter 7), the teacher assigns a reading passage to each group of students. Cards are used to assign different reading roles—roles that are rotated throughout the activity. When employing trio reading, the reader orally reads the selected paragraph or passage and the summarizer recounts or retells the portion of the story that was just read in his or her own words. The questioner creates questions about what was read and asks the reader to answer each question using complete sentences. In quad reading, the fourth student assumes the separate role of "answerer."

Trio/quad reading requires students to be skilled in forming questions and in retelling. Having students practice the component strategies before being assigned to trio or quad groups is important. For example, the teacher may first have students work in pairs to *Echo* read and then use *Question Cubes* to ask and answer questions of each other. After practicing these component strategies, students are organized into groups of three or four members.

Since struggling readers are often capable of listening and responding to grade-level text, these cooperative learning strategies help manage the amount of challenging content while still allowing them to participate by listening and responding orally. Being strategic, teachers can pre-select appropriate passages for struggling readers or provide pre-instruction to ensure accurate reading when it is the student's turn to be the reader. In either case the struggling reader is able to continue developing grade-level concepts, vocabulary, and responding skills.

CLASSROOM SUCCESSES USING INSTRUCTIONAL ASSESSMENT

Disheartened by the limited progress of struggling students in the typical classroom, many assessors and teachers were searching for ways to narrow the achievement gap. After learning about IA (known then as CBA) and how it facilitated high levels of task engagement and task comprehension, and after experiencing success with individual students, a few adventurous assessors and teachers eagerly expanded its principles and practices into group and whole class instruction.

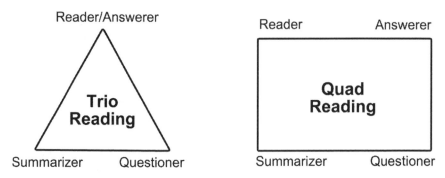

Figure 8.5 Trio/Quad Reading Structure

These early CBA efforts took root simultaneously in elementary schools across Pennsylvania in the early 1990s. Although each school adhered to CBA principles, the assessors and teachers of each school introduced and combined reading strategies in their own unique ways. As found in much of the research on highly effective teachers, these teachers "assembled a mosaic of classroom management and instructional strategies, arranging and rearranging the pieces according to the need of their student at any given time" (*English Update*, Spring, 1996).

While these initial whole class efforts were formative, two participating schools recorded the reading achievement test scores of students in their classes. The data was particularly meaningful since it provided an objective and comparative view of students' reading scores as measured by the Stanford Achievement Test (SAT).

East Elementary

The first school to expand assessment on a whole class basis was East Elementary, located in a suburban district in Pennsylvania. Over a three-year period the instructional support teacher had 50 percent of the teaching staff implementing aspects of CBA within their classrooms. As the principles became embedded into the fabric of the different classrooms, the school experienced a significant shift in performance.

Figure 8.6 shows the changes that occurred in the reading comprehension scores of 100 East Elementary students as measured by the SAT across a two-year period. The 1991-92 data depict a rather normal distribution of the reading comprehension test scores of the fourth-grade student population prior to implementing the CBA process. In contrast, the 1992-93 data demonstrate the shift in class performance that had developed in the reading comprehension scores for the same students one year later.

In comparing the reading comprehension test scores of students from 1991-92 to 1992-93, the largest percentage of decreases took place in the first three stanines, whereas the largest percentage of increases took place within the top three stanines. A more in-depth analysis indicated that a major upward shift occurred with a healthy percentage of students moving out of the first three stanines into the middle three stanines. A similar but even larger upward shift occurred in the percentage of students moving out of the middle three stanines into the top three stanines. East Elementary's

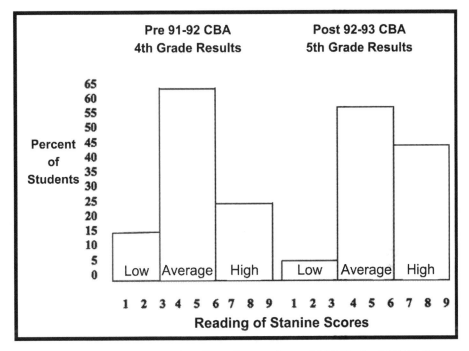

Figure 8.6 East Elementary: Pre-Post Comparison of 100 Students' SAT Scores Following Classwide CBA

experience is a practical example of moving from what Wiggins (1992) saw as a "Bell Curve" --at odds with the very purposes of education--to what Lazotte (1990) saw as a "J-Curve," or a skewed curve of competence.

West Elementary

Around the same time, we were invited to West Elementary, where they, too, had implemented their own CBA process targeting classes of students. The special education teacher, the instructional support teacher, and the reading specialist were all involved and willingly shared their remarkable experience of achievement after being challenged by the lack of student success. The special education teacher related the scenario as follows:

> *I was dissatisfied with the reading progress my students were making. Their rate of word acquisition was not adequate and I was seeing very little change in their comprehension. I had tried every trick I had been taught. I used up the students' time and my patience but it did not make a real difference in my students' reading.*

The special education teacher went on to describe her collaboration with the school's Instructional Support Teacher and Reading Specialist:

These two individuals began coming into my room and working with one group of students to develop a method of assessment that included activating prior knowledge, conducting a word search, and doing timed readings. They also devised, modeled, and introduced various fluency and comprehension strategies. Together, the three of us developed and refined the process that became known as Group CBA.

We needed a way of assessing more than one student at a time as well as a management system that would allow assessment and intervention activity to occur simultaneously. Cooperative learning strategies were taught for this purpose enabling students to work constructively in small groups and to guide their own learning. As they became familiar and comfortable with the process, they began taking ownership for their own learning.

As soon as one group was able to work independently, we added a second group to the process. The first group was instrumental in helping train the second group and so forth. The process went until multiple groups were using the group CBA process. As the year progressed, whenever a group introduced an activity--such as a new graphic organizer--that group would immediately want to share the activity with the other groups. The result was students teaching students.

Their assessment and intervention approach required several weeks of development and refinement and relied on learning centers to make it operational. Results of their teamwork quickly translated into sustained reading success and rapid gains in students' achievement, as seen in Figure 8.7. Like their sister school, West Elementary also recorded the SAT scores of students. But unlike East Elementary, the West scores were those of learning disabled (LD) students from two special education learning support classes. Figure 8.7 displays the fall and spring vocabulary and comprehension scores of these fifth- and sixth-graders. The fifth-graders were in their first year of receiving learning support via group CBA, while the sixth-graders were in their second year of receiving learning support via group CBA.

Examination of the data shows the gains achieved in both LD classes. Of the 60 students with pre-post test scores, 59 improved from fall to spring, with over half showing at least one year's growth in vocabulary and comprehension development. In fact, nearly half of the students showed two or more years of growth on at least one of the reading measures. The fifth-graders had gains in mean scores of 2.4 and 3.2 years, respectively, in vocabulary and 1.6 and 1.5 in comprehension. As a result of the improved reading performance, several students were assessed and released from special education services.

	Fifth Grade Learning Support				**Sixth Grade Learning Support**			
	Reading Vocabulary		Reading Comprehension		Reading Vocabulary		Reading Comprehension	
	Fall	**Spring**	**Fall**	**Spring**	**Fall**	**Spring**	**Fall**	**Spring**
Student A	2.2	4.3	2.9	3.5	2.4	5.1	2.6	4.7
Student B	2.6	5.2	2.8	4.3	3.7	8.5	3.6	5.5
Student C	2.9	4.7	3.2	3.6	4.4	5.6	3.0	4.5
Student D	4.5	8.1	2.9	6.6	5.1	10.0	6.8	7.9
Student E						6.0		4.5
Student F	4.3	8.1	2.9	5.1	6.0	11.2	5.5	12.4
Student G	2.4	5.4	2.4	5.0	4.7	9.1	2.8	5.8
Student H	3.2	5.0	2.9	3.2	3.0	5.1	3.0	3.6
Student I	7.0		4.5		3.0	5.4	2.7	2.9
Student J	2.7	5.0	2.7	4.5	3.5	7.1	3.1	4.7
Student K	2.9	4.1	2.3	3.3	3.5	6.0	3.8	6.8
Student L	3.7	6.6	2.8	4.4	4.4	9.1	4.1	5.1
Student M	3.7	5.7	3.8	5.9	2.1	3.5	3.5	4.1
Student N	3.0		3.5		3.3	5.6	4.1	5.4
Student O	2.9	4.1	3.2	3.8	3.0	7.1	4.1	4.9
Student P	3.5	6.6	2.8	8.2	2.9	5.1	4.1	3.8
Student Q	2.6	4.7	2.9	3.8	3.3	7.1	3.6	4.9
Student R		5.7		4.6				
Mean Totals	3.1	5.5	2.9	4.6	3.6	6.8	3.8	5.4
Mean Change		+2.4		+1.6		+3.2		+1.5

Figure 8.7 West Elementary Pre-Post Comparison of LD Students' SAT Scores Following Classwide IA

To celebrate their success, students developed a rap song with the aid of the three teachers. While the song stressed the importance of having the will to learn and a good attitude, one line in particular caught our attention-- "Ya made it happen without much pain." Here is the entire song:

Gather round kids cause it's time to read
and we gotta tell ya what you're gonna need.
The will to learn and a good attitude
will take ya far—now listen up dude.
Learn new words and what they mean.
Read your stories like a mean machine.

You'll understand what they're all about
and have some fun there is no doubt.
Drill your words and read your stories.
CBA reading is the end of your worries.
Chart your words and see that gain.
Ya made it happen without much pain.
Record your page and question share.
Write your own story if you dare.
You'll blow your mind with your new skill.
You'll love to read—man what a thrill.
You'll read all day and half the night.
Remember when reading was such a fight?
Your mom and dad will be real proud.
You'll want to shout this nice and loud.
If you wanna learn now how to read
Try CBA--it's what you need!

As word of the success spread, other teaching staff wanted to know what was being done differently to teach these students. When told about the concept of Group CBA, several teachers wanted to know how to replicate it into their classes. To assist them in this process, the original three educators described the general steps and provided a schedule of literacy activities—activities whereby small student groups rotated for daily instruction. The West Elementary daily plan is outlined in Figure 8.8.

North and South Elementary Schools

Two other early pioneer schools were North Elementary and South Elementary in central New York. As in the previous examples, the instructional support teachers in these schools spread the word about the CBA process. Upon learning about its principles, several classroom teachers volunteered to implement CBA in their classrooms on the condition that it would adhere to the school's literacy program, use its materials, and be accountable for students mastering their weekly literacy tests. Several refinements involving each weekly reading schedule occurred from year to year, eventually evolving into what became known as "Effective Reading Strategies," or the Five-Day Plan.

Five-Day Plan for Narrative Text

Figure 8.9 is an outline of a five-day plan using a narrative text entitled **_The Paper Bag Princess_** with first graders. Combined with effective reading strategies and organized around well managed structures, the five-day plan represents one of the best examples of teachers, support personnel, and students working collaboratively to ensure every student achieves success.

A critical strategy used in the five-day plan is that of expert parts. By strategically assigning students lines of text, a paragraph, a page, or a longer passage in a story, the expectation is that every student will be able to master the vocabulary and become an expert reader of the assigned segment when given practice time. Once the expert part is mastered, students are encouraged to continue to read as much of the story as they wish. Review and maintenance occurs with students re-reading their expert parts in order to become accurate and fluent, and to gain a better understanding of what they are doing and why.

Day 1. Day one begins with establishing expert groups of three or four students and assigning each group a limited number of pages to read from a story (i.e., expert parts). Each student is encouraged to master his or her expert part and continue to read as much of the story as they wish. Students engage in an individual **word search** of their assigned expert parts. Each student skims the text, looking for unknown words that are essential to understand their expert pages. Each student writes down four or five difficult or unknown words for their group to study. Since good and poor readers are represented in each group, the teacher encourages students to look for words they cannot pronounce, do not know the meaning, think someone else might need, or are proud to know. Each expert group selects five different words to chart on a group word-search poster, with each student writing down one expert word for their poster. They are instructed to use two-inch letters and to use their best penmanship. The group's assigned pages, together with their word-search posters, are displayed. The teacher uses the expert words from each poster to develop a chart to be used for vocabulary study in later lessons during individual and whole class practice during the week.

After listening to the teacher preview the story, the class engages in a *K-P-W-L* strategy, completing the first three columns on chart paper. This activity helps the teacher discover what the students know about the story, what they predict will happen, and what they want to know about the story. The final column--what was learned from the story--is completed later during the extension and/or review day.

Day one ends with the teacher reading the story or telling the story to the entire class. For homework, students are to study their new words and read their expert parts. Upon mastering their expert parts, they are encouraged to read further in the story.

Day 2. The second day begins with the teacher summarizing the story and embedding the vocabulary words from each group's word-search poster into a retelling of the story. Each student raises his or her hand when he or she hears their "expert word" used by the teacher in the story review. Words from the posters used to summarize the story reinforce and connect students' vocabulary words to the text. The teacher uses the poster words to identify the plot, characters, setting, events, and so on. Key words used by the author are added strategically, with the teacher explaining that just as the words students have chosen are important to the story so are words chosen by the author.

Students work in pairs to orally re-read their expert pages, engaging in *partner reading* and *forming questions*. Students read one page and then listen to their partners read the next page. Partners may offer help or suggest using a strategy to help with the reading. After re-reading their expert pages at least twice, students return to their groups to pick a what, when, where, or who card from their table. The card prompts the student to write a question that relates to the story. The questions on the card must start with the question word (e.g., Who said Prince Ronald was a bum?).

Day 1 (Cold Reading)

1. Introduce the story—talk about the title and illustrations—assess students' prior knowledge.
2. Assign different reading passages to the students in the group. Provide cards and markers for writing down unknown words (a word search).
3. Students skim-read their assigned passages. Unknown words are written on cards as students encounter them. Teacher observes how students interact with the content as they skim-read.
4. Group members assist in decoding and defining each student's unknown words.
5. Teacher conducts one-minute timed cold readings with individual students. (Allow the student to read a few sentences to 'warm-up" before taking the timed oral reading). Record reading patterns by taking a running record; after a four- or five-second delay, provide the student with an unknown word.
6. After completion of the students' cold readings, teacher models reading fluency by orally reading a passage to the group. The teacher may continue reading in order to cover additional content or to record the content on tape.
7. Students work independently to:
   • Construct a drill sandwich.
   • Record unknown words in a notebook and practice using unknown words in context.
   • Engage in question sharing.

Day 2

1. Teacher shares oral reading assessments with students.
2. Students chart results on individual Student Profile Charts.
3. In cooperative learning groups, students complete the following:
   • Paired reading using a rating form, i.e., "Dog Gone Good Listening."
   • Continued question sharing.
   • Tape recording and listening to assigned passage.
   • Silent easy reading.
4. Teacher begins fluency intervention activities (individually or in a group). Fluency interventions include one or more of the following strategies:

| Chunking | Echo Reading | Impress Reading |
| Choral Reading | Drop Word Reading | |

Figure 8.8 West Elementary Daily Plan

Day 3

1. Teacher continues fluency interventions.
2. Teacher directs comprehension activity (i.e., locating question words, main ideas, predicting outcomes, etc.).
3. Students work cooperatively to complete a hands-on comprehension activity.
4. Students continue working on the following:
   • Reviewing and revising drill sandwich.
   • Tape recording and listening to an alternate passage.
   • Repeated reading with partner using a rating form (i.e., "Dog Gone Good Listening").

Day 4

1. Teacher continues fluency interventions.
2. Teacher reviews comprehension skill from day three and interacts with students about their finished product.
3. Teacher continues work on comprehension skill.
4. Students (within their group) complete the following:
   • Paired reading (recording reading patterns on transparencies).
   • Tape recording and listening to passages.
   • Extension activity, i.e., creative story writing.
   • Silent easy reading.

Day 5

1. Teacher reviews comprehension skill and dialogues with individual students to assess their reading comprehension.
2. Individual groups share their extension activities with the teacher.
3. A written assessment of student progress is conducted.
4. Students continue the following:
   • Paired reading (recording reading patterns on transparencies).
   • Story extension activities.
   • Silent easy reading.

Day 6 (Second Reading)

1. Teacher conducts a second timed reading with assigned groups.
2. Teacher checks for fluency, oral reading patterns, and retention rate.
3. Teacher records information on Record Form.
4. Students record the number of correct words read per minute and oral reading errors on Student Profile Charts.
5. Students enjoy a fun "wrap up" activity (puzzles, word search, holiday activity pages, games, computer, etc.).

Figure 8.8 West Elementary Daily Plan (Continued)

Daily Activities Guide

Day One

1. Assign Expert Parts:
   Group 1: pg. 1-5
   Group 2: pg. 5-10
   Group 3: pg. 11-15
   Group 4: pg. 15-19
   Group 5: pg. 19-24
   Group 6: pg. 8-13
2. K-P-W-L Chart
3. Word Search/Poster
4. Teacher Orally Reads Story
5. Homework:
   Practice Expert Pages

Day Two

1. Story Review
2. Partner Reading/Questioning
3. Practice Word Chart
4. Mix-N-Match Vocabulary Words
5. Homework:
   Practice Expert Pages
   Practice Word Chart

Day Three

1. Tag Reading
2. Vocabulary Review:
   I Have/Who Has
3. Sentence Making
4. Skill Instruction:
   Consonant Clusters
5. Homework:
   Read Entire Story
   Practice Vocabulary Words

Day Four

1. Story Questions/Jeopardy
2. Sentence Study:
   #1 Read Sentence (Blank)
   #2 Pick Word to Match Blank
   #3 Read Completed Sentence
   #4 Help/Give Opinion
3. Snowball Game/Consonant Clusters
4. Vocabulary Review
5. Homework:
   Sentence Study
   Review

Day Five

1. Extension Lesson (when needed):
   Writing Activity
   Vocabulary Activity
   Computer Activity
2. Review & Test

Figure 8.9 North and South Five-Day Reading Plan Outline

After asking and answering questions, the teacher collects the students' questions for later use.

After partner reading is complete, students' expert words are placed on a class chart to be used for periodic review and practice. Each student is also given a personal copy of the *word chart* to keep track of the words they know (Figure 8.10). Additional practice is provided through a mix-n-match vocabulary activity. Each student is given a card with either a vocabulary word or a definition on it. Upon the teacher's signal, students exchange the cards until told to freeze. They look at their card and find the vocabulary word or definition held by another student that matches what they are holding. When all the cards are matched, the students take turns sharing, with one student reading the word and the partner reading the definition. If time permits, the activity is repeated for added practice. Day two ends with the **Mix-N-Match** activity. For homework, students continue reading their expert pages (and beyond) and studying the vocabulary words from the word chart.

Name_____ Date:_____				
Practice Words				
followed	beautiful	everywhere	unfortunately	fiercest
decided	princesses	chase	horses	smartest
breathed	another	meatball	magnificent	hundred
fantastic	married	dirty	whispered	dragon

Figure 8.10 Word Chart

Day 3. Day three begins with **tag reading**. The class is divided with students sitting in two or more circles and each student holding a book. One student in each circle begins to walk around their circle reading the story. At any point the reader tags another student who begins reading where the previous reader left off.   No one is to read longer than one minute.

Accuracy and automaticity with vocabulary is enhanced with the strategy ***Who has? I have!***   As described in Chapter 7, each student sitting in a circle is given a card with a vocabulary word written on one side and the definition of another vocabulary word written on the other side. One student begins by turning his or her card over and saying, "Who has?" followed by reading the definition of the vocabulary word. The other students look at their card to see if the definition matches their word. If it does, the student says, "I have," and reads the word, and so forth. To increase the opportunity for practice, students can be divided into small groups.

Each group is then given the ***word-search poster*** they made the first day. Using sentence strips, each student drafts a sentence that includes the expert word the student added to the poster.   Creating sentences using students' expert words helps students develop higher order thinking skills as they evaluate their sentences for content, meaning, spelling, and grammar.   The student edits the sentence and ensures it makes sense, relates to the story, displays good penmanship, and has correct capitalization, spelling, and punctuation.

The sentences are collected and later used during ***sentence study.*** To prepare for sentence study, the teacher recopies the sentences but omits the expert word and replaces it with a blank (i.e., cloze technique).   Students participate in round table discussions to hone their sentence-making skills and to receive positive feedback and analysis.

Day three ends with the teacher conducting a directed, short mini-lesson introducing a particular skill—in this example, identifying consonant-clusters. The teacher demonstrates the targeted skill or concept before students return to their groups for practice. For the current example, each student identifies a consonant-cluster found in the story and writes it down. Students take turns presenting what they believe to be a consonant-cluster to their group. Group members give a thumbs-up or thumbs-down if they agree or disagree. Afterward each group shares words they identified as consonant-clusters with the whole class.

Day 4. Students begin with a focus on comprehension by playing a game similar to Jeopardy. Using previously-generated questions, question cards are created and organized into a grid, each question reflecting different values. The students follow the process of the game by selecting questions of different values to ask and answer.

The sentences students constructed on Day three are returned for ***Sentence Study***. Each group receives a set of sentences with expert words omitted and a set of index cards each containing expert words. Group members assume roles to facilitate the activity. The first student reads the sentence, saying "blank" in place of the missing word while the second student physically places the correct matching word card in the blank space. The third student reads the complete sentence containing the expert word and the fourth student provides assistance or correction when needed. Student jobs are rotated with each new sentence. The groups rotate to the next table and repeat the same process. As sentence-making improves, an element of challenge can be added by having the students develop sentences composed of riddles, a mystery element that is one that students particularly enjoy.

After a brief review of the skill introduced in the mini-lesson of Day three (e.g., consonant-cluster skills), the teacher introduces the ***snowball game*** (see Chapter 7). The game ends by having students share their words and the consonant-clusters making up their words with the class. Day four concludes with the teacher reviewing the vocabulary words from the word chart with the class. Students read, review, and ask question about the story for homework.

Day 5. Extension activities vary from story to story, but usually involve creative ways to review the vocabulary, comprehension, or a targeted skill that was developed related to the story. In the current example, students are divided into three groups--creative writing, vocabulary bingo, and skill instruction.

- Creative writing. Students explore other stories that have similar themes or concepts—in this instance, stories that have dragons as main characters. They are reminded that dragons are imaginary creatures and are asked to brainstorm different ways to envision dragons as mythical creatures before they describe and draw their own dragons.

- Vocabulary Bingo. Students receive a bingo card from the teacher. Each card has different mixes of vocabulary words and definitions for playing the game.

- Skill Instruction. Target skills (e.g., consonant-clusters) are reviewed using a computer software game or similar activity. Students answer questions about the story and give examples of consonant-clusters as part of the computer game.

Day five ends with a review of the story and the essential skills taught in the story.

Test Day. The teacher constructs a test comprised of work completed by students throughout the week. In this example, the teacher incorporated ten fill-in-the-blank sentences written by the students during sentence study. Comprehension was assessed using questions developed during the Jeopardy game. Consonant-clusters consisted of matching parts of words and making new words. The goal was to construct an authentic test that matched the tasks students had generated throughout the week. This test was designed to assess how well the teacher taught the various skills and how much the students had gained and retained.

The number of days engaged in integrating class-wide assessment and instructional activities varies depending upon the skills taught and the amount of information covered. Many variations of this type of instructional planning and assessment can exist. For example, students could take the test with partners or with their learning groups. The goal is always to ensure that the conditions for learning are optimal, that the test is an accurate measure of what each student has learned, and that each student had a positive learning experience.

Five-Day Plan for Informational Texts

The planning process illustrated by North and South Elementary Schools represents the deliberate use of both structures and strategies to achieve quality outcomes for students through the application of CBA principles and practices when working with an entire class. These outcomes focused on improving the academic achievement for all students by creating optimal learning conditions working within narrative texts. However, the same structure can be used--and was used--with informational texts. Figure 8.11 illustrates how a social studies chapter on the Civil War was taught to fifth-graders using a variety of management structures and effective reading strategies over multiple days.

Central Elementary School

Our final example of using CBA on a whole class basis is not as detailed as the former examples. Instead, it addresses the pressures placed on schools to comply with newly-adopted state learning standards. This example demonstrates the amount of planning, organization, and implementation involved to raise fourth-graders' English Language Arts (ELA) Test Scores in a rural school where 50% of the students had initially received either marginal or unsatisfactory ratings.

In reviewing fourth-grade state assessment results, the support teacher identified difficulties related to students' ability to listen for precise information and to follow explicit directions. These patterns resulted in students misinterpreting test items and often providing only partial responses. Instead of the typical approach of trying

Extended Reading Plan
Chapter 19: The Civil War

A. Pre-Reading/Reading
1. Assign Expert Parts:
    Group 1: Lesson 1 (437-441)
    Group 2: Lesson 2 (444-447)
    Group 3: Lesson 3A & The
    Gettysburg Address (448-450)
    Group 4: Lesson 3B & 3C and
    (450-453)
    Group 5: Lesson 4A, 4B & 4C
    (454-457)
    Group 6: Lesson 4D & 4E
    (458-460)
2. K-W-L Chart
3. Word Search/Posters
4. Quad Reading on Expert Parts
5. Homework:
    Read expert parts

B. Comprehension/Vocabulary
1. Partner Reading/ Questioning
2. Story Review (summaries)
3. Vocabulary Bingo
4. Homework:
    Read Expert Parts
    Review 1st 8 pocket words

C. Fluency/Note-taking/Vocabulary
1. Tag Reading
2. Note-taking using
    Advanced Organizers
3. I Have, Who Has?
4. Fan & Pick
    Groups generate questions
    Teacher adds questions, if necessary
    Groups pass questions from group
    to group
5. Homework:
    Review 2nd 8 pocket words

D. Study Skills/Comp/Vocabulary
1. Magnet Words
    Key words/pictures
2. Fan and Pick
    Groups generate questions
    related to key words
    Teacher adds questions if
    necessary
3. Snowball Fight
4. Homework:
    Read over notes
    Study remaining pocket words

E. Review
1. Groups Share Notes & Discuss
2. Finish K-W-L
3. Mix-N-Match
4. Homework:
    Individual study

F. Show us what you know!
1. Review
2. Chapter 19 test

Figure 8.11 Class CBA Applied to Expository Text

to prepare students to take the annual state test by cramming discrete skills or simply practicing test taking skills, the support teacher thoughtfully targeted her teaching and guided practice to span several months of week-by-week instruction. Her approach not only helped students prepare and pass the state ELA test, but fundamentally increased the students' overall learning and achievement in general.

September

September activities focused on developing students' listening skills and skills at following directions. The teacher discussed the importance of listening, having a clear desk, focusing on the speaker, keeping lips closed, listening with both ears, and not watching a neighbor. Students then practiced following directions. Warm-up activities consisted of listening to 2-, 3-, and 4-step directions, then completing each step from memory. Learning to work sequentially was practiced by having students make things and do things that required following sets of steps, as in making a BLT sandwich. Students continued to practice listening and following directional words (e.g., first, second, then, etc.).

Graphic organizers were introduced to match different settings, details, sequences, characters, and feelings, and to compare and contrast characteristics they were examining. Instruction and practice were provided to construct a directional paragraph, first by showing how authors connected activities in a sequential order, and, secondly, by having students choose subjects of their choice to practice writing directional paragraphs. Writing conferences with the teacher were frequent, giving encouragement and feedback. Throughout these various activities, **QAD** was used (i.e., What is the question? What is the answer? What are the details? What comes first? What comes second? and so forth).

While teachers often complain, "Kids aren't listening and paying attention," students are seldom given opportunities to develop these skills. When properly instructed, these fourth-graders quickly learned that listening attentively and following directions explicitly provided the foundation for all ensuing activites.

October

October activities centered on note-taking, with students instructed on its importance. Students were encouraged to develop their own style in capturing key information, but not to write in complete sentences. They were taught to use key words and to construct graphic organizers to facilitate note-taking skills. Demonstrations were conducted with the classroom teacher reading part of a story and the support teacher modeling the process of note-taking on the board. Discussions followed concerning the support teacher's note-taking style, along with what her notes meant. The teacher would then read another part of a story, having each class member take notes. Students and teachers would discuss and compare their different note-taking styles. Parts of stories continued to be read orally, with students taking notes and answering comprehension questions from their notes.

A second focus involved locating details. The classroom teacher would read part of a story and the students would practice identifying important details by writing down only key words to stimulate recall. At other times they practiced identifying unimportant details. Discussions would follow by having students share their thinking. Students also practiced skimming materials to locate details quickly. The practice of locating details for note-taking purposes also made use of graphic organizers. For example, a graphic organizer might be used to develop character attributes. Students would discuss various attributes and then write paragraphs about an attribute of their choice. They frequently shared their written paragraphs and received helpful hints from their classmates.

Building upon the above activities, the teachers and students discussed the concepts of comparing and contrasting, how certain key words help identify comparisons, and how other key words help to draw contrasts. The teachers also used graphic organizers to model similarities and differences, followed by having student practice comparing and contrasting different attributes within their writing.

November

Comprehension was the primary focus of November activities. Fables, poems, and short stories were selected. Their structure and rich language were appropriate for students to practice locating main ideas and details, to interpret authors' intended messages, and for predicting and making inferences. These materials were also used to reinforce note-taking. Special attention was paid to using descriptive words or phrases to convey correct meanings.

Journal writing and reading encouraged students to share their experiences but also reinforced finding key information (order of events, likes and dislikes, etc.). Literature that called for following directions was used to systemically reinforce the skills of sequencing. The strategy of highlighting text was also introduced, modeled, and practiced to reinforce identifying main ideas and supporting details.

December

December was devoted to developing comprehension strategies, with particular attention to answering unaided and aided questions. Much of the focus was on restating questions before answering orally or in writing. Restating a question and answering it in written form was quite difficult for the students and required substantial practice. The teachers taught and modeled how to use decision-making when determining possible answers, how to read carefully, and how to use the process of elimination. Practice opportunities and direct feedback were given to ensure the use of complete sentences when writing answers.

Activities involved reading letters, short stories, and news articles. Each of these activities required students to construct short written responses focusing on events, sequences, time lines, and details. Because it was December, all written activities were kept short and involved either individual or class discussions concerning how students arrived at their answers.

January

January consisted of reviewing previously taught skills in preparation for taking the state ELA test. Students were reminded that the previous activities were designed to provide them with the background and skills to be comfortable and confident in taking the test. Samples of previous ELA test questions were reviewed, discussed, and practiced, and some test areas received added attention. For example, students were taught, in responding to test bullets, that these were indications that the author wants specific things addressed. In addition, test rubrics of how written work would be scored were introduced and discussed. Different writing samples were used with students telling how they would score different writing samples.

January also focused on stretching students' written language into different types of genres (e.g., descriptive, persuasive, journal, etc.). Following grammar rules was stressed, as were writing complete sentences, using descriptive words, and making logical connections in paragraph writing. Fables were used to reinforce identifying main ideas and supporting details. Poetry was used to reinforce note-taking and comprehension, and analogies were used for students to explore what was being connected or compared.

Central Elementary Results

Clearly, there was much effort and planning that went into this year-long effort by the staff at Central Elementary. But it was worth it. When the state ELA test was administered to the following year's fourth-graders, results showed that not a single fourth-grader received an unsatisfactory rating and only a small percentage (21%) received a marginal rating. More striking, while only 50% of the students had achieved the required decent or competent rating the previous year, 79% received decent or competent rating after participating in the year-long CBA process (see Figure 8.12). While this example compares the performance of two different groups of fourth-graders on the state ELA test, achieving these results is a testament to what highly-effective, dedicated teachers can accomplish and again reinforces the goal of creating a J-curve competence. Not all situations require such an aligned and intense year-long focus, but the upshot is that with careful planning and thoughtful organization of strategies and structures students can consistently achieve success.

Year	(1) Unsatisfactory	(2) Marginal	(3) Decent	(4) Competent
1999	5% 2 students	45% 17 students	39% 15 students	11% 4 students
2000	0% 0 students	21% 8 students	58% 22 students	21% 8 students

Figure 8.12 Fourth-grade Pre-Post ELA scores

SUMMARY

Jespersen and Fitz-Randolph (1977) made the following observation concerning time: "We can spend it, save it, waste it or kill it; but we can't destroy it or even change it, and there's never any more or less of it." (p. 3). There is only so much time available in school, so assessment must be a means to help use that time effectively. The examples in this chapter illustrate how time was efficiently and effectively employed to meet the literacy needs of many students using group and whole class instructional assessment. Furthermore, these examples demonstrate that assessment activities need not be limited to one-on-one practices in order to guide the successful instruction of students, especially those who struggle in their reading development and who have achieved little prior reading success.

This chapter is not intended to be comprehensive but was written to stretch one's thinking about how the principles and practices of IA have been applied to support group and whole class instruction. The examples provided illustrate both the flexibility and the range of planning and implementation that were undertaken. Each example emphasizes the use of a variety of effective literacy strategies, managing learning via cooperative learning structures, and teaching students to engage in self-assessment and self-monitoring activity to guide their own learning as well as group learning. Equally important, they confirm the National Research Council's findings (Snow, Burns, & Griffin, 1998) that struggling students do not necessarily need a different means of support; what they need is *effective* support! The various examples demonstrated ways of providing teachers and students with the types of effective support needed in regular classrooms by thinking beyond the teaching techniques and classroom structures typically available.

One relevant point gleaned from this chapter is that the teachers in these examples were not satisfied with maintaining the status quo, but willingly devoted time and energy over the long term to implement what they saw was an approach that had great promise to guide instruction effectively and efficiently. They were not satisfied with setting limited goals and achieving marginal success. Instead, they were convinced that by maintaining the instructional match and being strategic with their instruction, week-by-week and month-by-month, they could be instrumental in narrowing the achievement gap. The outcomes from the student data clearly show that they consistently worked toward this end.

Of course, the real challenge in implementing group and class assessment practices rests with the willingness of teachers to shift the focus of their instruction from being overly teacher-centered to being more peer-mediated, allowing students to take ownership for self-assessment and for guiding their own learning. Effective teachers delegate responsibilities rather than micro-manage instruction and learning. They skillfully transfer instructional routines by strategically giving the responsibility for learning directly to students in order "to stimulate and nourish students' own mental observations of knowledge and to help them grow in their capacity to monitor and guide their own learning and thinking" (Resnick & Klopfer, 1989, p. 4). Working in this manner enhances the level of student involvement while giving teachers and support personnel time to observe and interact with students about their learning and thinking. In the final analysis, effective classroom support is not so much about providing classroom teachers relief from certain students, but more about supporting classroom teachers in managing instruction so students are successful in their classrooms.

In conclusion, this chapter was written to stimulate thinking about different ways of working shoulder-to-shoulder in order to keep students actively engaged and excited about learning in the regular classroom. For assessment to play an integral role in facilitating instruction in the classroom, it must adhere to the realities of the classroom. These realities require planning and structuring the learning environment so that students can work together, learn from each other, and engage in cooperative and self-assessment activities. In the end, students need to be given sufficient opportunities to analyze, synthesize, discuss, and think about what they are reading rather than continuing to perform poorly (Allington, 2002).*

---

*   Acknowledgements: We would be remiss if we did not recognize a number of dedicated teachers who expanded the application of IA to make this chapter possible. We wish to thank Mary Ann Webb for her pioneering work in exploring whole class assessment and its effect on improving students' SAT scores. The same can be said for Gloria Noerr, John Knopick, and Irma Stein for developing and sharing their group IA process, and to Carla Auten and Nannette Rusczyk for their pioneering work in integrating assessment and instruction into weekly plans. We wish to thank Laurie Comfort and Sara Vakienar for, more recently, refining the Effective Reading Strategies approach and Berneda Rhodes for strategically tying whole class assessment to ELA Standards. Without the ingenuity of these people, we would not have been able to share examples of effective group and whole class assessment practices nor to illustrate the flexibility exhibited in weaving assessment and instruction into regular classroom routines.

Chapter 9

Instructional Accountability: Practical Guidelines and Procedures

If educators want better learning and better learner feelings, then they ought to offer students more learning success and fewer learning failures.

(Block, 1980, p .97)

In undertaking any meaningful endeavor, individuals need to be accountable—productive, responsible, and answerable to the vested interests of others. No less is expected of students, teachers, and support and administrative personnel. Schools must be accountable to parents by providing their children with high quality instruction, and policy makers must be accountable to taxpayers by ensuring that learning standards are upheld and that essential resources are provided to support high-quality instruction.

However, we question why the role of assessments has been so narrowly focused on providing data largely to stake-holders who are furthest removed from the classroom, at the expense of providing data that directly benefit teachers and students in the classroom. In Chapter 1, we discussed why accountability systems favor the use of "assessments of learning." Initially, it makes sense to assess student outcomes after teachers have had time to impart information and help develop essential skills, and students have had time to learn and apply their newly acquired knowledge and skills. However, the use of norm reference and Common Core learning standards to assess the year-end performance of students does little to support developing instructional accountability. These types of data have limited value in directly informing and guiding instruction on a daily basis.

Ongoing tensions between practices of assessments *of* learning and assessments *for* learning are not new (Edwards, Turner, & Mokhtari, 2008). In fact, Valencia (1990) lamented how we have grown weary from trying to accommodate what have been seen as two competing practices and from witnessing how disconnected summative assessment data are from data that truly inform and guide instruction. What is needed instead is an assessment system that honors the alignment of assessment and instruction. Given this current era of accountability and high-stakes testing, Elmore (2003) further laments how much easier it is to measure performance than it is to measure practice. While high-stakes testing allows for the measurement of performance, it contributes little to support instructional practice. In fact, the excessive use of high-stakes testing robs teachers and students of opportunities to truly demonstrate instructional accountability.

As we have discussed previously, assessments of learning adhere to normative and standardized formats that require formal development and administration. To assure trustworthiness and ensure stable scores, test developers religiously embrace the properties of test validity and reliability—meaning that tests actually measure what is intended, and do so consistently. Upholding these two test properties requires test developers to establish rigid administrative protocols. Deviation from how each test is to be administered would result in obtaining unreliable scores and would invalidate the test's results. Yet it is the very rigidity built into obtaining valid and reliable test scores that denies teachers the freedom to interact with students, to think about and reflect upon their responses, and to use insights gained from these interactions to pursue more fruitful lines of inquiry leading to more appropriate instruction for students. From the standpoint of teaching and learning, these are the very features that are relevant and truly enable teachers and students to be accountable. This is the standard that needs to be upheld instead of teachers being handcuffed by rigid measurement systems and procedures.

Formal testing is touted as reliable and valid when comparing student test scores against what experts have established as standards of acceptable performance. When musing about the validity or trustworthiness of formal tests, however, Popham (2009) notes that assessment validity "doesn't refer to the accuracy of a test.... Rather, it refers to the accuracy of score-based inferences about test takers" (p. 77). Of course, such inferences are possible as long as these inferences conform to the test's *standard error of measurement*--a statistical property that tells the assessor the probability that the student's score falls within a range of one standard error 95% of the time, or within a range of two standard errors 68% of the time. It is interesting that such inferences are allowed in formal testing within the bounds of *standard errors of measurement,* yet the very inferences that really matter--inferences that come from astute observations and from directly interacting with students as they are being assessed--are considered outside what standardized testing procedures allow. These are the very types of inferences that make a real difference when it comes to informing and guiding instruction.

MAKING ASSESSMENT ACCOUNTABLE

Since beginning our work, our focus has been on creating and maintaining the instructional match to gain valid and reliable data in order to deliver quality instruction. As detailed in Chapter 3, this practice is grounded in the principles of effective learning and teaching. When learning tasks are suitably matched to the student's entry skills, as illustrated in the learning triangle (see Figure 3.3), a path is formed that enables the student to achieve consistently high levels of performance.

Understanding the role of the instructional match extends well beyond the clichés of meeting the needs of struggling readers. We realized years ago that unless greater control was exercised--beyond routine attempts at leveling books and assigning lower level books to poor readers--creating and maintaining the instructional match would remain tenuous. Using selected passages to simply determine a struggling student's reading level, and then matching reading material to the student on that basis, provides a false sense of accountability because this practice often results in an imprecise approximation. From our experience, matching reading materials in this manner has been in use for years with only limited success. Such attempts have never proven precise enough to answer the question, "Why are struggling readers in constant jeopardy of mismatched instruction?"

In searching for the answer, we discovered that the main obstacle to securing instructional-level conditions was not due to misidentifying where the skills of struggling readers were breaking down, but instead the problem was found in the inherent variability of reading materials themselves. No matter how basic the reading material, the fluctuating selection of words and language concepts typically exceeded the entry skills of most struggling students. This fluctuation constantly violated the limits of working memory, making it extremely difficult for the assessor to create and maintain instructional-level conditions sufficient for the student to achieve any semblance of reading success, or for the assessor to determine precisely what the student knew and was able to do.

What results from the variability found in materials is a cycle of inadequate assessment, mismatched instruction, and aching frustration. In contrast, when insights gained from relevant assessment data are used to match instruction to the ongoing learning needs of students throughout the school year, achievement improves and accountability becomes evident. This is illustrated in Chapter 8. The process consists of identifying precisely what the student knows and can do, using the information to create learning conditions that match the student's needs, and scaffolding and refining instructional strategies to ensure that meaningful learning occurs for the student over the long term.

Assessment, instruction, and accountability are essential components of teaching and learning, but they are not separate and distinct components. Their functions are interrelated, having the over-arching goal of consistently and effectively informing and guiding instruction. With this perspective in mind, the remaining sections address how these components relate to creating better reading experiences, delivering instruction to poor readers, and making better use of the reading curriculum materials available. In addition, there are critiques offered about what we view as distracting practices that inversely perpetuate mismatched curriculum and instruction and interfere with the ability of struggling readers to achieve consistent reading success. These various points apply to students of all ages, backgrounds, languages, and cultures.

For Students

Assessment practices that repeatedly compare the performance of one student to another--against established norms or standards--in order to identify student's deficiencies may serve the overall goals of a state or school district, but those practices fail to serve the real learning and instructional needs of teachers and students. The rigid administrative protocols for collecting normative and standardized test data are impersonal and are impervious to the harm they often inflict.

Not to be misunderstood, we are not against the formal testing of students (e.g., Common Core State Standards). We recognize that process serves some important educational functions, but we are concerned with the excessive use of high-stakes testing conducted under the guise of accountability. With the push to achieve high test scores, it is easy to lose sight of the instructional side of assessment and, in the process, forfeit the learning needs of the struggling student. When assessment loses sight of the student, it fails to inform the teacher about what the student knows, fails to build instruction based upon what the student can do, and fails to unleash the learning potential that allows the student to flourish. Accountability necessitates attention to several critical points and cautions against some common distractions.

Assessment should help, not harm students.

In writing the *Standards for the Assessment of Reading and Writing* (1994) the joint task force of the International Reading Association and the National Council for the Teachers of English identified this central point as their first standard. They noted that assessments have life-altering consequences that can increase or decrease students' opportunities and motivation to learn by eliciting positive or negative feelings toward others and toward themselves as learners.

Although the joint task force was referring to the life-altering consequences of high-stakes testing, the daily feedback struggling students receive in the classroom is a powerful contributor to their habitual feelings of discouragement and inadequacy. The evolving and cumulative effect of constantly falling behind and feeling inadequate defines them as the have-nots of school, a distinction which constantly works against them. As Mirman, Swartz, and Barell (1988) noted, "It is not only the cognitive mismatch but also a personal one that highlights the discrepancy between life and school" for these students (pp. 141-2).

Assessments should elicit the best from the student.

It is often stated that parents are sending all their children to school; they are not keeping their best and brightest at home. Similarly, children are not withholding their best efforts in school. They want to perform well and be accountable. IA has responsibility to see that this happens. It is unrealistic for students to be accountable when the conditions for learning result in frustration and failure.

Assessors and teachers inadvertently work against the needs of struggling students when they constantly focus on what students do not know and what they have trouble learning. Collecting data of this sort merely confirms areas of learning difficulty, but the data are not precise enough to establish appropriate starting points for delivering and managing instruction effectively and efficiently for these students.

Experience has shown that professionals are quick to identify when and where a student is struggling in comparison to other classmates, but slow to recognize that the most reliable source of data for scaffolding appropriate instruction is what the student knows and what the student can actually do. This indispensable source of information not only helps the assessor and teacher pinpoint the reading skills of the student, but provides clues concerning how the student thinks and approaches reading.

Students perform best when assessed under instructional-level conditions.

Wanting to honor the alignment of assessment and instruction, IA strives to match its purposes to the learning skills of students. This alignment requires the presence of instructional-level conditions as a precondition for assessing students. Providing these conditions enables students to accurately demonstrate what they know and what they can do as the starting point for creating and maintaining the instructional match.

Jacob's Case. While the following reading passages may appear equivalent in difficulty, they illustrate what typically occurs when a student is asked to read under mismatched versus instructional-level conditions. The first passage, taken from an end-of-unit test, was used to assess Jacob's reading fluency. Word substitutions and insertions were noted, unknown words were underlined, and a one-minute, timed reading was recorded. Seven errors occurred as Jacob read 50 words, giving him a fluency score of 43 words read correctly per minute. An error rate for the entire passage was 14 percent.

> The lion liked to <u>thing</u> of <u>hisself</u> as the King <u>for</u> the <u>Forest</u>. One day he <u>caught</u> a mouse.
>
> "You can't eat me," said the mouse. "I'm a <u>magic</u> mouse. All the animals in the forest are afraid of me."
>
> "I don't <u>believe</u> you," said the lion.
>
> "<u>Will</u>, then just (1 minute) follow me," said the mouse.

In contrast, there were only three unknown words *(i.e., strange, positive,* and *Mr. Bond)* in the second passage Jacob was asked to read, resulting in an error rate of 3 percent. Reading at his instructional level, Jacob achieved a reading fluency rate of 93 correct words per minute, a rate that included successfully decoding the three unknown words.

> "Are you Detective Tom? Min said.
>
> "I am," said Tom. "What can I do for you?"
>
> "I have to find a missing letter." Min said. "It was supposed to go to my mom, but she didn't get it."
>
> "How can you be <u>positive</u> this specific letter to your mom is missing?" said Tom.
>
> "There were two letters for my mom," said Min. "I definitely slid them into the letterbox. She got one, but she didn't get two.

Now, that was <u>strange</u>."

"I think I can solve your case," Tom said. You can be my assistant. We'll go to the letterbox to find information. We can't solve this case with no information.

Min and Tom went to the letterbox. Tom saw something <u>strange</u>.

"Now, that makes me think," he said.

"What is it?" Min said.

"This letterbox is very full," Tom said. "Maybe some letters fell out."

"Are you positive?" said Min.

"No," said Tom, "But here comes Mr. Bond. We can talk with him." Mr. Bond had no information. "Some letters did drop out of the box," he said. "I think I got them all." Then Mr. Bond got back to his job.

Excerpt from **The Case of the Missing Letter**

Both passages used for assessment purposes on the same day appear to be equivalent in difficulty. However, the first passage was at a frustration level (86% known words), while the second reflected an appropriate match (97% known words).

Unfortunately, too many schools narrowly focus on measuring students' oral reading rate, directing teachers to record and compare students on this metric. But what is the teacher to actually record? In Jacob's case, if the teacher were directed to only record his oral fluency rate, would the teacher record 43 correct words per minute or 93 correct words per minute? Omitted from such a recording is any reference to how the error rate affected the student's reading rate and comprehension.

This example illustrates several compelling reasons why creating instructional-level conditions is an important *first* step *before* assessing what the student knows and can do. For instance, IA snapshots, taken under instructional-level conditions, allow the student to perform at his or her best. They enable the assessor to gather ongoing information about how the student orchestrates his or her skills concerning the essential reading dimensions. More importantly, when the snapshots are taken under instructional-level conditions, the IA controls for passage variability, allowing the assessor to better pinpoint which reading dimension needs support. Further, they guide the assessor's selection and use of appropriate reading strategies and materials.

Once instructional-level conditions are in place and appropriate instruction is underway, the second purpose of assessment provides confirming and corrective feedback as part of ongoing instruction. The third purpose of assessment is then employed to monitor and measure the student's reading progress. This practice of reordering and implementing the purposes of assessment represents a growth model that ensures each student will be able to function under optimal learning conditions.

Self-assessment enhances and enriches student learning.

Assessment is not the sole property of the assessor and teacher. For sustainable growth, ownership needs to be transferred to the student. The student's role is "to strive to understand what success looks like, to use feedback from each assessment to discover where they are now in relation to where they want to be and to determine how to do better the next time" (Stiggins, 2007, p. 23). As teachers increase their understanding of how instructional-level conditions support student learning, and how mismatched experiences hinder learning success, they are in a position to share this understanding with their students.

This point was exemplified in an observation of a fifth-grade science lesson where the teacher asked for a volunteer to orally read a portion of the text in class. To the teacher's surprise, Jason, a learning disabled student, raised his hand. With reservation the teacher called on Jason, knowing that he might experience some reading difficulty. After turning to the designated page, Jason said to the teacher, "Before I read this, I need to look for what I know and what I need." This comment took the teacher by surprise, raising questions about what he meant by looking for what he knew and needed, and where he learned such a strategy. After answering the questions, Jason returned to reviewing the material and then proceeded to read the text successfully to the entire class. Jason had learned about self-assessment from another teacher and internalized the practice of looking for what he knew and what he needed before reading, and used the practice throughout the school day.

Jason's case is a prime example of a student taking charge of his own learning by being actively engaged in self-assessment. To be effective problem solvers, students must be able to identify what they know, and what they need, and to apply learning strategies appropriately when tackling challenging situations. They need to examine and reflect upon what they are learning, ask searching questions, and engage in conversations with teachers and peers in order to gain the most from their learning experiences, all of which are important metacognitive attributes.

Distractions in assessing for student learning

The larger educational community holds to the belief that testing is the best way to prove that student achievement is improving, and--by fiat--that instruction is improving. While we recognize that annual testing has become an expected way of life for students, the overemphasis on high-stakes testing has both a temporal and financial cost for students. The amount of time that is dedicated to actual testing and to test preparation robs students and teachers of valuable instructional time. Likewise, there is a financial cost to testing that must be weighed when judging its value, including the actual cost to administer, score, and report test results. For instance, Supovitz (2009) notes that sales of published tests rose from $260 million in 1997 to over $700 million in 2008, not including the "myriad of supporting and other test preparation materials and services offered by smaller vendors" (p. 212). With resources so scarce in today's schools, the costs of testing cannot be overlooked when judging their contributions.

High-stakes testing is seen by many as an objective way of determining how students are performing. However, the excessive amount of testing and test preparation is anything but objective when assessing struggling students. Obsession with test preparation and testing has failed miserably in narrowing the achievement gap and ensuring that students who struggle receive high-quality instruction. While the literature reveals that the use of high-stake testing does increase a focus on the content to be taught, little research exists to support the view that it has substantially, or meaningfully, altered the delivery of instruction (Diamond, 2007; Supovitz, 2009).

For Instruction

Just as assessment must remain accountable to supporting student learning, it must also remain accountable to fostering the design and delivery of effective instruction. Assessment and instruction need to work in an integrated and fluid manner, continually gathering and providing relevant data that allow teachers to pinpoint and focus instruction as efficiently and effectively as possible.

Activating prior knowledge is essential to instruction.

In spite of how important prior knowledge is to student learning, traditional assessment practices remain passive toward activating such prior knowledge as an essential entry condition for delivering quality instruction to struggling readers. For all practical purposes, the process of linking new knowledge to the student's prior knowledge has been left to the discretion of the teacher. Fortunately, this passive position on behalf of assessment has not adversely affected most school-age children. Their learning backgrounds and experiences appear sufficient for them to manage the daily academic rigor needed to maintain instructionally-matched conditions with reasonable consistency.

The same cannot be said for the struggling reader. Remaining passive does not help the classroom teacher discern how best to use the student's prior knowledge to support the student's reading development. Assessment must assume an active role in creating the type of learning conditions that enable the struggling reader to perform at his or her best. We are once again reminded of this important point in the following statement made by the NRA/NCRE joint task force on assessment.

> The quality of information is **suspect** when tasks are too difficult or too easy, when students do not understand the tasks or cannot follow the directions, or when they are too anxious to be able to do their best or even their typical work. In these situations students cannot produce their best efforts or demonstrate what they know. Requiring students to spend their time and efforts on assessment tasks that do not yield high quality, useful information results in students losing valuable learning time. Such a loss does not serve their interests and is thus an invalid practice *(Standards for the Assessment of Reading and Writing, 1994, p.14).*

The message could not be clearer! Assessments that use reading materials which do not permit students to perform at their best produce questionable results and are not in the best interest of learning and teaching. For students to perform at their best, the amount of challenge must be at the student's instructional level or the assessment data will be suspect and invalid.

Creating instructional-level conditions optimizes student learning and teaching.

Assessments must ensure that reading material conforms to the instructional--and not the frustration--level of the student. This does not mean it is inappropriate to use grade-level texts in assessing entry-level skills and teaching struggling readers. Instead, there are options to using peer-expected texts, just as there are options to using other material. When such options are applied strategically they create conditions that enable struggling readers to perform at optimal levels. When selecting reading material, the challenge level of the material should conform to the parameters described in Figure 3.10. These parameters reflect the working memory limits of school-age students in general and, as such, provide an optimal window for learning. The parameters act as guidelines for managing the level of difficulty of reading material (see Chapter 3).

Unless instructional-level conditions exist, there is no assurance that assessment data will accurately reflect what the struggling reader actually knows and is able to do. Without these conditions, "even an evidence based program may not result in student progress" (Rosenfield, 2008, p. 1647). Therefore, the first IA decision question to address is: *Does the student possess the language, conceptual background, and sight-word vocabulary to read and comprehend the selection?* When the reading selection is too hard, the amount of unknown information will inhibit the performance of the student and give a distorted picture of the student's actual reading skills. When the selection is at the student's instructional-reading level, the student is in an advantageous position to integrate new information and to problem-solve when needed in order to read and understand the selection.

Initial impressions are not always the real problem.

When sharing concerns about a student, teachers will initially describe the student as having major reading problems. This is not surprising, as the teacher's observations are often not much more than "glimpses" within large group settings of the student reading under frustrating conditions, or based upon testing that simply compares the student to some standard. However, once instructional-level conditions are in place, and IA snapshots are conducted, initial impressions often change. Frank's case is an apt example.

Frank's Case. Frank was a hard-working, conscientious, likeable sixth-grader. His teacher stated that he had dogged determination to complete his assignments and to do well in school. Her most pressing concern was how slowly he read, often taking twice as long as his peers to complete assignments. In spite of being a slow reader, once he finished a reading assignment he was able to answer both literal and inferential questions and was described as having good comprehension. With the school year coming to a close, his teacher was worried about how he would cope upon entering junior high because he was such a slow reader. She brought the concern to an IA training cohort, engaged in a year-long professional training to develop and refine skills in conducting instructional assessments.

After talking with his teacher and gaining a better understanding of her concern, the training cohort proceeded to conduct an IA snapshot. The snapshot confirmed the positive features stated by the teacher. Frank was able to listen to and comprehend peer-expected text. A word search indicated that word recognition and word meaning were easily within his instructional reading level and did not interfere with his ability to read and understand grade-level material. To explore what the teacher expressed as her primary concern, a sample of his oral reading was collected, giving the training cohort a clearer picture of what his contextual reading looked and sounded like. While a fluency rate of 150 words-read-per-minute was a fair expectation for sixth-graders, Frank read at approximately 60 words-per-minute.

A second IA snapshot, following the same assessment steps but using a different sixth-grade selection, revealed a similar picture of Frank's performance. Again, his listening comprehension remained strong, as did word recognition and word meaning, but fluency remained sluggish. When asked for details, a member of the training cohort replied that he read the passage at 60 words-per-minute while committing only three errors, for a fluency rate of 57 correct words-read-per-minute.

The cohort was challenged to share other observations about Frank's performance as to the seven essential reading dimensions. This question caused a lapse of discussion, necessitating additional guidance before an accurate accounting of Frank's performance was gained. The ensuing conversation between the trainer and the cohort went something like this: "What I heard you say was that Frank read 60 words-per-minute with three errors; tell me more about the errors." Members of the cohort quickly identified the three words that gave Frank difficulty, which prompted the trainer to say, "Tell me more about what you notice about the three difficult words." After some review, the cohort concluded that Frank decoded each of the words and that once he was able to pronounce them correctly he knew precisely what they meant. The trainer then said, "So you are certain that he decoded each of the three words?" The group offered further clarification indicating that while he relied primarily on decoding, he also appeared to use context clues to ensure that each word made sense in the context in which it appeared. The trainer mused for a while then asked, "How long did it take Frank to decode the three words?" This final question was not expected and could not be answered by the cohort. After allowing time to think about the significance of the question the trainer replied, "It took Frank 35 seconds."

The additional data stimulated a good deal of reflection and redirected the cohort's discussion about what else might be at the root of Frank's primary reading problem. Some of the questions that developed were as follows: 1) If it took him 35 seconds to decode three words and only 25 seconds to read 57 words, then how fast did he read the 57 words? 2) Was he really a slow reader or a slow decoder? 3) Would the primary concern change from focusing on reading fluency to word study and, particularly, to decoding? 4) Did he rely on some type of "sound-it-out" system that inhibited his reading fluency? 5) While he immediately knew the meaning of each word once the word was decoded, was he using an inefficient decoding strategy for his age level? The data from the two assessment snapshots had sparked these and other questions, leading the cohort to conduct additional snapshots to clarify how decoding was limiting Frank's fluency. Only after probing the questions and correctly identifying the problem were they able to decide on how to proceed and what instructional strategies would be effective to minimize and possibly alleviate the problem.

Instruction requires analysis and narrowing of problems.

Frank's case is a prime example of why an effective reading assessment cannot rely on one-shot, initial impressions if real accountability is to be achieved. Without the teacher and the cohort recognizing the value that comes from conducting multiple snapshots and taking time to pause, ponder, and discuss what they were seeing between each assessment snapshot, they would not have realized that Frank's reading problem was less related to fluency and more related to decoding.

The objective of each assessment snapshot is to narrow and identify what is contributing most to the student's reading difficulty. An instructional match will not materialize without the assessor and teacher having a firm grasp of the exact nature of the difficulty. Once they are clear about where to focus instruction, there still remains the need to determine what corrective actions are to be taken and what instructional strategies are to be applied—strategies that are aligned with the assessment data. Beyond this, the assessor and teacher have responsibility for bridging what the student knows with what is new so that meaningful connections are made by the student. This means that the margin of challenge must be managed to ensure that there is a match between what the student knows and what is being taught, and that instructional-level conditions are maintained so that learning can occur comfortably and with high success.

Unlike formal and standardized assessments that are administered under strict guidelines and designed to tease out right and wrong responses, IA follows a process that is flexible and student-friendly. The purpose is to understand how the student thinks, works, and problem-solves when the conditions for learning and responding are optimal. Simply noting errors or correct responses, as Burns (2005) discovered, is not as important as understanding the thinking and reasoning that led the student to respond in a particular way. For this reason, struggling readers are encouraged to share what they know, to show what they can do, and to not worry about being right or wrong.

Instructional assessment is a way of thinking.

We can all improve our observation skills; we can all hone our skills at looking for clues, asking questions, and pursuing lines of inquiry to gain more insight. Honing such skills, however, is made easier when the assessor and teacher work shoulder-to-shoulder in the classroom, reflecting upon their observations and sharing their thinking. Such on-the-spot experiences foster immediate feedback, stimulate questions as they arise, give direction as to where and how to proceed, and resist becoming bogged down by formal and standardized procedures. For instance, in Frank's case, the training cohort would never have seen how he approached decoding had they simply followed the structured assessment protocol recommended for recording one-minute reading fluency rates. They would have simply told Frank each unknown word after a three-second delay. Without taking the opportunity to view, ponder, and explore how his approach to decoding was contributing to his reading, the cohort would have simply continued to address Frank's instructional need as a reading fluency problem, not correctly identifying Frank's decoding needs.

We are not suggesting that assessments occur without structure. What we are saying, instead, is that formal procedures can interfere with real opportunities to pursue important areas of inquiry. For assessments to be relevant, valid, and timely, built-in flexibility is necessary. Having said this, the IA process adheres to a sequence of steps. These steps, though, merely provide a framework for viewing how the student's reading skills are orchestrated with respect to the different reading dimensions. While they outline how a reading snapshot is to be performed, the structure is broad enough to permit the assessor and teacher to delve more deeply into the student's thinking and reasoning in direct relation to each essential dimension. This approach creates a much more strategic instructional picture of the student's reading skills and reading needs.

Effective instruction keeps the big picture in mind.

Reading is fundamentally about gaining meaning within the context of what is read. Reading should never be reduced simply to counting the number of words the student reads per minute. While rapid word recognition reflects mastery of a set of discrete skills, it does not automatically transfer to meaningful reading. In distinguishing between the development of growth constructs and skill mastery, Pearson (2006) observed that as educators we strive for the mastery of discrete skills (e.g., letter-sound correspondence, letter patterns, word recognition) so we can get to the real substantive areas of reading (i.e., comprehension, reasoning, critical thinking). Pearson further noted, "We teach [growth constructs] not with the expectation that they get learned to mastery…but with the expectation that they are the real stuff of literacy" (p. xii), which are constantly being honed and refined as the learner matures.

The distinction between skill mastery and the development of growth constructs is an important topic because much of the focus of reading assessment today has gravitated toward mastering discrete skills. This shift is based on the assumption that skill mastery frees the student to concentrate on comprehending—the heart of real reading. As a test to this assumption, millions of dollars were funneled into Reading First schools without achieving significant improvement in the reading comprehension of students. According to a report of the Institute of Education Sciences, the comprehension test scores of students in Reading First schools were no different from other first-, second-, and third-graders in non-Reading First schools (Institute of Education Sciences, 2008).

What are the instructional implications? For one thing, reading comprehension does not just naturally happen as the result of the sequential development and mastery of reading sub-skills (see Cramer & Rosenfield, 2008). While various aspects of understanding are embedded in all areas of reading, the development of comprehension is a holistic enterprise and not an additive one. The development of reading sub-skills should not be over emphasized at the expense of the other reading dimensions. The reading dimensions are so interdependent that when a change occurs in one aspect of reading it is likely to produce a corresponding change in other aspects. As Chall and Curtis (1987) cautioned, the "emphasis should always be placed on the relationship among the different abilities—accuracy in word recognition and analysis, word meanings, background knowledge, and reading comprehension—rather than on each in isolation" (p. 787). To gain a valid picture of how the different reading dimensions affect one another, it is essential for assessments to be conducted in context. How the student orchestrates his or her skills while actually reading provides insights into what the student truly knows and needs. The assessment methods used by the assessor and teacher to create the instructional match--and how the student responds to the match-- tell how well the student is getting the instruction he or she truly needs.

While it is important for the assessor and teacher to gain a comprehensive view of the student's overall reading skill, it is equally important for the student to understand what reading is all about. It is important for students to view comprehension, inquiry, reasoning, and critical thinking as the real substance of reading. Obviously, students need to make sense of what they read, but they also need opportunities to reflect upon, analyze, and openly discuss and express their views with others concerning what they read. They need to examine the different ways authors express ideas, including how information is connected, and how inferences are conveyed. Given this context, struggling readers should receive the same opportunity as their non-struggling peers to be actively engaged in reading.

Distractions that influence instructional decisions

Certain assessment practices work against providing high-quality instruction for the struggling student. Assessment practices that focus narrowly on identifying what the student is unable to do and what the student does not know will result in poor performance. Likewise, using reading material that is too difficult will only serve to highlight the student's deficiencies. Assessment materials that are poorly matched predispose the assessor and teacher to look for what is wrong with the student and, in the process, create an invalid picture of the student's performance. Mismatched conditions will result in the student being unable to perform at his or her best. Equally important, mismatched conditions during assessment will create difficulty for the assessor and teacher in identifying an appropriate starting point for instruction.

Rushing to solutions is another area that adversely affects assessment's role in instructional planning and delivery. What is assumed to be the problem and what is the actual problem are often different. Initial conversations, observations, and interpretations of the presented problem can be misleading when practitioners are in a rush to solve the problem. Rushing to solutions bypasses the need for a thorough analysis of multiple snapshots to pinpoint the problem and begin instruction. Problem identification requires analysis, thinking, and reflection around data leading in the right direction. Too often, this process is short-circuited when individuals offer suggestions and provide intervention strategies that are premature. Offering suggestions and applying strategies prematurely result in frustration for both the student and teacher, while ultimately sacrificing valuable instructional time.

Another distraction involves "taking the easy road" by focusing assessment only on the mastery of reading sub-skills. This does not negate the value of assessing progress on a range of sub-skills, but it is too easy to focus on, and to be satisfied with, achieving short-term goals and lose sight of the real purposes of reading. To be effective, as Covey (1989) said, we need to "begin with the end in mind." Assessing the mastery of various sub-skills is relatively easy compared to assessing qualitative changes taking place in the student's comprehension, reasoning, and critical thinking. Yet, these qualitative abilities are what are most important to reading performance.

Assessors and teachers should not be satisfied with poor readers merely attaining short-term goals, nor should they believe that mastery of a range of reading sub-skills is what produces an effective and proficient reader. At times, the literature surrounding literacy is confusing because it often refers to sub-skills as "enabling skills," suggesting that there is a definite sequence of enabling steps which contributes directly to the development of a mature reader. This line of thinking suggests that students who have difficulty mastering enabling skills are considered at risk of reading failure.

This inaccurate view has been reinforced by different national initiatives and reports, including one by the National Reading Panel (2000). The Panel's summary report advised school districts to develop a comprehensive system of reading instruction involving phonemic awareness, phonics, vocabulary, fluency, and comprehension. This sequential view, to the chagrin of the literacy community, reinforced the development of discrete skills at the expense of not adequately focusing on the more substantive areas of reading. In spite of opposition, proponents of this enabling view have maintained that the sequential mastery of discrete skills is foundational to the development of effective and efficient reading. Adherence to this view has caused assessment too often to focus narrowly on those sub-skills easiest to measure. Regrettably, much of assessment's woes today come from targeting certain discrete skills once considered to be less important but now viewed as the more important measures for determining reading development and accountability (Goodman, 2006).

To a large degree, what is now considered assessment are sets of one-minute samplings of discrete skills used to reflect the student's reading difficulties, reading progress, and reading comprehension. The more qualitative areas of comprehension, reasoning, critical thinking, and problem solving have been largely replaced by the easier and more quantifiable reading skills of fluency, decoding, and vocabulary. Proponents of this form of data collection believe it to be an accurate reflection of how well a student reads and also believe that fast reading is essentially good reading—an assumption that is seriously questioned (Goodman, 2006; Cramer & Rosenfield, 2008; Shelton, Altwerger, & Jordan, 2009).

Despite flaws regarding the normative practice of collecting one-minute reading samples, no issue related to this practice has inflamed members of the reading community more than the creation, distribution, and use of DIBELS (Dynamic Indicators of Basic Early Literacy Skills, Good & Kaminski, 2002). This widely disseminated test uses a series of timed measures that purport to reflect the five key domains cited by the National Reading Panel (2000). From our own perspective, we see DIBELS as an attempt to stretch one-minute reading assessment procedures well beyond what they are capable of achieving. Others concur, and offer a more scholarly and critical review of attempting to extrapolate a student's reading performance from a series of one-minute fluency readings (Altwerger, Jordan, & Shelton, 2007; Goodman, 2006; Pressley, Hildren, & Shankland, 2005; Shelton, et al., 2009). This reductionist practice does not enable the assessor and teacher to determine the most important functions of reading, which are to determine how a student thinks and makes sense of print. As Flurkey (2006) stated, thinking is a normal function of reading and thinking takes time. Each time the student speeds up or slows down, the student is exercising the flexibility needed to monitor an understanding of what he or she is reading.

While we support the development of expressive and fluent reading, much more is gained by taking a flexible approach to developing reading fluency. Adhering to a strict assessment protocol where only grade-level material is used to assess a student's oral reading rate and using grade-level norms to compare where the student ranks is too restrictive. This only perpetuates a flawed practice, especially where poor readers are concerned. Whenever a struggling reader is assessed under conditions of frustration, the results of reading fluency, as well as the results from other reading dimensions, are suspect. Rather than following a normative assessment protocol, greater care should be exercised in helping struggling readers see how reading fluency and reading flow work and how they are affected by frustration and by independent and instructional reading conditions. This would help everyone understand why instructional assessments are conducted under instructional-level conditions. Such conditions allow the student to exert his or her best efforts and at the same time enable the assessor and teacher to see how the different reading dimensions are affected as the student reads versus worrying only about how fast and correct the student reads.

For Selecting Learning Tasks

Assessment has a role in ensuring the selection, creation, and use of appropriate reading material, just as it has a role in ensuring ongoing student learning and the delivery of effective instruction. Unfortunately, the selection of reading tasks is often considered a procedural step dictated by the curricula or the administration of a placement test. But as Bloom (1976) discussed, tasks represent mediating variables and, without careful consideration, can become barriers to successful learning and teaching experiences.

Learning tasks are normative.

Learning tasks make explicit demands upon the student regardless of whether or not the student is able to meet those demands. Once reading material is printed, the print does not change, but requires the same ability to decipher the words and to interpret the content from whoever reads it. The reading requirements are the same for everyone, similar to the way standardized normative tests are administered. When new content is introduced, it is assumed that the student has sufficient prior knowledge and experience to read and understand the content or that the student will need additional background information. Unfortunately, this first assumption is what permeates most grade-level thinking, particularly as students advance through school. This is not a helpful assumption for struggling readers. Such students are eager to tell assessors and teachers what they know when given a chance within comfortable reading circumstances. It is up to the assessor and teacher to create the conditions that give them this chance.

Learning tasks must align with what the student knows and needs.

We have repeatedly stated that learning tasks should not be too hard or too easy, but should be just right for the student. This is as true for the assessment of reading as it is for the teaching of reading. The initial role of assessment is one of creating "just right" conditions to enable the student to demonstrate what he or she knows and can do with respect to the reading dimensions. The assessor and teacher must accurately capture how the student performs.

Regrettably, this view is not adhered to in educational channels. The typical view consists of aligning a district's curricula with the established core learning and requiring students to meet those standards. However, when the reading difficulties of the student are examined, it is easy to understand why the curricula should be aligned and matched to the student needs and not vice versa. This does not mean losing sight of the big picture and ignoring the state learning standards. Both forms of alignment are necessary. To be truly accountable, learning tasks need to be appropriately matched to the student's entry skills, allowing the student to remain productive as he or she works toward achieving mastery of the literacy standards.

Matched material is not the same as leveled material.

The concepts of instruction level and of matching material at the student's reading level have become almost synonymous with the practice of labeling books at so-called readability levels. Placing the student in a leveled book is based on the assumption that if a student is assigned the right level book most of the student's reading problem will naturally disappear, which may or may not be the case. Having suitable reading material available represents only the starting point for establishing the instructional match.

Assuring that reading material contains an appropriate margin of challenge allows the assessor and teacher to assess what the student knows and can do while exploring the student's real reading concerns. If the language and vocabulary of the material are too far removed from the student's ability to process the information, the data resulting from the assessment will likely mask the student's reading problems because several domains may appear as major concerns. These situations interfere with the task of providing an accurate analysis of the data and can easily lead to inaccurate problem identification followed by the use of faulty instructional strategies, as illustrated in the following case.

Pattie's Case. Pattie was a pleasant third-grader of Latino descent and, while Spanish was spoken in the home, Pattie and her parents had a fair command of the English language. While she was able to read third-grade-level material, her classroom teacher indicated that Pattie was essentially a "word caller" who had great difficulty retelling what she read. Her retelling contained simple ideas expressed in few words. While she had ideas about what she wanted to say, communicating those ideas was limited, often expressed in incomplete and disconnected thoughts.

An IA snapshot confirmed that Pattie had sufficient word recognition and word meaning skills to engage in the third-grade text. A word search and an oral reading of the following passage revealed only five unknown words—*image, satisfied, fedora, detective,* and *brim.* Of the five unknown words, she knew the meaning of the words *satisfied, detective,* and *brim* when told the words.

"Here," said Binky. He reached into his pocket and flipped a quarter into the bowl.

"There's just one thing," he added, glaring at Arthur.

"What's that?"

"Don't tell anybody I gave. It's bad for my image."

"Okay," said Arthur.

Binky seemed satisfied, at least for the moment.

"Hey, Arthur!" yelled Buster as he ran down the hall.

"What's with the goofy hat?" asked Arthur.

"This hat is not goofy," said Buster. "It's a fedora—part of my new detective kit. I've been snooping—ah, looking for crimes."

"Have you found any?"

"No." Buster pushed back the brim of his hat. "But I did pick up some secret information." He peered to the left and right, making sure no one else was listening.

"You promise this will go no further?"

Arthur nodded.

Buster leaned forward. "Third-grade picnic this Friday," he whispered.

*(From **Arthur Accused**, Krensky & Brown, 1998, pp. 4-5)*

When asked to tell what she had read, she responded, "It's about quarters." When asked to tell more she replied, "There was a picnic." Her teacher indicated that these answers were typical of her unaided responses. When prompted with guided questions, such as, "Where did he flip the quarter?" or "What did Buster wear that was goofy?" the questions needed to be specific to generate a response. Her written work mirrored her story retelling.

Pattie's limited response prompted her teacher to place her in a lower-level text, thinking that the easier text would improve her responses. As shown in the following passage, the text contained mostly simple sentences.

Tim the Terror!

I have this little brother. His name is Tim. Mom wants me to like him, but I don't.

He takes all of my toys. Then he breaks them into little pieces.

It all started when Tim was a baby. He couldn't talk, but he made loud "Give me!" noises.

"Waaaaahhhhh!" he screamed, when he wanted one of my things.

When I didn't give it to him, he screamed louder.

(From Stop Taking My Things, Weeks, 2000)

Using the easier text resulted in no change in how Pattie responded. However, the use of "Tim the Terror" did create an "ah ha" moment for the teacher. She realized that the easier text actually reinforced the types of simple sentences Pattie produced rather than creating appropriate models of more complex and compound sentence structures routinely found in third-grade material. She also recognized that if the instructional goal was to model how an author uses descriptive language and structures to create more complex sentences, then *"Tim the Terror"* was not a suitable model. The easier text did not match what the teacher saw and what the assessor confirmed as Pattie's major problem--that of responding with fragmented ideas using few words to retell stories.

This case reinforces an earlier point that reading materials are merely tools. It also highlights the point that reading tasks are not neutral, that decisions to select and introduce a different text can either support or hinder reading development, and that placement of a student into leveled material does not always create instructionally-matched conditions. In Pattie's instance, placement into a lower-level text perpetuated the very problem identified as her major need—the development of fuller and more complex language. Establishing an appropriate match requires strategically using assessment data to accurately identify appropriate reading materials and intervention strategies geared to the learning needs of the student.

Reading programs and materials are instructional tools.

While reading programs and materials are central to providing effective assessment and instruction, they are merely tools, and no single tool works satisfactorily in every situation. It has always been our position that when a specific book or program provides measurable benefits for a student's reading development, then the book or program should remain a viable, useful tool. It is only when the book or program is not benefiting the student, and may be actually contributing to the student's reading struggle, that the book or program needs to be adjusted or changed.

While commercial publishers espouse the belief that their reading programs meet the needs of all children, the variability issues make this impossible. Once material is printed, the same demands are placed on whoever reads it, regardless of their reading skills. Teachers would be in an almost impossible position if they did not have access to an array of reading materials and programs to use in attempting to reach the reading needs of different students. However, it is ultimately the effectiveness of the teacher in selecting and using materials and programs appropriately with struggling readers that accounts for the real differences in the reading progress these students make, rather than a particular book or program.

Reading must remain contextual.

Much of what we have written is centered on creating conditions for learning that enable students to perform to the best of their abilities. Once these conditions are established, the student must actually read for the assessor and teacher to gain a thorough picture of how reading skills are being applied by the student. The more the student interacts with and reads matched literature, the clearer the assessment picture becomes. Naturally, as the student reads and participates in well-planned literacy activity within the context of daily instruction, the better the assessment situation (Brozo & Hargis, 2003), and, we should add, the better the instructional situation. Whether the literacy focus is on creating greater understanding of the author's intent or on improving a reading sub-skill, the student will benefit most when the activity is folded directly back into the content, keeping the activity as contextual as possible.

Distractions to Selecting and Creating Learning Tasks

At times, teachers rely too heavily on books and programs to bring about real changes in improving the reading performance of students. While books and programs are important resources in helping teachers differentiate instruction, it is the process of selecting and fine-tuning provided by teachers that makes the difference in how well materials are used by students. It is simply not sufficient to rely on assigning a particular grade-level program or to choose a book based on its estimated difficulty level to keep the struggling reader actively engaged and progressing comfortably. Texts require constant regulation to make sure the challenge level conforms to the conditions described in the optimal learning window.

Quality instruction does not happen by just adjusting or replacing the learning task, as commercial publishers would have you believe. Using printed material to assess the student's reading skills necessitates a careful analysis of the data to ensure that instructional decisions are appropriate. The choice of what reading material to use, either before or after the assessment, should not be left to trial and error. Although the use of reading material is central to the instructional assessing process, following the steps of the IA process keeps the level of difficulty in check and makes it possible to get the most out of the material as well as the student. Once the assessor and teacher know precisely what the student knows and can do, it is relatively easy for them to look ahead, to look behind, or to use other material to anticipate what is known and unknown and to determine when additional selections are warranted.

The passage of the Reading Excellence Act (1998) called for using the findings of scientifically-based research to enhance instruction and improve student reading development in grades K-3. Since its passage there has been scrambling by curriculum developers to show evidence that their programs are research-based. We definitely support valid research and its infusion into the development of reading materials, but we do not want people to get carried away thinking that the answer to the reading needs of struggling students can be found in the use of "evidenced-based" reading programs as opposed to the skills of effective teachers. Publishers would like nothing more than to create programs that they could advertise as "teacher-proof" in order to take the teacher out of the instructional equation. There is little research, however, to support using one program over another. What constitutes a scientifically-based/evidence-based program is sketchy at best. In fact, Allington (2005) stated that he knows of:

> no research suggesting that the use of any commercial core reading program reliably produces better results than the use of locally developed core reading programs. Indiscriminate use of any core program such that all children in a grade are placed in a single strand, text, or grade level contradicts everything research and practice has taught us about matching students with curriculum appropriate to their level of development. The same is true for adoption of a single intervention program for struggling readers. Children differ. Struggling readers differ. Any curriculum decision that fails to acknowledge this must be considered unscientific (p. 18).

SUMMARY

It is hard to deny that a number of educational efforts "have missed the mark by emphasizing lock-step accountability, assessments that provide little or no information to improve instruction or lead to literacy reform efforts" (IRA, 2009, p.4). In contrast, this chapter provided an opportunity to highlight what instructional accountability truly means. It addressed a number of points central to creating conditions that lead to reading success for students and in doing so provided an opportunity to ponder, question, and think about a number of concerns not typically associated with assessment but integral to effective and efficient instruction.

Instructional Assessment and instructional accountability are not about testing. Instead, they are about finding out what the student knows, what the student can do, how the student thinks, and what works for the student regardless of how the student is functioning at a particular time. Instructional assessment and accountability are about creating learning conditions that enable the student to perform consistently to the best of his or her ability. They provide the path to meaningful instruction by starting where the student is able to function and succeed so that the ongoing scaffolding of instruction benefits the student over the long haul. Instructional assessment and instructional accountability are about thinking, about being inquisitive, about reflecting, and about sharing what is learned from the student's ongoing performance. They are integral to instruction, using the data gained from each snapshot to fine-tune ongoing learning and teaching. Central to the function of each is creating an atmosphere where the student sees comprehension, reasoning, and critical thinking as the primary goals and the substance of real reading.

REFERENCES

Adams, M. J. (1990). *Beginning to read: Thinking and learning about print.* Cambridge, MA: MIT Press.

Adams, M. J. & Bruck, M. (1995, Summer). *Resolving the great debate. American Educator,* 19 (2), 7, 10-20.

Adams, M. J., Foorman, B. R., Lundberg, I., & Beeler, T. (1998). *Phonemic awareness in young children.* Baltimore: Paul H. Brookes.

Algozzine, B., & Ysseldyke, J.E. (1983), Learning disabilities as a subset of school failure: The oversophistication of a concept. *Exceptional Children,* 50, 242-246.

Allard, H. & Marshal, J. (1977). *Miss Nelson is missing.* Boston: Houghton Mifflin.

Allington, R. L. (1990, March). Curriculum and at-risk learners: Coherence or fragmentation? *PRISE Reporter,* 21(3), 1-2.

Allington, R. L. (1998). *Ten principles for looking at reading/language arts lessons in your classroom.* Paper presented at the Preventing Early Learning Failure Conference, Northville, MI.

Allington, R.L. (1999, August). *Reading strategies in the primary grades.* Presentation delivered at the Prevention of Early Learning Failure Conference, Livonia, MI.

Allington, R. L. (2001). Teaching children to read: What really matters. In B. Sornson (Ed.) *Preventing early learning failure.* Alexandria, VA: Association for Supervision and Curriculum Development.

Allington, R. L. (2002, June). What I've learned about effective reading instruction from a decade of studying exemplary elementary classroom teachers. *Phi Delta Kappan,* 83, 740-747.

Allington, R. L. (2005, October/November). NCLB, Reading First and whither the future? *Reading Today, 23* (2), 18.

Allington, R. L. & McGill-Franzen, A. (1989). Different programs, indifferent instruction. In D. K. Lipsky & A. Gartner (Eds.) *Beyond separate education: Quality education for all* (pp. 75-98). Baltimore: Paul H. Brookes.

Allington, R. L. & McGill-Franzen, A. (1996, August/September). Why is Congress caving in on IDEA reform? *Reading Today, 14* (1), 6-7.

Altwerger, B., Jordan, N., & Shelton, N. R. (2007). *Rereading fluency: Process, practice and policy.* Portsmouth, NH: Heinemann.

Anderson, R. C. & Pearson, P.D. (1984). A schema-theoretic view of basic processes in reading comprehension. In P. D. Pearson, R. Barr, M.L. Kamil, & P. Mosenthal (Eds.), *Handbook of Reading Research* (pp. 255-291). New York: Longman.

Applegate, A. J., Applegate, M. D., McGeehan, C. M., Pinto, C. M. & Kong, A. (2009, February). The assessment of thoughtful literacy in NAEP: Why the states aren't measuring up. *The Reading Teacher, 62* (5), 372-381.

Archer, A. L., Adams, A., Ellis, E. S., Isaascon, S., Morehead, M. K. & Schiller, E. P. (1987). Working with mildly handicapped students: Design and delivery of academic instruction. *Academy for Effective Instruction*, Reston, VA.: The Council for Exceptional Children.

Arnold, V. (1987). Close to Home. New York: McMillan.

Bear, D., Invernizzi, M., Templeton, S., Johnston, F. (2008). *Words Their Way: Word Study for Phonics, Vocabulary and Spelling Instruction.* Upper Saddle River, N.J.: Pearson Education.

Betts, E. A. (1946). *Foundations of reading instruction.* New York, American Book.

Black, P. & Wiliam, D. (1998, October). Inside the black box: Raising standards through classroom assessment. *Phi Delta Kappan, 80* (2), 139-148.

Block, J. H. (1980). Success rate. In C. Denham & A. Lieberman (Eds.) *Time to learn* (pp. 95-106). Washington, D.C.: National Institute of Education.

Bloom, B. S. (1976). *Human characteristics and school learning.* New York, McGraw Hill.

Borg, W. R. (1980). Time and school learning. In C. Denham & A. Lieberman (Eds.) *Time to learn* (pp. 33-72). Washington, D. C.: National Institute of Education.

Borkowski, J. G. & Muthukrishna, N. (1992). Moving metacognition into the classroom: "Working models" and effective strategy teaching. In M. Pressley, K.R. Harris & J.T. Guthrie (Eds.), *Promoting academic competence and literacy in school* (pp. 477-501). San Diego, CA: Academic.

Brookhard, S., Moss, C. & Long, B. (2008, November). Formative assessment that empowers.

Brozo, W. G. & Hargis, C. (2003, November). Using low-stakes reading assessment. *Educational Leadership, 61* (3), 60-64.

Buehl, D. (2001). *Classroom strategies for interactive learning.* Newark, DE: International Reading Association.

Building a more complete picture. In G. Duffy & P. Anders (Eds.), *Reading in the middle school* (pp 124-153). Newark, DE: International Reading Association.

Burns, M. (2005, November). Looking at how students reason. *Educational Leadership, 63* (3), 26-31.

Burns, M.K. (2007, September). Reading at the instructional level with children identified as learning disabled: Potential implications for response-to-intervention. *School Psychology Quarterly, 22* (3), 297-313.

Burns, M.K. (2004). Empirical analysis of drill ratio research: Refining the instructional level for drill tasks. *Remedial and Special Education, 25* (3), 167-173.

Caine, R. N. & Caine, G. (1994). *Making connections: Teaching and the human brain.* Menlo Park, CA: Addison-Wesley.

Carillo, L. W. (1964). *Informal Reading—Readiness Experiences.* San Francisco, Chandle Publishing Co.

Chall, J. S. & Curtis, M. E. (1987). What clinical diagnosis tells us about children's reading. *The Reading Teacher, 40* (8), 784-789.

Checkley, K.. (2003, January). Closing the achievement gap: It's everybody's job. *Education Update, 45* (1), p. 1.

Chetty, R., Friedman, J., & Rockoff, J. (2011). *The long-term impacts of teachers: Teacher value-added and student outcomes in adulthood.* (Working Paper No. 17699). Cambridge, MA: National Bureau of Economic Research.

Clymer, T. (1963). The utility of phonic generalizations in the primary grades. *The Reading Teacher*, 16, 281-309.

Coldsmith, D. (1993). *Thunderstick.* New York, NY: Bantam Books.

Cole, A. D. (1998). Beginner-oriented texts in literature-based classrooms: The segue for a few struggling readers. *The Reading Teacher, 51* (6), 488-501.

Cook, W. W. & Clymer, T. (1962). Acceleration and retardation. In N. B. Henry (Edts.) *Individualized Instruction.* Chicago, IL., 1962 *Yearbook of the National Society of the Study of Education.*

Cooter, K. S. & Cooter, R. B. Jr. (2004). One size doesn't fit all: Slow learners in the reading classroom. *The Reading Teacher, 57* (7), 680-684.

Coulter, W.A. & Coulter, E. M. B. (1991). *Curriculum-based assessment for instructional design: Training manual.* New Orleans: LSU Medical Center.

Covey, S. R. (1989). The 7 habits of highly effective people. New York, NY: Simon & Schuster.

Cramer, K., & Rosenfield, S. (2008). Effect of degree of challenge on reading performance. *Reading and Writing Quarterly, 24*, 1-19.

Crowley, G. & Underwood, A. (1998, June 15). Memory. *Newsweek, 131* (24), 38-39.

Cunningham, A. E. & Stanovich, K. E. (1998). What reading does for the mind. *American Educator*, 22, 8-15.

Cunningham, P. M. & Allington, R. L. (1999). Classrooms that work: *They can all read and write*. New York, NY: Addison-Wesley Longman.

Dempster, F. N. (1981). Memory span: Sources of individual and developmental differences. *Psychological Bulletin*, 89, 63–100.

Denham, C. & Lieberman, A. (Eds.). (1980). *Time To learn*. Washington, D. C.: Department of Education, National Institute of Education, 7-32.

Deno, S. L. (1985, November). Curriculum-based measurement: The emerging alternative. *Exceptional Children, 52* (3), 219-232.

Diamond, J. B. (2009, October). Where the rubber meets the road: Rethinking the connection between high-stakes testing policy and classroom instruction. *Sociology of Education, 80* (4), 285-313.

Dochy, F., Segers, M., & Buehl, M. M. (1999). The relation between assessment practices and outcomes of studies: The case of research on prior knowledge. *Review of Educational Research, 69* (2), 145-186.

Dolan, W. P. (1994). *Restructuring our schools: A primer on systematic change*. Kansas City, MO: Systems and Organizations.

Dombey, H. & Moustafa, M. (1998). *Whole to part phonics: How children learn to read and spell*. Portsmouth, NH:Heinemann.

Doran, H. C. & Fleischman, S. (2005). Challenges of value-added assessment. *Educational Leadership, 63* (3), 85-87.

DuFour, R. P., Eaker, R., & DuFour, R.B.(Eds.). (2005). On common ground: *The power of professional learning communities*. Bloomington, IN: Solution Tree.

Dunn. L. (1968). Special education for the mildly retarded: Is much of it justified? *Exceptional Children 35*, 5-22.

Edwards, P. A., Turner, J. D., & Mokhtari, K. (2008, May). Balancing the assessment of learning and for learning in support of student literacy achievement. *The Reading Teacher, 61* (18), 682-684.

Ehri, L. C. (1992). Reconceptualizing the development of sight word reading and its relationship to recoding. In P. B. Gough, L.C. Ehri, & R. Treiman (Eds.), *Reading Acquisition* (pp. 107-144). Hillsdale, NJ: Erlbaum.

Ellis, E. S. (1997, November/December). Watering up the curriculum for adolescents with learning disabilities. *Remedial and Special Education, 18*(6), 326-346.

Elmore, R. F. (2003, November). A plea for strong practice. *Educational Leadership, 61* (3), 6-10.

English Update (Spring 1998). Effective early literacy teachers bring low achievers' scores way up, p. 9S (http://ceka.albany.edu).

Fielding, L., & Pearson, P.D. (1994). Reading comprehension: What works. *Educational Leadership, 51* (5), 62-68.

Fielding, L., & Roller, C. (1992, May). Making difficult books accessible and easy books acceptable. *The Reading Teacher, 45* (9), 678-685.

Fisher, C. W., Berliner, D. C., Filby, N. N., Marliave, R., Cahen, L. S. & Dishaw, M. M. (1980). Teaching behaviors, academic learning time and student achievement; An overview. In C. Denham & A. Lieberman (Eds.) *Time To Learn* (pp. 7-32). Washington, D. C.: Department of Education, National Institute of Education.

Flood, J., Lapp, D. & Fisher, D. (2005, April-June). Neurological impress method plus. *Reading Psychology, 2* (12), 147-160.

Flurkey, A. (2006). What's "normal" about real reading? In K. Goodman (Ed.). *The truth about DIBELS: What it is, what it does* (pp. 40-49). Portsmouth, NH., Heinemann.

Forbes, R. & Roller, C. M. (1991). The relationship of instructional level placement and the informal reading inventory to the process instruction of reading. *Iowa Reading Journal, 4* (2), 3-9.

Fountas, I. C. & Pinnell, G. S. (1996). *Guiding reading: Good first teaching for all children*. Portsmouth, NH: Heinemann.

Gates, A. (1930). *Interest and ability in reading*. New York, NY: Macmillan.

Gickling, E. E. (1977). Controlling academic and social performance using an instructional delivery approach. *Programming for emotionally handicapped: Administrative considerations.* Washington, D.C.: CORRC/MERRC Conference Proceedings, George Washington University.

Gickling, E.E.. (1990). Orientation to the instructional assessment process. Special Education Division, Pennsylvania Department of Education, Harrisburg, PA.

Gickling, E.E. (Dec. 1996), Instructional assessment manual. In P. Enggren & J.F. Kovaleski (Eds.)*The instructional support system of Pennsylvania*, (Vol. 215, pp. 5-31). 200 Anderson Rd., King of Prussia, PA.: PRISE/EISC.

Gickling, E. E. & Armstrong, D. L. (1978, November). Levels of instructional difficulty as related to on-task behavior, task completion, and comprehension. *Journal of Learning Disabilities*, (11) 9, 559-566.

Gickling, E. E. & Havertape, J. F. (1981). Curriculum-based assessment. In J. A. Tucker (Ed.). *Non-test based assessment*. Minneapolis, MN: The National School Psychology Inservice Training Network, University of Minnesota.

Gickling, E. E. & Rosenfield, S. (1995). Best practices in curriculum-based assessment. In A. Thomas & J. Grimes (Eds.). *Best practices in school psychology, volume III*, (pp. 587-595). Bethesda, MD: National Association of School Psychologists.

Gickling, E. E., Shane, R. L., & Croskery, K. M. (1989). Developing mathematics skills in low-achieving high school students through curriculum-based assessment. *School Psychology Review, 18* (3), 344-355.

Gickling, E. E. & Thompson, V. P. (1985, November). A personal view of curriculum-based assessment. *Exceptional Children, 52* (3), 205-218.

Gill, T. J. (1992). Focus on research: Development of word knowledge as it relates to reading, spelling, and instruction. *Language Arts*, 69, 444-453.

Glass, G. V. (1983). Effectiveness of special education. *Policy Studies Review, 2*, 65-78.

Good, R. H., & Kaminski, R. A. (Eds.). (2002). *Dynamic indicators of basic early literacy skills (6th ed.).* Eugene, OR: Institute for the Development of Educational Achievement.

Goodman, K. S. (2006). *The truth about DIBELS: What it is, what it does*. Portsmouth, NH: Heinemann

Graves, M. F. (Oct./Nov., 1998). Beyond balance. *Reading Today, 16* (2), p. 16.

Graves, M. F. & Watts-Taffe, S. (2008, November). For the love of words: Fostering word consciousness in young readers. *The Reading Teacher, 62* (3), 185-193.

Gravois, T. A. & Gickling, E. E. (2002). Best practices in curriculum-based assessment. In A Thomas & J. Grimes (Eds.), *Best practices in school psychology, volume IV* (pp. 885-898). Bethesda, MD: National Association of School Psychologists.

Gravois. T. A. & Gickling, E. E. (2008). Instructional assessment: Best practices in instructional assessment. In A. Thomas & J. Grimes (Eds.), *Best practices in school psychology:Volume V*, (pp. 503-518), Bethesda, MD: National Association of School Psychologists.

Gravois, T. A., Gickling, E. E. & Rosenfield, S. R. (2008) *Training in instructional consultation, assessment and teaming*. Baltimore, MD: ICAT Publications.

Gravois, T.A., Gickling, E. E. & Rosenfield, S. (2011) ICAT: *Training in instructional consultation, assessment and teaming*. Baltimore, MD: ICAT Publishing.

Gravois, T.A., & Nelson, D. (2015). Best practices in instructional assessment of writing. In A. Thomas & P. Harrison (Eds.). *Best practices in school psychology VI* (pp. 203-218). Washington, DC: NASP.

Griffith, L. W. & Rasinski, T. V. (2004, October). A focus on fluency: How one teacher incorporated fluency with her reading curriculum. *The Reading Teacher, 58* (2), 126-137.

Guskey, T. R. (2003). How classroom assessment improves learning. *Educational Leadership, 60* (5), 6-11.

Guskey, T. R. (2005, February). Mapping the road to proficiency. *Educational Leadership, 63* (3), 32-38.

Hammerberg, D. D. (2004, April). Comprehension instruction for socioculturally diverse classrooms: A review of what we know. *The Reading Teacher, 57*(7), 648-659).

Hargis, C. H. (1982). *Teaching reading to handicapped children*. Denver, CO: Love Publishing.

Hargis, C. H. (1987). *Curriculum based assessment: A primer*. Springfield, IL: Charles C. Thomas.

Hargis, C. H. (1997). *Teaching low achieving and disadvantaged students*. Springfield, IL: Charles C. Thomas.

Hargis, C.H. (2006, January). Setting standards: An exercise of futility? *Phi Delta Kappan, 87* (5), 393-395.

Hargis, C. H., Terhaar-Yonkers, M., Williams, P. C., & Reed, M. T. (1988). Repetition requirements for word recognition. *Journal of Reading, 31* (4), 320-327.

Harry, B. & Klingner, J. (2007, February). Discarding the deficit model. *Educational Leadership, 64* (5), 16-21.

Hasbrouck, J. E. & Tindal, G. (Spring, 1992). Curriculum-based oral reading fluency norms for students in grades 2-5. *Teaching Exceptional Children, 24* (3), 41-44.

Hasbrouck, J. & Tindal, G. A. (2006, April). Oral reading fluency norms: A valuable assessment tool for reading teachers. *The Reading Teacher, 59*(7), 636-644.

Hattie, J. (2011). *Visible learning for teachers: Maximizing impact on learning.* New York, NY: Routledge.

Heckelman, R. G. (1966). Using the neurological impress remedial reading technique. *Academic Therapy, 1*, 235–239.

Heckelman, R. G. (1969). A neurological-impress method of remedial-reading instruction. *Academic Therapy, 4*, 277–282.

Henderson, E. H. (1990). *Teaching spelling (2ⁿᵈ ed).* Boston, MA: Houghton Mifflin.

Herron, J. (2008, September). Why phonics teaching must change. *Educational Leadership, 66* (1), 77-81.

Hillerich, R.L.(1978). *A writing vocabulary of elementary children*, Springfield, IL: Charles C. Thomas,.

Holdaway, D. (1979). *The foundations of literacy.* Portsmouth, NH: Heinemann.

Hollingsworth, P. M. (1970). An experiment with the impress method of teaching reading. *The Reading Teacher, 24*, 112–114.

Hollingsworth, P. M. (1978, March). An experimental approach to the impress method of teaching reading. *The Reading Teacher, 31* (6), 624–626.

Howard, M. (2009). *RTI from all Sides: What every teacher needs to know.* Portsmouth, NH: Heinemann.

Howe, K. B. & Shinn, M. M. (2002, August). *Standard Reading Assessment Passages (RAPS) for use in general outcome measurement: A manual describing development and technical features.* Eden Prairie, MN: Edformations.

Hudson, R. F., Lane, H. B., & Pullen, P. C. (2005, May). Reading fluency assessment and instruction: What, why, and how? *The Reading Teacher, 58* (8), 702-714.

Hutchins, P. (1968). *Rosie's walk*, New York: Macmillian.

Individuals with Disabilities Education Improvement Act of 2004 (2004). H.R. 1350. Retrieved April 22, 2013 from http://thomas.loc.gov/cgi-bin/query/z?c108:h.r.1350.enr:%20

Institute of Education Sciences, National Center for Education Evaluation and Regional Assistance. (2008, April). *Reading First Impact study: Interim report* (Publication No. NCEE 20084016). Retrieved from http://ies.ed.gov/pubsinfo.asp?pubid:NCEE20084016

Instruction-Based Assessment: Where have we been and where have we yet to go? An interview with Dr. Ed. Gickling (2005). Richmond, VA., Virginia Department of Education, Office of Student Services, Office of Special Education.

International Reading Association (2009). *Keeping the promise to all students Reading Today, 26* (3), pp. 4-5.

IRA/NCTE Joint Task Force (1994). Standards for the assessment of reading and writing. Newark, DE: International Reading Assoc. & Urbana IL: National Council of Teachers of English.

Jensen, E. (1998). *Teaching with the brain in mind.* Alexandria, VA: Association for Supervision & Curriculum Development.

Jespersen, J. & Fitz-Randolph, J. (1977). *From sundials to atomic clocks: Understanding time and frequency.* New York, NY: Dover.

Johns, J. L., Lenski, S. D., & Elish-Piper, L. (2002). *Teaching beginning readers: Linking assessment and instruction.* Dubuque, IA: Kendall Hunt.

Johnston, F. R. (1998, May). The reader, the text, and the task: Learning words in first grade. *The Reading Teacher, 51* (8), 666-675

Kagan, S. (1994). *Cooperative learning.* San Clemente, CA: Resources for Teachers.

Kavale, K. A. (1988). The long-term consequences of learning disabilities. In M. C. Wang, M. C. Reynolds, & H. J. Walberg (Eds.). *Handbook of Special Education Research and Practice* (Vol. 2, pp. 303-344). New York, NY: Pergamon Press.

Keeping the promise to all students (December 2008/January 2009). Reading Today, 26 (3), pp. 4-5.

Kirschner, P. A. (2002). Cognitive load theory: Implications of cognitive load theory on the design of learning. *Learning and Instruction,* 12, 1-10.

Kotz, J.C. & Purcell, K.F. (1987). *Chemistry and chemical reactivity.* Philadelphia, PA: Saunders College.

Kovaleski, J. F., Tucker, J. A., & Duffy, D. J. (1995, June). School reform through instructional support: The Pennsylvania initiative, part I: The Instructional Support Team (IST). *NASP Communiqué, 23,* 1-8.

Kozol, J. (1991). *Savage inequalities: Children in America's schools*. New York, NY: Crown Publishers.

Krensky, S. & Brown, M. (1998). *Arthur accused*. Boston, MA: Little, Brown.

Kuhn, M. (2004, December). Helping students become accurate, expressive readers: Fluency instruction in small groups. *The Reading Teacher, 58* (4), 338-344.

LaBerge, D. & Samuels, S. J. (1974). Toward a theory of automatic information processing in reading. *Cognitive Psychology, 6*, 293-323.

L'Amour, L. (1987) *The Haunted Mesa*. New York, NY: Bantam Books.

Lane, K. S. (1975). The modified Dale-Chall formula: A statistical comparison with two other readability formulas on intermediate level basal readers. Master's Thesis, University of Tennessee-Knoxville.

Langer, J. A. (1984). Examining background knowledge and text comprehension. *Reading Research Quarterly, 19* (4), 468-481.

Lezotte, L. W. (1990). Effective Schools. Presentation at a North Carolina Department of Education workshop in Raleigh, NC, and in A. Thomas & J. Grimes (Eds.) Best Practices in School Psychology III. Washington, DC: The National Association of School Psychology, (p. 325-336).

Lipsky, D. K. & Gartner, A. (1989). *Beyond separate education: Quality education for all*. Baltimore, MD: Paul H. Brookes.

MacQuarrie, L. L., Tucker, J. A., Burns, M. K., & Hartman, B. (2002). Comparison of retention rates using traditional, drill sandwich, and incremental rehearsal flash card methods. *School Psychology Review, 31* (4), 584-595.

Marston, D. & Magnusson, D. (1985, November). Implementing curriculum-based measurement in special and regular education settings. *Exceptional Children, 52* (3), 266-276.

Marzano, R. J. & Marzano, J. S. (2003, September). The key to classroom management. *Educational Leadership, 61* (1), 6-13.

Marzano, R. J., Marzano, J. S. & Pickering, D. J. (2003). *Classroom management that works: Research-based strategies for every teacher.*. Alexandria, VA: Association for Supervision and Curriculum Development.

Mason, B. J. & Bruning, R. (1999). Providing feedback in computer-based instruction: what the research tells us. http://dwb.unl.edu/Edit/EB/MasonBruning.html (Accessed 07/23/06).

McNamee, G. D. & Chin, J. (2005, November). Dissolving the line between assessment and teaching. *Educational Leadership, 63* (3), 72-76.

Meichenbaum, D. & Biemiller, A. (1992). In search of student expertise in the classroom: A metacognitive analysis. In M. Pressley, KR. Harris & J.T. Guthrie (Eds.). *Promoting academic competence and literacy in school* (pp. 3-56).

Miller, D. (2002). *Reading with meaning: Teaching comprehension in the primary grades*. Portland, MA: Stenhouse.

Miller, G. A. (1956). The magical number seven, plus or minus two: Some limits on our capacity for processing information. *The Psychological Review, 63* (2), 81-97.

Mirman, J. A., Swartz. R. J. & Barell, J. (1988). Strategies to help teachers empower at-risk students. In B.Z. Presseisen (Ed.) *At-risk students and thinking: Perspectives from research* (pp. 138-156).

Moustafa, M. (1997). *Beyond traditional phonics*. Portsmouth, NH: Heinemann.

National Governors Association Center for Best Practices Council of Chief State School Officers (2010). *Common core state standards*. Washington, DC: National Governors Association Center for Best Practices, Council of Chief State School Officers.

National Reading Panel (2000). *Report of the National Reading Panel: Teaching Children to Read: An evidence-based assessment of the scientific research literature on reading and its implications for reading instruction*. Washington DC: U.S. Department of Health and Human Services, National Institute of Child Health and Human Development.

Neef, N., Iwata, B., & Page, R. (1980). The effects of interspersal training versus high density reinforcement on spelling acquisition and retention. *Journal of Applied Behavior Analysis, 13*, 153-158.

Nelson, D. (2013). *Reading, writing, ans comprehension skills of intermediate elementary students*. (Unpublished dissertation). University of Maryland, College Park

New Zealand Staff Ministry of Education (1992), *Dancing with the pen: The learner as a writer*. Katonah, NY: Richard C. Owen.

Obama, B. (2004). D*reams from my father: A story of race and inheritance*. New York, NY: Three Rivers.

O'Neil. J. (1996, September). On emotional intelligence: A conversation with Daniel Goleman. *Educational Leadership, 54* (1), 6-11.

Osborn, M. P. (2002). *Revolutionary war on Wednesday*. New York, NY: Scholastic Book.

Palincsar, A. S. & Brown, A. L. (1984). Reciprocal teaching of comprehension-fostering and comprehension-monitoring activities. *Cognition and Instruction, 1*, 117-175.

Papandrea, J. A. (2003). *Fixing the hole in the pipe: Moving beyond pre-referral toward changing the system* (Unpublished dissertation). Andrews University, Berrien Springs, MI.

Paratore, J. R. & Indrisano, R. (1987, April). Intervention assessment in reading comprehension. *The Reading Teacher, 40* (8), 778-783.

Pascual-Leon, J. (1970). A mathematical model for the transition rule in Piaget's developmental stages. *Acta Psychologica, 32* (1), 301-345.

Pearson, P. D. (2006). Forword. In K.S. Goodman (Ed.) *The truth about DIBELS: What it is, what it does* (pp. v-xiv). Portsmouth, NH: Heinemann,.

Pennsylvania Department of Education (1990). *Reading Assessment Handbook*, Harrisburg, PA.

Popham, W. J. (2005, November). Can growth ever be beside the point? *Educational Leadership, 63*(3), 83-84.

Popham, W. J. (2006, February). Assessment for learning: An endangered species? *Educational Leadership, 63*(5), 82-83.

Popham, W. J. (2008). The assessment-savvy student. *Educational Leadership, 66* (3), 80-81.

Popham, W. J. (2009, February). Unraveling reliability. *Educational Leadership, 66*(5), 77-78.

Pressley, M., Hildren, K., & Shankland. R. (2005). *An evaluation of end-grade-3 dynamic indicators of basic literacy skills (DIBELS): Speed reading without comprehension, predicting little* (technical report). East Lansing, MI: Literacy Achievement Research Center, Michigan State University.

Public Law 94-142. Education for All Handicapped Children Act. 94th Congress, S. 6 (1975).

Rambeau, J. & Rambeau, N. (1967) *Jim Forest and the bandits*. San Francisco, CA: Field Educational.

Rasinski, T. V. (2003). *The fluent reader: Oral reading strategies for building word recognition, fluency, and comprehension*. New York, NY: Scholastic Professional Books.

Reading Excellence Act (1998). Public Law No. 105-277.

Resnick, L. B. & Klopfer, L. E. (Eds.). (1989). *Toward the thinking curriculum: Current cognitive research*. Alexandria, VA: Association for Supervision and Curriculum Development.

Roberts, M. L., & Shapiro, E. S. (1996). Effects of instructional ratios on students' reading performance in a regular education program. *Journal of School Psychology, 34*, 73–91.

Roberts, M.L., Turco, T.L., & Shapiro, E.S. (1991, December). Differential effects of fixed instructional ratios on students' progress in reading. *Journal of Psychoeducational Assessment, 9* (4), 308-318.

Rohrbeck, C.A., Ginsburg-Block, M.D., Frantuzzo, J.W., & Miller, T.R. (2003). Peer-assisted learning interventions with elementary students: A meta-analysis review. *Journal of Educational Psychology, 64* (2), 240-257.

Romano, T. (2004, October). The power of voice. *Educational Leadership, 62* (2), 20-23.

Romberg, T. A. (1980). Salient features of the BTES framework of teacher behaviors. In C. Denham & A. Lieberman (Eds.), *Time to learn* (pp. 73-93). Washington, DC: Department of Education, National Institute of Education.

Rosenfield, S. (2008). Best practice in instructional consultation and instructional consultation teams. In A. Thomas & J. Grimes (Eds). *Best practices in school psychology V* (pp. 1646-1660), Bethesda, MD: The National Association of School Psychologists.

Rosenfield, S. A. (1987). *Instructional consultation*. Hillsdale, NJ: Lawrence Earlbaum Associates.

Rosenfield, S. A. & Gravois, T. A. (1996). *Instructional consultation teams: Collaborating for change*. New York, NY: Guilford.

Routman, R. (1991). *Invitations: Changing as teachers and learners K-12*. Portsmouth, NH: Heinemann.

Samuels, S. J. (1997, February). The method of repeated readings. *The Reading Teacher, 50*(5), 376-381.

Sanders, W. (1988, December). Value-added assessment. *The School Administrator*, 24-27.

Schell, L. M. (1988, October). Dilemmas in assessing reading comprehension. *The Reading Teacher, 42* (1), 12-16.

Scherer., M. (2005, November). Reclaiming testing. *Educational Leadership, 63* (3), 9.

Shapiro, A.M. (2004, Spring). How including prior knowledge as a subject variable may change outcomes of learning research. *American Educational Research Journal, 41*, 159-189.

Shapiro, E. S. & Elliott, S. N. (1999). Curriculum-based assessment and other performance-based assessment strategies. In C. R. Reynolds & T. B. Gutkin (Eds.). *The Handbook of School Psychology*, third edition (pp. 383-408), New York, NY: John Wiley & Sons.

Shelton, N.R., Altwerger, B., & Jordan, N. (2009, April). Does DIBELS put reading first? *Literacy Research and Instruction, 48* (2), 137-148.

Skrtic, T. (1991). The special education paradox: Equity as the way to excellence. *Harvard Educational Review, 61* (2), 148-206.

Slavin, R. E. (2003). *Educational psychology: Theory and practice*. New York, NY: Pearson Education.

Slavin, R., E., & Madden, N.A. (1989, February). What works for students at risk: A research synthesis. *Educational Leadership, 46* (5), 4-13.

Slavin, R.E., Chamberlain, A., & Daniels, C. (2007). Preventing reading failure. *Educational Leadership, 65* (2), 22-27.

Smith, F. (1978). *Reading without nonsense*. New York, NY: Teachers College Press.

Snow, C.E., Burns, S., & Griffin, P. (1998). Preventing reading difficulties in young children. Washington, D.C.: National Research Council, National Academy Press.

Spady, W. G. (1984). Organizing and delivering curriculum for maximum impact in making our schools more effective. Paper presented during the Proceedings of Three State Conferences, Phoenix, AZ.

Sparks, D. (2005). Leading for transformation in teaching, learning, and relationships. In R.P. Dufour, R. Eaker, & R.B. Dufour (Eds.). *On common ground: The power of professional learning communities* (pp. 155-175). Bloomington, IN: Solution Tree.

Stahl, S. A. (1992, April). Saying the "p" word: Nine guidelines for exemplary phonics instruction. *The Reading Teacher, 45* (8), 618-625.

Standards for the assessment of reading and writing (1994). International Reading Association and National Council of Teachers of English Joint Task Force on Assessment. Newark, DE: International Reading Association.

Stanovich, K. E. (1993-1994, December-January). Romance and reality. *The Reading Teacher, 47* (4), 280-291.

Stiggins, R. (2005). Assessment FOR learning: Building a culture of confident learners. In R.P. DuFour, R.B. Eaker, & R. DuFour (Eds.). *On common ground: The power of professional learning communities* (pp. 65-84). Bloomington, IN: Solution Tree.

Stiggins, R. (2007, May). Assessment through the students' eyes. *Educational Leadership, 64* (8), 22-26.

Strommen, L. T. & Mates, B. F. (1997, October). What readers do: Young children's ideas about the nature of reading. *Reading Teacher, 51* (2), 98-107.

Supovitz, J. (2009, May). Can high stakes testing leverage educational improvement? Prospects from the last decade of testing and accountability reform. *Journal of Educational Change, 10* (2-3), 211-227.

Templeton, S. (1995). *Children's literacy: Contexts for meaningful learning.* Boston, MA: Houghton Mifflin.

Thaler, M. (1989). *The teacher from the black lagoon.* New York, NY: Scholastic.

Thompson, V. P. & Gickling, E. E. (1992, March-April). A personal view of curriculum-based assessment: A response to "critical reflections..." *Exceptional Children, 58* (5), 468-471.

Thompson, V. P., Gickling, E. E., & Havertape, J. F. (1983). The effects of medication and curriculum management on task-related behaviors of attention deficit disordered and low-achieving peers. In R.B. Rutherford (Ed.), *Monograph in behavior disorders: Severe behavior disorders of children and youth* (pp. 86-97). Arizona State University.

Tobias, S. (1994, Spring). Interest, prior knowledge and learning. *Review of Educational Research, 64*, 37-54.

Tomlinson C. A. (2008, November). The goals of differentiation. *Educational Leadership, 66* (3), 26-30.

Tomlinson, C. A. (2007, December/2008, January). Learning to love assessment. *Educational Leadership, 65* (4), 8-13.

Toppa, G. (2005, October 19). Math proficiency rises but reading stagnates: National tests are mixed bag. *USA Today*, 7D.

Tucker, J. A. (1985). Curriculum-based assessment: An introduction. *Exceptional Children, 52*, 199-204.

Tucker, J. A. (1988). Isn't that special. Barrien Springs, MI.

Tucker, J. A. (1989). Basic flashcard techniques when vocabulary is the goal. Unpublished teaching materials, University of Tennessee at Chattanooga, Chattanooga, TN.

Vacca, J.A.L., Vacca, R.T., & Gove, M.K. (1991). *Reading and learning to read, 2nd ed.*. New York, NY: HarperCollins.

Valencia, R. R. & Villarreal, B. L. (2003). Improving students' reading performance via standards-based school reform: A critique. *The Reading Teacher, 56*(7), 612-621.

Valencia, S. (1990, January). A portfolio approach to classroom reading assessment: The whys, whats, and hows. *The Reading Teacher, 43* (4), 338-340.

Valencia, S. W. (1990, September). Alternative assessment: Separating the wheat from the chaff. *The Reading Teacher, 44* (1), 60-61.

Valencia, S. W., McGinley, W., & Pearson, P. D. (1990). Assessing reading and writing. In G.G. Duffy (Ed.). (pp. 124-153). *Reading in the middle school, 2nd ed*. Newark, NJ: International Reading Association.

Valencia S. & Pearson, P. D. (1987, April). Reading assessment: Time for a change. *The Reading Teacher, 40* (8), 726-732.

Vygotsky, L. (1978). Mind in society: *The development of higher psychological processes*. Cambridge, MA: Harvard University Press.

Walmsley, S. A. & Allington, R. L. (1995). Redefining and reforming instructional support programs for at-risk students. In R. L. Allington & S. A. Walmsley (Eds.) *No quick fix: Rethinking literacy programs in America's elementary schools*. New York, NY: Teacher College Press.

Wang, M. C., Haertel, G. D. & Walberg, H. J. (1993, Fall). Toward a knowledge base for school learning. *Review of Educational Research, 63* (3), 249-294.

Wang, M. C., Reynolds, M. C. & Walberg, H. J. (Eds.). (1987). *Handbook of special education research and practice*. Oxford, England: Pergamon Press.

Weeks, J. (2000). *Stop taking my things*, Leichhardt, NSW, Australia: Blake Education.

Wiggins, G. (1989, May). A true test: Toward more authentic and equitable assessment. *Phi Delta Kappan, 70* (9), 708.

Wiggins, G. (1992). Foreword. In R. A. Villa, J. S. Thousand, W. Stainback, & S. Stainback (Eds.). *Restructuring for caring and effective education: An administrative guide to creating heterogeneous schools* (pp. xi-xvi). Baltimore, MD: Paul H. Brookes.

Wiley, D. E. & Harnischfeger, A. (1974, April). Explosion of a myth: Quantity of schooling and exposure to instruction, major educational vehicles. *Educational Researcher 3* (4), 7-12.

Will, M. C. (1986, February). Educating children with learning problems: A shared responsibility. *Exceptional Children, 52* (5), 411-415.

Willingham, D.T. (2009). *Why don't students like school? A cognitive scientist answers questions about how the mind works and what it means for the classroom.* San Francisco, CA: Jossey-Bass.

Wolfe, P. & Brandt, R. (1998, November). What do we know from brain research? *Educational Leadership, 56* (3), 8-13.

Wong, S., Groth, L. & O'Flahavan, J. (1995, December/January). Classroom implications of reading recovery. *Reading Today, 13* (3), 12.

APPENDIX A

Instructional Reading Assessment Summary

Student: _____   Snap Shot: _____   Text:_____

Select Material	○ Peer Expected	○ Other
	○ Unfamiliar	○ Familiar
	○ Narrative	○ Expository
	Observations:	

Build the Relationship	*Observations:*

Read to the Student (3A)	*Unaided*	*Aided (5W)*	*Forced Choice*	*Visual/ Referent*
	Observations:			

Word Search 3:1 (3B)	*Observations:*

Decision Questions:

Does the student possess the language and prior knowledge to understand the content based on the retelling and responses?

    Yes   No   Maybe

Based on the word search does the student possess sufficient sight vocuabulary to read the selection?

    Yes   No   Maybe

Options Used

○ Teach   ○ Look ahead/behind ○ Segments

○ Transition   ○ Teacher made   ○ Other material

Sample Reading (3C)	Fluency:	Rate: _____ WPM	Quality:
	Word Study Strategies Used:	Words/Miscued/ Attempted:	Strategy Employed:

Assess Comprehension (3D)	Unaided	Aided (5W)	Forced Choice	Visual Referent
	Observations:			

Decision Question:
Which reading dimension requires further "snap shots' or immediate instructional support?

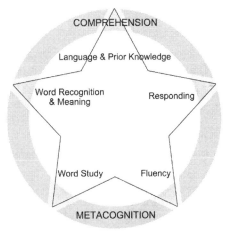

Can the following questions be answered?
1. *What does the student know?*
2. *What can the student do?*
3. *How does the student think?*
4. *How does the student approach what s/he is unsure of?*
5. *As a teacher, now what do I do?*

Instructional Reading Assessment Summary

Student _____   **Snap Shot #** _____   **Date** _____

Select Material	○ Peer Expected	○ Other
	○ Familiar	○ Unfamiliar
	○ Narrative	○ Expository
Text used:	*Observations:*	

Build the Relationship	*Observations:*

Read to the Student	**Retelling**	*Unaided*	*Aided (5W)*	*Forced Choice*	*Visual/ Referent*
Unaided (*Tell me what you know about...Tell me more*)	Main idea				
Aided Questions (*Who, What, When, Where, Why, How*)	Characters				
	Setting				
Forced Choice (e.g., *Who was speaking, the mother or the daugher?*)	Sequencing				
Visual Referent (e.g., *Look back in the text...Look at the picture...*)	Details				
	Pred./Infer.				
	Listening Comprehension				
	Prior Knowledge				
	Language Concepts				

Word Search	*Known:* *Unknown:*
Ration of 3 easy:1 hard (fast) *Check for meanings* *Does not allow for word study strategies* *What does the student know?* Sight words Known and unknown words Prior knowledge Language concepts	

Decision

Does the student possess the language and prior knowledge to understand the content based on the retelling and responses?
Does the student possess sufficient sight vocabulary to read the selection based on the word search?

☐ Yes = Go ahead with assessment   ☐ Maybe = Read more and do another Word Search

☐ No = Make content adjustment

Options

○ Teach a few words/concepts   ○ Look ahead/behind   ○ Content segments
○ Transitional stories   ○ Teacher made   ○ Other material

Sample Reading	☐ Instructional Level		☐ Independent Level

Fluency timing
Running record
Self corrections
Know and unknown words
Sight words
Word analysis skills

Fluency Rate: _____ WPM	Quality:

Word	Word Study Strategy

Assess Comprehension	**Retelling**	*Unaided*	*Aided (5W)*	*Forced Choice*	*Visual/ Referent*
Unaided (*Tell me what you know about...Tell me more*)	Main idea				
Aided Questions (*Who, What, When, Where, Why, How*)	Characters				
	Setting				
Forced Choice (e.g., *Who was speaking, the mother or the daugher?*)	Sequencing				
Visual Referent (*e.g., Look back in the text...Look at the picture...*)	Details				
	Pred./Infer.				

Observations:

Decision

Which reading dimension(s) require(s) further "snapshots" or immediate instructional support?

Can the following questions be answered?
1. *What does the student know?*
2. *What can the student do?*
3. *How does the student think?*
4. *How does the student approach what s/he is unsure of?*
5. *As a teacher, now what do I do?*

Reading Dimensions	Strength	Need	Find out more...
Language/Prior Knowledge			
Responding			
Fluency			
Word Study			
Word Rec. and Meaning			

Appreciation is extended to Tim Neall and Vicki Fornasar, Instructional Consultation Team facilitators in Prince William County, Virginia, for sharing these forms with us.

Index

A

C

H

I

R

S

Made in the USA
Lexington, KY
08 September 2016